THE GENERAL NEXT TO GOD

William Booth, 1829-1912, first General

THE GENERAL
NEXT TO GOD

THE STORY OF WILLIAM BOOTH
AND THE SALVATION ARMY

Richard Collier

Collins

ST JAMES'S PLACE, LONDON
1965

To
The Men And Women
of
The Salvation Army

While women weep as they do now, I'll fight;
while little children go hungry as they do now,
I'll fight; while men go to prison, in and out,
in and out, as they do now, I'll fight—I'll
fight to the very end!

WILLIAM BOOTH

Contents

Illustrations

Illustrations

The Long Shadow

It was midnight when Hazel Hoffman came awake to darkness, uneasy and alone—and within seconds, she knew why. Her husband, Brigadier Franklin W. Hoffman, Salvation Army, had tiptoed from the bedroom of their snug cretonned apartment at No. 349, Bowery, New York, to admit a caller—and the voice drifting up from three flights below, a voice gripping on to sanity, suggested nothing but trouble.

It was Friday, 10th April, 1964, and the date is fixed in Hazel's mind only because on this day, a hundred years before, William Booth, pawnbroker's apprentice, founder of the unique Christian brigade of which she made part, was born in Nottingham, England. There was nothing else to single out the day from the gruelling routine she and Franklin had faced since they took over The Army's Bowery Corps four years earlier : the nightly service in the small cream-tiled chapel, where powerful blowers sucked the sour air from the room every six minutes, the shuffling parade of lost tormented faces, the struggle to persuade some two hundred alcoholics a year among the Bowery's 25,000 strong legion of the lost to turn over their wills and their lives to God.

But in the small hours of this day, as Hazel will always recall, the burly, granite-jawed Franklin returned to the apartment with an air of quiet triumph. It was Tom, an alcoholic artist estranged from his wife, whose frantic knocking had roused him—one of twenty men currently " drying out " as inmates of the Bowery's hostel. Three weeks back, the Hoffmans had despaired ; helpless to resist his craving, Tom had vanished to make one with the unofficial dead in the Bowery's sleazy streets. Subsequent treatment at the city's

Bellevue Hospital had sobered him up ; it could not reach the sickness in his mind. At midnight, for the second time in hours, he had crept from Bellevue, teetering on the brink of delirium tremens, somehow covering the thirty intervening blocks to seek his only friends—the Hoffmans.

Yet what had clinched Franklin's decision to let Tom stay, he told Hazel later, was the sudden advent of Jim, an inmate sticking staunchly by his pledge, awakened by the foot-in-the-door anguish in Tom's voice. Hearing the Brigadier's plea that accommodation was at a premium, Jim's solution bespoke Christian compassion : " Let him spend the rest of the night with me in *my* room. I know what he's having to fight."

As Franklin Hoffman hastened back to tell his wife the news, he saw a sight which seemed to promise a brighter future : Tom, openly hostile to prayer until now, was kneeling in silent thanksgiving beside his new-found friend.

For exactly one hundred years, Salvationists like Hazel and Franklin Hoffman, unarmed soldiers of what one journal styled " an immense federation of hearts and consciences " have regarded such happenings as routine. Outlawed by Russia, Red China and all Iron Curtain countries, they are still a global Army two million strong, fighting the good fight in seventy-one countries, nursing the walking-wounded of civilisation, operating under forty-plus territorial commanders, watched over by 25,000 officers. Non-sectarian and non-political, they spread the Gospel in 147 languages, everywhere from Dickensian slums to glittering £175,000 neighbourhood centres, in marriage guidance clinics, day nurseries, boys' and girls' summer camps, business girls' home-from-homes. Known variously as the Sidewalk Soldiers, the Tambourine Troops, or just the " Sally Ann," The Army, through its investigation bureau, has laboured to restore 250,000 missing persons to their families as tirelessly as their emergency teams, in August, 1955, battled the aftermath of " the worst flood since Noah " that followed Hurricane Diane across New England.

The Army works round the globe and round the clock. As the Hoffmans re-lived the small-hours' tensions of that day over their usual hasty luncheon, others were returning to the battle-line; in Hamburg, Germany, 3,000 miles away, it was already 7 p.m. At No. 15, Talstrasse, Major Walter Flade was finishing his evening meal—ham, black bread, salt fish, catsup—and girding himself for what lay ahead. To-night the stocky smiling Flade would lead his shock troops through strange terrain for a 48-year-old ex-insurance clerk and Whermacht medical orderly—the savage neon-lit six-acre labyrinth of the St. Pauli red-light district. Of The Army's 16,700 global outposts few lay in tougher territory—and Flade knew it.

On the street called The Great Freedom, outside the Erotic Night Club, the Boudoir and the Tabu, Salvation songs like " I worship the power of God's love " would strive against the tom-tom throb of jazz—though often, to the club bouncers' fury, customers lured out by the sweet-voiced harmony thought better of returning. Only on the dimly-lit Herbertstrasse, most infamous street in all Europe, boarded and barred to all under sixteen years, would a brooding silence reign. For two hundred yards, behind heavy glass window-panes, street girls in filmy black underwear sat as rigid as wax models under the dim red lighting, silent, watchful. Until Flade's joyful melodies rang out on the spring night, only one sound broke the eerie silence : the steady scrape of prowling feet as customers weighed up their choice.

But Flade would not despair; like every other Salvationist he held no man or woman beyond redemption. Only a few months back, one such girl, faced with the burden of an illegitimate child, had come to his Talstrasse headquarters begging for help. After leading her to acceptance of Christ, the Major had found her a job in a packing factory; her baby was well cared for now, in a Salvation Army home. Another had quit her place in the window to join the Salvationists there and then in the street. She, too, was now a factory-worker who had found peace with God.

To-night, like every other Salvationist, Flade would pray for converts—but if converts did not come, his faith was armour against discouragement. His life, like that of all his colleagues, pivoted on an unseen axis : the redemptive purpose of God, the instinct, in great things and in small, to champion the needy and downtrodden. In February, 1962, Flade's work for Hamburg's flood victims had made front-page headlines ; some sixth sense had made him cling on for two months to clothing for three hundred people, unclaimed orders donated by a friendly dry cleaners'. Those garments had proved the answer when hundreds of Hamburg's citizens fled naked and shivering from the onrushing waters of the Elbe River—but for the most part Flade's daily round was a world away from such headline-screaming catastrophes : as unsung as the twenty-three million cut-price meals, the eleven million beds to the homeless, that the Army supply each year.

One woman alone has served over a million such meals. In Paris, as the clocks on this night showed 7.30 p.m., Major Georgette Gogibus was as always in the galley of the barge *Peniche*, 1,000 tons, once the *Louise Catherine* out of Rouen, seeing the white windmill of a pleasureboat's searchlight raking the twilight from below the Austerlitz Bridge. Across the steely waters of the Seine, the guide's commentary came clearly : " And moored there, *mesdames et messieurs*, you see the barge of *l'Armée du Salut*, where every night more than a hundred poor men are given free lodging. . . ."

Ten yards away, on the Quai Bernard, Major Georgette's guests queued patiently beneath the plane trees : men who all day had tramped the streets seeking work, searching garbage cans for scraps of food. Some were Yugoslav refugees from Tito's régime, others from Algeria, more still the *clochards* (tramps) of the Paris slums, whose dirt-glazed hands had never handled above a franc at a time. Some were too old to work, some work-shy, others students in quest of jobs. But at day's end, as for fourteen years past, all had turned to the light and warmth of Major Georgette's floating hostel, their ever-present refuge in time of trouble.

Standing at the checkpoint by the narrow gangplank, a lone woman who passes each night among 150 men, Georgette knew no fear. Hadn't she sought to help others ever since she yearned to follow in the footsteps of her father, a chemist—

before realising that this Army offered the chance to make up other more potent prescriptions ? Before lights out, at 9 p.m., the kindly bespectacled Major might, as on another night, have saved an Army deserter from an overdose of barbiturates, advanced a man money towards a doctor's fee, found a third casual work to tide him over. Only when the men lay dead to the world in their double-decker bunks below would Georgette's tall slight figure pass along the darkened aisle to her cabin in the stern. Then, setting her small blue enamel alarm clock for 6.30 a.m., she dropped to her knees. She had given these men their soup and savoury rice ; now she must give them her prayers.

At this moment, in her quiet cabin, Georgette Gogibus was close to God—and close in her way of life to two million other Salvationists. Like them she saw the Bible as divinely inspired. Like them she believed in the Trinity, in the salvation of all believers " by faith through grace," in " the immortality of the soul, in the resurrection of the body, in the general judgment at the end of the world." Like them she strove for " personal holiness," a second and deeper sanctification through which even the desire to sin is washed away.

As with the others, an ironclad military discipline governed her life. The Army's midnight-blue uniform spells total abstinence from liquor and tobacco. As ordained ministers, officers live in Army-owned houses and cannot marry outside the service. Even The Army's eighth General, 65-year-old Frederick Coutts, as a soldier of the South Croydon, Surrey, Corps—what would be called the congregation in other churches—is regularly visited by his C.O., who prays with him as with any other soldier. His " cartridge "—a weekly contribution towards Corps expenses—is " fired " regularly whether at home or abroad. Regardless of rank, no officer has an inalienable right to pay or draws above £25 a week— with a captain's £5 a week as more common.

And there were few soldiers, on their founder's birthday, who didn't think, however fleetingly, of money. Despite its £23 million assurance society, its bank with £3 million in deposits, The Army's slogan—" With Heart to God and Hand to Man "—involves mammoth operational expenses : over £3 million annually in New York City alone. At 56 Broomfield Street, Poplar, East London, within sight of dockland's cranes, Major Marion Dunn, the dark vivacious Corps commander, was on this day as perplexed as any. Making ends meet was proving as stern a test of faith and ingenuity as at any time in twenty-one years' service.

Six months earlier, in October, 1963, had come an assignment which coupled an honour and a challenge : the chance to infuse new life into Poplar, the world's oldest surviving Salvation Army Corps, lapsed into decline after wartime devastation. Major Marion took over to find a Corps in sore financial straits, the windows of its Kerbey Street mission hall grimed and broken. The roof leaked ; doors swung drunkenly from their hinges. There was seating for close on two hundred—button hard wooden benches, not chairs.

Though an appeal to headquarters—the six-story brick-and-stone tower in Queen Victoria Street, London, which is The Army's High Command—would have yielded a grant, Major Marion was made of sterner fibre. Summoning her local officers, the uniformed laymen who undertake duty in a corps, she announced bluntly : " From now on, we're going to pay our way."

And by 8 p.m. on Friday, 10th April, drawing up final details for Sunday's services in her small pin-neat Broomfield Street maisonette, Marion could look back over six months in which unflagging faith, work and prayer had moved a mountain of difficulty. The Corps had piled up no more debts ; its hall she had scrubbed and polished and burnished with her own hands. At Christmas she had led her soldiers, by now fifty strong, through the wintry streets, singing carols that weighed down her collection box with £50 worth of silver.

She had bought curtains and carpeting, and an electric sewing machine to teach her Girl Guides dressmaking, before praying long and earnestly to God for the money to pay for them—and always a donation had arrived in time, never once had God failed her. She had toured the long yellow-brick terraces where the dockers lived, seeking children like a blue-uniformed Pied Piper—and now she had a Sunday School class of fifty. Best of all, she had combed the junkshops for cast-off brass instruments, and now, in the sooty red-brick hall, a band of twelve was somehow learning, with eight battered instruments, to play the music of God.

As they bent to their tasks across the world, these five blue-clad apostles—Marion Dunn, Walter Flade, Georgette Gogibus, Hazel and Franklin Hoffman—did not think to question the invisible bond that linked their endeavours. To bring human souls to God through prayer and good works was the one thought in their minds. Yet a shadow did lie across all their lives, like the shadow from a sundial : a long shadow cast by a man who one hundred years ago strode through East London's streets on the brink of an awful realisation.

"Darling, I've Found my Destiny"

1865

He came up Mile End Road, East London, as the saffron light of evening flooded the sky, a tall black-bearded man in dark frock coat and wide-brimmed hat, moving fast against an urgent floodtide of humanity.

Outside the drab red-brick façade of The Blind Beggar tavern he halted. From beneath his arm he drew a book and, incongruously, in a high voice, gave out the verse of a hymn. In an instant, faces were glued to the pub's glass windows; a ragged unwashed throng pressed curiously about the stranger, whose 6 feet 1 inch made him, by London's cockney-sparrow standards, seem a towering giant. His pale eagle face with its long straight nose and firm chin was dominated by piercing grey eyes of almost frightening intensity.

" There is a Heaven in East London for *everyone*," they heard him cry, " for everyone who will stop and think and look to Christ as a personal Saviour."

From the pub there came only a spattering volley of jeers and oaths, but those within the circle were listening despite themselves. The preacher's voice was an unfamiliar Midlands sing-song, but infusing it they sensed a strange new ring : a love for all mankind. Then from the rear a rotten egg came whizzing to find its mark and the subtle spell was broken. With the yolk trickling slowly down his pallid cheek the stranger paused, and prayed. Then, pulling his hat over his eyes, he walked rapidly westwards.

It was the first sultry week of July, 1865—twenty-eight years since Victoria was crowned Queen, fourteen since Prince Albert's Great Exhibition in Hyde Park, twenty-three acres of cast-iron and glass, had confirmed Britain as the world's most powerful nation and London as the focal point of the world. But to this man, the Rev. William Booth, London was an alien unfamiliar city. Sixteen years back, a pawnbroker's apprentice who yearned to be an evangelist, he had paced the streets south of the Thames ; later, briefly, he had preached there and found his bride. But the East London streets through which he strode now were outlandish soil to all. The well-to-do merchants of Mayfair and Belgravia knew as little as William Booth of this labyrinth of half a million souls.

But as the 36-year-old Booth moved west towards his lodgings, the realisation that this was a crucial night in his life came home with stunning force. Only the urgent promptings of the East London Special Services Committee, a small revivalist mission which had booked the itinerant evangelist for a week's preaching engagement in nearby Whitechapel had led him to postpone a campaign in Derbyshire. But why go as far afield as Derby ? For all the crusading years of his life, he had sought a human jungle. Now he walked in its midst.

Shoulders stooped, long arms swinging, the preacher's raking stride carried him now through a ragged, shrieking, fighting population. Match-sellers and orange-women blocked his path ; Irish flower-girls, bare feet marbled with dirt, whined and cajoled. He thrust past hulking labourers, women clad only in soiled petticoats. Children with wolfish faces foraged at his feet, gobbling up heaps of decaying plums in the street-market's garish light.

To-night the ruler-straight length of Mile End Road was a vortex of light and colour—light wavering from candles stuck in huge turnips, light flaring from fish-tailed gas jets above coarse scraps of meat. The pitiless rays focused on sights that a man as impressionable as Booth could never forget, and again the thought flashed through his mind: Where can you find such heathen as these?

He saw five-year-olds blind drunk at tap-room doorways; mothers forcing beer from white-chipped jugs down babies' throats. Outside pub after pub silent savage men with ashen faces, coats piled nearby, lunged and struck and toppled heavily and watching women, faces animal with passion, screamed " Strike ! Strike ! " Beyond the intense white glare of naphtha, men passed furtively, blood-soaked handker-chiefs cloaking the shivering bodies of dogs that had lost a fight. Goldfinches, blinded with red-hot cambric needles to make them sing the better, twittered in cramped cages.

It did not shock those who made part of it: East London was their world. As children they fashioned their toys from its garbage—often herring backbones, trailed on pieces of string. As adults the streets were their eating place—breakfast doled out by the hot-baked-potato man, supper from the hot-eel seller with his black-ribboned hat and white apron. Even at midnight Mile End Road would be awake and clamorous as weary children trailed forth for their parents' supper—a wedge of Gloucester cheese, a fresh tobacco-pipe, more beer.

If the cheese was tinted with red lead to simulate high-priced red Double-Gloucester, the poor would not complain. In the same way they accepted other adulterations: street-sold lemonade spiked with oil of vitriol, flour doctored with pipe-clay, cocoa gritty with earth. When two farthings could un-balance a weekly budget, none dared set too high a store on quality. In July, 1865, this city of three million souls num-bered more than 100,000 paupers. Three wet days saw 30,000 street vendors on the brink of starvation.

No stranger to poverty after thirteen years as a Methodist Circuit Minister in Britain's mean streets, William Booth felt his heart go out like a father's to these people.

Grimly, like a hunter on safari, he tramped west—faster and faster, despite the crush. A conviction was mounting within him and he sought to see the worst. On all sides the crowd jostled him . . . Yankee foremastmen from the windjammers with tarry trousers and case-knives strung from their girdles

... soldiers on furlough, their scarlet coatees gaping open ... bearded Jewish old-clothes vendors ... young costermongers in brass-buttoned cord jackets and green neckerchiefs ... street-girls in poppy-red Garibaldi blouses.

The noise was shattering, a Babel of sound. Flower sellers bawled " All a-growin' and a-blowin'," barely audible above the sharp clatter of night cabmen's wheels, the slow rumble of empty hearses returning from Bow Cemetery. Sun-burned Italian organ-grinders, churning out *Traviata*, vied with the sad plaint of the ballad-singers' " Swanee River." Booming above it all came the deep bass of St. Paul's Cathedral bells farther west.

Incredibly, London was still, in many ways, a rural city. A man perched on the glittering 1,850-foot eminence of the Crystal Palace tower would have seen, looking north and east, a plateau polka-dotted with sooty red brick, extending as far west as Bayswater Road, no farther north than Camden Town. Three miles north-west of Piccadilly, Notting Hill was virgin parkland where the turf-cutters culled their spoils. Milk was hawked from street to street by countrywomen wearing clean white stockings and straw bonnets. Those early abroad saw drovers trudging to Smithfield Meat Market by St. Paul's behind herds of foggy-breathed bullocks.

Yet the city, as William Booth knew, was growing apace. Since he had first paced its streets almost a million souls had flooded in to crowd its stinking tenements and alleys, many of them countrymen who had forsaken the land. East London, a travesty of the villages which had been Hackney, Stratford, Bethnal Green, Stepney, Bow and Bromley, now held over 290 people to the acre—" a great large muck-heap what the rich grows their mushrooms on," was one pauper's bitter comment. For many life was an unremitting year-long struggle to maintain overt respectability—penny bunches of mignonette kept in cracked jugs on the windowsill, calico blinds to mask the squalor within, marriage certificates hung primly beneath the clock.

But day by day more families lost heart, contracting out of the battle. In the dark alleys near the docks, the sick, the dying, often the dead, lay side by side on the bare floors of fireless rooms covered with tattered scraps of blanket. Their children's cradles were gooseberry sieves ; their swaddling clothes the same threadbare jackets in which the parish buried them. Their homes smelt of red herrings, stale bedding and last week's rain.

The whole city stank. As fast as William Booth moved on this July night, he couldn't escape it : an unholy compound of cattle-hides, firewood soaked in turpentine, stale corduroy and leaking gas. Other smells, unforgettable to the fastidious Booth, blanketed the warm air—gin, onions, dung, frying batter, the grey sudsy water that puddled the stone setts, the curling, coiling smoke from three million chimneys.

Even the Thames, still a great public highway, where twenty river-steamers plied at rush-hours, was nicknamed " The Great Stink." Almost 370 sewers flushed into its yellow-grey water. Between Westminster and London Bridge, a sticky black bank of sewage, six feet deep, stretched one hundred feet into the main channel—creating a stench so appalling that in summer no M.P. could use the House of Commons Library.

Next year, cholera would strike again, as it had done three times since 1832—and the lights burning all night long in the windows of Whitechapel's London Hospital would give silent testimony that the poor, as always, were bearing the brunt.

Towards 8 p.m. on this July evening, it came home to William Booth that in these 2,000 miles of London streets dwelt thousands of souls irretrievably damned.

Eight miles west of Mile End, at 31 Shaftesbury Road, Hammersmith, West London, Catherine Mumford Booth anxiously awaited her husband's return. At 36, she was still the gentle, slightly-built woman with lustrous dark-brown eyes and mobile mouth with whom Booth had fallen desperately in love thirteen years ago—yet to-night she was sorely troubled.

For four years now, ever since Booth, his heart and mind drawn increasingly to the unchurched masses of Britain's cities, had resigned his position in the Methodist ministry, their future had grown daily more precarious. Nor was it for themselves alone that Catherine worried. Upstairs their six children—from Bramwell, aged nine, to Marian, just fourteen months—slept peacefully, as yet untroubled by the problem of winning bread from a hard world.

Towards midnight, as Catherine later recalled, a key grated abruptly in the lock and Booth, his eyes shining, strode into the living-room. " Darling," were the first words that burst from his lips, " I've found my destiny," and even as he spoke Catherine felt the cold hand of uncertainty touch her heart.

As a ten-year-old in Wilford Meadows, a green tract of pasture beside Nottingham's Trent River, where crocuses made golden splashes in springtime, William Booth had played soldiers with his friends—and William, as he later confessed, was usually the Captain. This innate quality of leadership, though early in evidence, was to desert Booth entirely for the next quarter-century. He was a man tossed by the wind, seeking an outlet for a talent he could not express.

So great was Booth's enthusiasm as an angler that, armed with a volume of Sir Walter Scott, he would squat on the banks of the Trent from five a.m., hoping for a bite—yet his lack of success was such a byword one family joke became paramount. Solemnly an old uncle would set a plate with a snow-white napkin in the small square hallway of the Booth house—in readiness for the non-existent catch.

Born on 10th April, 1829, at 12 Nottintone Place, a red-brick six-room terrace house in the Nottingham suburb of Sneinton, the son of Samuel and Mary Moss Booth, William was from the first no stranger to poverty. When Booth was only thirteen, his father, a money-minded small-time builder whom his son recalled as " a grab—a get," faced ruin. A mortgage was called in, and all plans for making William a gentleman at Mr. Biddulph's school were swiftly abandoned. Within a year Booth senior had died of the shock—but not before apprenticing his gangling teenage son to a Unitarian pawnbroker, Francis Eames, in Nottingham's slummy Goose Gate.

Darling, I've Found my Destiny

These were the hungry years after Waterloo : years of bad harvests and worse taxes, when the time-honoured Corn Laws, designed to protect the landowner at the expense of the poor, kept bread prices high and bellies empty. As a boy, Booth saw the iron railings fronting his father's house wrenched from their sockets by starving rioters battling armed troops. He saw ragged men and women smash their way into bakers' shops before fleeing, their arms crammed with loaves. All Britain, cried the Conservative M.P. for Shrewsbury, Benjamin Disraeli, is divided into " the two nations."

And nowhere was this a greater truth than in Nottingham itself. One nation, which Booth came to love as he grew to manhood, packed the city's 8,000 back-to-back houses, where stocking-weaving, the chief home industry, was so hard-hit by French competition that often only prostitution stood between its women weavers and death. The other crowded the stands at Nottingham's Trent Bridge to see William Lillywhite demonstrate the new-style bowling in a Notts *v.* All-England cricket match for £100 a side, or crammed the guinea stalls of the Mechanics' Hall to hear the " Swedish Nightingale," Jenny Lind. Chartism smouldered—so called from the " People's Charter " of its militant reformers who demanded Parliamentary reform, cheaper bread and votes for working people. Young as he was the import of these demands was not lost on William Booth.

For in these years, the three golden brass balls drew whole families like a magnet—often the pawnbrokers' was the sole bastion that stood between a family and eviction. Under " the sign of the swinging dumplings," Booth learned more than the pricing of adzes, cotton umbrellas and printed shawls or the deft handling of the black calico bags of pawn tickets. He learned as from a primer what poverty did to people. If one in fourteen was being relieved from the rates, self-respect, he found, died hard. Sunday silk handkerchiefs went first to the pledge-counter ; wedding-rings came last.

A tall pale-faced boy with raven-black hair and flashing eyes, Booth's own religious upbringing was sketchy, to say the least. Though his father, for appearance's sake, insisted that

William and his sisters, Ann, Mary and Emma, regularly attended church, Samuel Booth almost never entered a place of worship. Mary Moss Booth, his mother, who after her husband's death took over a small Goose Gate haberdashery store, was of small help either. " Be good, William," was her sole counsel, " and all will be well."

Fiery, passionate, impulsive, it was not surprising that " Wilful Will," as Nottingham's citizens called him, was won, as a teenager, to the " Methodists." So nicknamed because of the stern rules of upright conduct formulated by their eighteenth-century founder, John Wesley, the warm ardour of their services in the tall Wesleyan Chapel on Broad Street struck a vibrant chord in Booth. Wesley had believed in acts of penance and emphasised the confessional but he went much further : he sought to reclaim men without religion, the down-trodden and desperate who cursed life itself. To bring home God's love for the forsaken, this fragile little minister, despite his diffident spirit, had taken the revolutionary step of preaching in the open air to crowds of drunken miners, a pile of stones as his pulpit.

" You are the sons of God, the heirs of eternal life," Wesley told his grimy cynical congregations, whose lexicon contained no such words as " forgiveness," " redemption " or " hope," and at first, with quaking memories of the French Revolution, Church and State denounced him as a firebrand. They recoiled from his vehemence, his use of unordained laymen to preach God's word ; they saw his encouragement of working-class unorthodoxy as one fraught step towards mob-rule. Only slowly did his crusade for decency, honesty and goodness win sympathisers. For the poor, Wesley opened a labour factory, a free medical dispensary and a bank ; he visited some of the vilest English gaols to minister to the unfortunates. Until his death at eighty-eight, he never ceased to stress that body, mind and soul alike were intended to bear the image of God.

This was the human hero that Booth held always before him in his long groping towards the stars. " There is one God," he would avow, " and John Wesley is His prophet."

Though his name was later synonymous with some of the

most astonishing conversions in the annals of latter-day religion, Booth's own conversion was simple and undramatic. Around eleven p.m. on a night in 1844, trudging home from a meeting through unpaved streets, a sudden spiritual exaltation flooded his whole being. He saw, with the clarity that Saul of Tarsus saw the light on the Damascus Road, that he must renounce sin—all and every sin—and atone to others for the wrongs that he had done them.

There was that silver pencil-case he had gained from friends through a trick—and the many times he had filched apples and cheated at marbles. Wasn't he fast becoming a pocket edition of his father—a boy giving grudgingly, when he gave at all ?

Within days, his conscience unburdened by repentance and confession, Booth had become as doughty a champion of right-living as Bunyan's Valiant-for-Truth. Although pawn-shops officially closed at midnight on Saturdays, the booming trade often kept the assistants working into the small hours of Sunday. This, Booth now told his employer, Francis Eames, was no longer possible. If need be he would start work again from Sunday midnight—but Sunday work was against all Christian principles.

" You'll work with the rest of us until we shut up shop," Eames told him curtly, " or you can leave."

Booth, standing rock-steady by his principles, at once joined the growing ranks of Nottingham's unemployed. This was not easy for his widowed mother, but nor was it easy for Eames, who had lost his most valued employee. Within days, after wrestling with his pride, the pawnbroker surrendered. From now on Booth was the one apprentice to finish work on the stroke of Saturday midnight. Yet, when Eames departed shortly on a tour of the Continent, it was William who took charge of the shop.

Many revivalists held the Chapel's devotees spell-bound during the " Hungry Forties." Always a ready pupil, Booth took something from them all. From men like the Rev. James Caughey, a lean black-cloaked Irish-American minister from Burlington, Vermont, he learned the hypnotic value of a subdued opening that warmed by degrees to white-heat. Others like Isaac Marsden of Doncaster, Yorkshire, showed him that precepts went home hardest in the form of simple parables. Passing one morning along a Nottingham alley, Marsden espied a housewife busy at her wash-tub. Sorrowfully he hailed her : " I say, missus, if your heart is not washed cleaner than those clothes, you'll *never* get to Heaven."

From the first it was the poor people who crowded his own pledge boxes for six days out of seven that drew Booth like a lodestar. Already, along with his friend, Will Sansom, handsome young son of a well-to-do lace manufacturer, he was treading in Wesley's footsteps—carrying the war against sin and misery into the open air. Perched on a chair or a barrel in a red-brick alley they would preach, undismayed, to a crowd of three at most, exhorting them to join a meeting in a nearby cottage. One such cottage in Nottingham's Kid Street was the unpromising amphitheatre for Booth's first sermon ; poor women had carried their own chairs to its parlour and an inverted box flanked by flickering candles served as lectern.

Those who heard it never forgot this sermon with its gentle parable of a mother watching her child's first efforts to walk. Would she shout and scold at it, or sit unmoved if it fell and hurt itself ? It was fully as hard, Booth said, for a man to follow Christ. Harsh words were no help when a man was failing ; the answer was a concerted effort by all to help him walk straight.

Yet if the need was there Booth could use words to scourge. Standing in Red Lion Square, hemmed in by a gang of loafers, he flayed their guilt unmercifully : all the world's suffering and sorrow came from sin like theirs. His voice, powerful even then, cut like a stockwhip : " I want to put a few straight questions to your souls. Have any of *you* got a child at home without shoes to its feet ? Are *your* wives sitting now in dark houses waiting for you to return without money ? Are you going away from here . . . *to spend on drink money that your wives need for food ?* "

But time and again, in the vast cold barracks of Broad

Street Chapel, Booth noted one thing lacking. Their sermons done, revivalists like Caughey and Marsden, following time-honoured Methodist procedure, would urge people to the communion rail—called also the mourner's bench, a kind of Protestant confessional—in public acceptance of Christ. Yet the poorest and most degraded never came forward. Nor were they present even at Booth's own street sermons.

Booth, of course, knew where they congregated—down in "The Bottoms," one of Nottingham's cruellest slums, where men shunned church as they shunned prison. These lost sheep he now set out to find.

Those who made part of Broad Street congregation never forgot that electric Sunday in 1846 : the gas jets, dancing on whitewashed walls, the Minister, the Rev. Samuel Dunn, seated comfortably on his red plush throne, a concord of voices swelling into the evening's fourth hymn :

> *Foul I to the fountain fly;*
> *Wash me, Saviour, or I die*

The chapel's outer door suddenly shattered open, engulfing a white scarf of fog. In its wake came a shuffling shabby contingent of men and women, wilting nervously under the stony stares of mill-managers, shop-keepers and their well-dressed wives. In their rear, afire with zeal, marched " Wilful Will " Booth, cannily blocking the efforts of the more reluctant to turn back. To his dismay the Rev. Dunn saw that young Booth was actually ushering his charges, none of whose clothes would have raised five shillings in his own pawnshop, into the very best seats ; pewholders' seats, facing the pulpit, whose occupants piled the collection-plate with glinting silver.

This was unprecedented, for the poor, if they came to chapel, entered by another door, to be segregated on benches without backs or cushions, behind a partition which screened off the pulpit. Here, though the service was audible, they could not see—nor could they be seen.

Oblivious of the mounting atmosphere, Booth joined full-throatedly in the service—even, he later admitted, hoping this devotion to duty might rate special commendation. All too soon he learned the unpalatable truth : since Wesley's day, Methodism had become " respectable."

The service done, Booth found himself facing a drumhead meeting of deacons under the Rev. Dunn and their instructions left no room for doubt. In future, if Booth brought such a flock to chapel they would enter by the side door—and sit in their appointed seats.

Head bowed, Booth accepted the rebuke—but in many ways, it would seem, this first gesture came to symbolise the entire credo of the army of men and women who would one day hail him as its founder.

In truth, Booth's headstrong actions alarmed the chapel brethren. Though many were sincere men, their beliefs were fixed, immutable. Like Booth's own mother and sisters they saw no prospect of salvation for the drunken outcasts spawned by Britain's Industrial Revolution. Even the astonishing conversion of " Besom Jack," a drunken broom-seller whose wife was reduced to begging used tea-leaves from neighbours, did nothing to reassure them. " Besom Jack," first of many colourful converts wholly convinced of sin, became one of Booth's most devoted followers—but even his conversion, the deacons noted, had taken place in the open street, where Booth and his little band often knelt to pray for the passers-by.

" They gave me plenty of caution," Booth recalled grimly later, " quaking and fearing at every new departure, but never a word of encouragement to keep me on. But I went forward all the same."

If this was true, few save the dogged Booth could discern visible progress. At nineteen, his six years' apprenticeship ended ; he joined the swelling ranks of the unemployed whose lot Prince Albert deplored in a personal letter to the Prime Minister, Lord John Russell. But the Royal concern was of little help in finding Booth a job. Twelve fruitless months later, he decided, like many provincial lads, to seek his fortune in London. At this stage of his life, the thought of being other than a lay preacher had never occurred to him. An only son, his first charge was to support his mother and sisters.

Bitter disillusion followed. Try as he might, Booth found

Fourteen years of poverty and preaching lay between the expulsion of William Booth and his wife Catherine Mumford by the Methodists and the foundation of the Salvation Army

Among the most important of early Salvationists were (top left and right) Bramwell, Booth's eldest son (the earliest known photograph); Frederick Booth-Tucker, India's trail-blazer, whose soldiers lived like fakirs. (Bottom left and right), Switzerland's pioneer, Arthur Booth-Clibborn; "Fiery Elijah" Cadman, onetime chimney sweep, creator of the term "Hallelujah Army"

just one vocation open to him : the pawnbroking trade he had hoped to quit for ever. And his new master, who furnished bed and board above the shop in Walworth, a grimy stucco desert south of the River Thames, drove a tighter-fisted bargain than Francis Eames. " I was practically a white slave," was Booth's bitter summing-up.

All through 1850, Booth's liberty, aside from Sunday, narrowed down to two scant hours a week. Even on the Sabbath the shop doors were bolted and barred sharp at ten p.m. Often Walworth Chapel, to which he was attached as a lay preacher, sent him as far afield as Greenwich, eight miles south. Sunday after Sunday, following a long day of services, the youngster's weary legs pounded the pavements, breath sobbing from his lungs as he strove to reach the shop before lock-up time.

He was barely of age, yet already the long weeks of thirteen-hour days, the fusty pawnshop air, the sour food, were taking their toll. Dyspepsia was a nagging ever-present torment. Years later, collating data for this period of his life, he blocked in a sub-heading " LONDON " and, as if by reflex, added one word : " Loneliness."

And just as in Nottingham, Booth's Walworth Chapel sermons struck a jarring note with the well-to-do congregations. " They smell of the shroud," one minister tut-tutted. Despite Booth's conviction that thousands of unsaved men and women passed daily to eternal damnation, the feeling grew that he was a reformer, whose presence spelt trouble. His refusal to give up open-air preaching on nearby Kennington Common set the seal on it. At quarter's end, the Chapel declined to renew the ticket every Methodist needs to retain church membership.

But one man, Edward Harris Rabbits, a rebel against the Church's orthodox methods, had heard Booth's preaching and liked it. The youth's pulpit style—fiery, ardent, pulling no punches—was a tonic in itself. Moreover, Rabbits was a man accustomed to call the tune. As owner of a £60,000 chain of South London boot stores, begun with the borrowed half-crown convention demands, even his store managers became, without option, local preachers—with the accent on brimstone and fire.

In June, 1851, after inviting Booth to dinner at his home off Walworth Road, Rabbits wound up the meal abruptly : " You must leave business and wholly devote yourself to preaching the Gospel."

Booth shook a despairing head. " There is no way for me," he replied. " Nobody wants me." Even a tentative application to sign on as Chaplain in a convict hulk bound for Botany Bay—a ministry from which most clerics fought shy—had been turned down.

Rabbits disagreed. The Reformers, whom he represented, wanted him, and as an evangelist, though, as Booth truly said, he could not live on air.

" How much *can* you live on ? " he asked thoughtfully, and Booth, after careful calculation, reckoned that twelve shillings a week would secure lodgings and keep him in bread and cheese. But this estimate Rabbits pooh-poohed.

" Nonsense," he rallied him. " You cannot do with less than twenty shillings a week, I am sure. *I* will supply it, for the first three months at least."

Booth, as Rabbits was perhaps the first to see, was obviously meant for better things and wider horizons. Armed with a few sticks of second-hand furniture, he quit the pawnbroker's shop for two cramped rooms in a widow's house near the Elephant and Castle tavern, afire with zeal to preach the Gospel of Christ. But no overnight transformation in his new congregations became apparent. No one even cursed or reviled him, as the Nottingham roughs had done ; for the most part they just stared at him, shuffling their feet self-consciously. For so young a man, most felt secretly, his sermons were both excitable and long-winded.

Only Fate's intervention now saved Booth from joining London's ever-growing army of might-have-beens. On Good Friday, 10th April, 1852, Rabbits, meeting the young preacher outside his lodgings, coaxed him to a meeting of the Reformers in Cowper Street, off City Road. On that afternoon, his twenty-third birthday, Booth fell in love with Catherine Mumford.

Darling, I've Found my Destiny

Despite their brief acquaintance a strange affinity had grown up between the tall hollow-cheeked Booth and the dark petite Catherine, daughter of a local coach-builder and his wife. At their first meeting, following a service in a nearby hall, Booth, of course, could scarcely know that this girl, despite her twenty-three years, was so shrewd a judge of sermons that even Rabbits set much store by her verdicts. It was at a tea-party given by Rabbits for local Reformers that he first became keenly aware of Catherine—when the host, anxious to show off his prodigy's paces, urged William to recite an American temperance poem.

At first Booth had demurred. Never in the conventional sense a sociable man, he was acutely uneasy in social gatherings. Nor was he, at this stage of his life, a total abstainer; he had no wish to disconcert the guests. Only the gentle musical voice of the dark-eyed girl pleading from the sofa overcame his qualms.

The reluctant cynosure of all eyes, Booth launched painfully into

THE GROG-SELLER'S DREAM
A grog-seller sat by his bar-room fire,
His feet as high as his head and higher . . .
Foolish and fuddled, his friends had gone,
To wake in the morn to a drunkard's pain,
With bloodshot eyes and a reeling brain . . .

An aching silence followed—until one moderate drinker, taking umbrage, launched into a white-hot defence of his habits. But afterwards Booth could never remember much of the noisy argument which ensued. All he remembered was that Catherine's clear determined voice had rung out above the others, defending the principles he had expounded. And, when the guests, shortly afterwards, filed into the dining-room for supper, the wine remained untasted. Everyone was at pains to stress how much they preferred water.

But this third meeting with Catherine, on Good Friday, proved the turning point in both their lives. The meeting over, Booth offered to escort Miss Mumford home to Brixton by hackney coach. Soon it was plain that the lurching carriage, the animated conversation, was exhausting the delicate girl To Catherine's delight the masterful Booth summarily forbade her to talk.

There were many things about Catherine Mumford Booth could not then know. A Derbyshire girl whose family had moved to South London, all her life had been a battle against ill-health : spinal curvature at the age of fourteen, incipient tuberculosis four years later. Amazingly, at twelve years old, she had already read her Bible several times. At twelve, she could worst her father in argument, on an adult level, over the Catholic Emancipation Bill.

But Catherine, as Booth would discover, was no precious parlour intellectual whose sympathies with the poor stopped short of true involvement. In Boston, Lincolnshire, where she spent her youth, the citizens would long remember the dainty little girl with flashing eyes who threw aside hoop and stick to walk beside a drunken man the constable was frogmarching to the lock-up. To prove that there was just one friend in the jeering mob that hounded him, Catherine Mumford had made her first recorded protest.

Booth, of course, knew none of this until much later. He knew only that, after accepting her parents' invitation to stay the night, he left the Mumfords' house at Russell Street, Brixton, next morning " feeling . . . wounded." For Booth had fallen deeply in love and knew that he was loved in return. Yet how could a man support a delicate wife on twenty shillings a week ?

Booth liked best to illustrate the progress of their orthodox Victorian courtship by recalling the time he and Catherine's mother were chatting in the Russell Street drawing-room. Suddenly an anguished cry of " William ! " rent the air. Hastening into the garden, Booth was horrified to find that his beloved had been stung by a wasp—yet mingled with his distress was a certain inner glow. It was, it dawned on him, the first time that Catherine had ever used his Christian name—and she had called for *him*, not Mrs. Mumford.

" Conceit, you see," Booth would wind up dryly.

Darling, I've Found my Destiny

For Booth, inspired by his chosen love, the next thirteen years were to prove an eventful odyssey. Already, before 1853 had dawned, he and Catherine, after obtaining her parents' willing consent, had become engaged—a daring step, for Booth's fortunes now seemed at lowest ebb. Following differences of opinion, Edward Rabbits did not renew the three-month contract : to live at all Booth began to sell his furniture, drawing on his meagre savings. Time and again, Catherine fought to bolster his crumbling morale : " Never mind. Do not give way. God loves you. He will sustain you."

But for Catherine, Booth acknowledged, he could never have fulfilled his great life's work. Her tact, her keen intellect, her maturity, were needful checks to Booth's mercurial spirit. Where Booth's heart ruled him Catherine was cool, level-headed. Her long reasoned letters—often 2,500 words, twelve folios long—were fresh reasons for battling on when black despair or self-pity seized him.

Often it seemed a one-way courtship—conducted, through sheer necessity, on paper. In 1852, the Reformers gave Booth charge of the Spalding circuit, south Lincolnshire, a hundred miles from London; for the next eighteen months, trudging on foot or rattling in a gig over the flat fenlands of his twenty-seven mile wide parish he had little time for love-letters. But Catherine, with time on her hands, wrote almost daily, worrying about William's health (" don't sit up singing until twelve after a hard day's work "), advising him, sometimes rebuking, always promising hope for the future (" we will make home to each other the brightest spot on earth, we will be tender, *thoughtful*, loving and *forbearing* . . . yes, we will ! ").

Already, to Catherine, William was a man of destiny ; to him she was a haven from the world's troubled seas and his distress signals were frequent. " I want a sermon on the Flood, one on Jonah, and one on the Judgment. Send me some bare thoughts ; some clear startling outlines. Nothing moves the people like the terrific . . ."

Strangely, their one lovers' quarrel centred round an issue which later knew no stronger champion than William Booth :

the equality of the sexes. An avowed feminist, Catherine penned a blistering retort to a minister who publicly dismissed women as the weaker sex, forwarding a copy to her fiancé on circuit. But Booth, to her entire mortification, took the Minister's part.

Catherine would have none of it. " Oh prejudice, what will it not do ! " she raged, " That . . . woman is in any respect except physical strength and courage inferior to man I cannot see *cause* to believe, and I am sure no one can prove it from the word of God." Like many a lover before and since, Booth was forced to compromise. " I would not encourage a woman to begin preaching," he wrote bravely, then added a hasty rider, " although I would not stop her on any account . . . I would not stop you if I had power to do so, although I should not like it."

He ended in conciliatory mood ; her remarks on woman's position he would read yet again. " I am for the world's salvation ; I will quarrel with no means that promises help."

By great good fortune, their wedding—on 16th June, 1855, at Stockwell New Chapel, South London—saw Booth already established as a Dissenting Minister. Despite his triumphs at Spalding the young couple had faced their future clear-sightedly : only a systematic study of theology in a training college could establish Booth as a truly ordained minister. Secretly Booth hankered after Spalding, where the simple rural congregations idolised him—" Oh, the stagnation into which I had settled down," he confessed later—but Catherine was adamant. It was she who had taken the vital step of pressing him to return and enrol at a small crammer's run by a breakaway sect of their church, the Methodist New Connexion, at Albany Road, Camberwell, South London. There, under the Rev. Dr. William Cooke, Booth, the red-hot evangelist, wrestled to master Greek and Latin grammar and saw less of Catherine than ever. At Dr. Cooke's, he recorded ruefully, students rose each day at five a.m.

A warm-hearted old man, who looked like a well-to-do farmer, Cooke soon saw that Booth was no ordinary theo-logical student. On the day of his enrolment, preaching in the local Brunswick Chapel, he made fifteen converts. His sermons were charged with thunderous fervour; once, picturing the world's sinners as like shipwrecked men whom only Christ could save, he leapt on to the seat at the back of the pulpit, wildly waving his pocket handkerchief by way of a distress signal. He spent more hours away from his books than any student should. Yet so impressed was Cooke with the youngster's love of mankind that months before due time he proposed the 23-year-old Booth as a London Circuit Superintendent.

But Booth, after the years of prayer and preparation, now held back; he doubted his own ability. At length a compromise was reached : Booth became deputy superintendent, quit of all business ties, free to devote himself to evangelism. And his masters made another concession. Most New Connexion ministers were free to marry only after four years' probation—yet Booth's star now shone so brightly that permission to marry Catherine was granted after one year. Their honeymoon was in true Booth tradition—one week's relaxation at Ryde, Isle of Wight, then a whirlwind revivalist tour of Guernsey.

Already at twenty-six many felt that Booth was driving his frail body close to breaking point; to Catherine it seemed she had married not a man but a human dynamo. Others showed equal concern. At nineteen, a doctor had warned Booth that a man with a nervous system like his needed a frame like a bullock and a chest like a prize-fighter to survive : twelve months as an evangelist would kill him. Seven years later, when Booth's working pace approached fever-pitch, an insurance company reported sadly that only an increased premium could ever induce them to insure his life.

Booth, massaging his chest with cold water, swallowing raw eggs for breakfast, paid the larger premium without a murmur. He was to go on paying it for almost sixty years.

At first the young couple had no settled home; Booth was accepted as the New Connexion's travelling campaigner. A fixed stipend of £2 a week left little room for luxuries. Before long Catherine's health cracked under the strain of makeshift lodgings, unheated trains, and endless chapel services. Often William had to leave her behind as he journeyed and Catherine confessed : " I feel as if part of myself were wanting."

Lincoln . . . Bristol . . . Bradford . . . Manchester . . . Sheffield—within months all these cities felt the cyclone impact of Booth's personality. " No Flying Scotsman is fast enough for me," he wrote, in the years when George and Robert Stephenson's locomotives were laying a trail of steam and sulphur across Britain. Already he was exploring a new and notable technique : after the service, when penitents came to the communion rail, two officials were now on hand to conduct them to the vestry. Names, addresses, personal details—all were noted down, before a proven convert took full charge of each penitent.

It was as if Booth, remembering his very first sermon of the mother and her child, was fearful lest his converts should falter.

But through the eighteen-fifties, the old story of Broad Street Chapel was repeated time and again. Once, in a space of months, Booth made over 1,700 converts, an average of twenty-three a day, but soon the Connexion leaders saw him as going too far, too fast : his methods were lusty American rather than Victorian English. After his whirlwind revival meetings, the organisation of converts and the routine of follow-up was left to local officials ; it was Booth, shuttling from town to town, who got the press-notices, the fanfare. One critic spoke for all : " He is taking the cream and leaving the skimmed milk for others."

In 1857, the Connexion cut short Booth's country-wide travels. He was given charge of one of their least-promising circuits, the grimy little milltown of Brighouse, Yorkshire. But if Booth's sphere of influence was narrowed to regular pastoral work they could not entirely tie his hands. Always before him he held Wesley's eleventh rule for his helpers : " You have nothing to do but save souls . . . go always not only to those who need you, but to those who need you most."

Darling, I've Found my Destiny

At Brighouse, the Booths came closer than ever before to the masses who needed them. They agitated for a law to prohibit girls under twenty from working in the factories before one p.m. They battled to improve the lot of the " half-timers," seven-year-old mill girls working a fourteen-hour day, with only the whiplash of an overseer's strap to keep them awake. Their own first child, christened William Bramwell after a famous preacher, had been born a year earlier.

Though Booth chafed against fixed circuit work, close friends hinted that this arrangement was only temporary. It would not hurt to propitiate the powers-that-be. But in 1858, the year that he became a fully ordained minister, Booth was given yet another circuit, this time Gateshead, a bleak industrial suburb of Newcastle-on-Tyne.

Once more, contrary to his better judgment, he obeyed— but time and again his eyes would stray from the thousand-strong congregation of Gateshead's Bethseda Chapel to the miles of mean slate roofs beyond the chapel's windows. The thought obsessed him : " In how many of those houses is the name of Christ never mentioned ? Why am I here, with this crowded chapel of people who *want* to hear the message ? Why am I not outside, bringing the message of God to those who *don't* want it ? "

Two years passed—memorable mainly for the fact that Catherine herself began to preach. One morning in the chapel, a strange compulsion seized her : before the service was over she must rise and speak. " You will look like a fool and have nothing to say " an inner voice taunted her, but Catherine heard this as the Devil's voice and this time the Devil had over-reached himself. " That's just the point," she retorted, " I have never yet been willing to be a fool for Christ. Now I *will* be one."

From the pulpit Booth now glimpsed a perplexing sight : abruptly his wife had left her seat and was walking slowly towards him down the aisle. A stifled buzz of comment arose from a thousand voices ; over the past two years Catherine's timid bashful nature had become a byword. At once, all solicitude, Booth was at her side. " What is it, my dear ? "

Like all the rest of the congregation he concluded that Catherine was ill.

" I want to say a word," Catherine heard herself reply, her voice made higher by nervousness. Booth himself was so astonished that he could only announce meekly : " My dear wife wishes to speak." Then he sat down.

" I dare say many of you have been looking on me as a very devoted woman," Catherine told the rapt congregation, " but I have been disobeying God . . ." And she went on : she, who had never ceased to proclaim woman's right and duty to preach, had striven against the divine revelation. Greatly wondering, Booth saw now that many of the congregation were weeping.

But Booth's swift practical mind was working overtime : despite his earlier misgivings here was an attraction that would pack the chapel out for months to come. No sooner had Catherine finished speaking than he hurried to her for a whispered consultation before once more hastening to the pulpit. " To-night," he exclaimed triumphantly, " My wife will be the preacher."

It was a revolutionary step. Though Catherine's fame as " The Woman Preacher " was destined to endure for twenty-eight years and to spread far beyond Gateshead, many leading Methodists shook their heads. Most Victorian women lived in a world of sandalwood fans, white kid-gloves and tortoise-shell card cases ; a respectable woman who raised her voice in public risked grave censure. And soon after, when Booth fell ill and Catherine took full charge of Bethseda Chapel, already-existing doubts were reinforced. These independent Booths needed curbing.

By May, 1861, Booth was facing one of the greatest crises of his life. Both he and Catherine knew that their own future would be one of the most hotly-debated points at the New Connexion's Annual Conference in Liverpool's Bethseda Chapel. Booth had more than a shrewd idea that his special request—to be relieved from a circuit minister's duties and set apart as an evangelist—would be rejected out of hand.

But not until Saturday, 25th May, one week after the Conference had opened, was the burning question of Booth's future at last raised. By now the members were tired and fidgety; through the chapel's wintry gloom, the voices debating the young man's petition were edged with anger. One minister stated flatly that Booth's request was "against all reason and authority." "It would be bad for him and bad for the circuit," snapped another. Now Dr. William Cooke, principal of Booth's old seminary, stepped in as peacemaker. If Booth took over the Newcastle circuit, couldn't he, by special arrangement with his officers, occasionally take time out for evangelistic work elsewhere? With sinking heart Booth heard this amendment carried by a large majority. He was trapped.

As Superintendent Preacher of the Newcastle circuit, Booth could, of course, grant himself permission to conduct revival meetings anywhere else in Britain—but how could any responsible man leave the Connexion's largest toughest circuit to his juniors? They had given him his freedom—and clamped bars about him.

Now a startling incident occurred—startling because, minutes earlier, the President, Dr. Henry Crofts, determined to thrash out Booth's future in camera, had ordered the public gallery cleared. Yet now, from far above, a voice challenged their verdict: "No—never!" Catherine Booth, after vacating her gallery seat, had still lingered by the door at the head of the stairs—and suddenly her anger and disappointment could no longer be contained.

"Are the doors not closed?" cried Dr. Crofts, outraged, "Close the doors!"

Her protest made, Catherine withdrew but when the conference ended, Booth took up his hat and left the chapel, to find her waiting in the porch. Several ministers sought to detain him, but Booth brushed them quietly aside, not speaking: his heart was too full for words. Within two months he had resigned from the Connexion.

He was thirty-two years old with four children, and his prospects seemed more hopeless than they had ever been.

But whatever the New Connexion's stand, the Booths' star-potential was undeniable. An invitation from sympathisers to conduct a short revival at Hayle, Cornwall, grew by degrees to a mammoth eighteen-month campaign, unparalleled since Wesley's day. To hear William Booth and his wife preach, fishermen rowed ten miles across dark and choppy seas; villagers tramped for miles over the hills. "Business is no longer carried out," a local noted. "The shopkeepers and their customers are all busily engaged in the Booth meetings . . ." At these meetings, Booth claimed, seven thousand Cornishmen found peace with God.

"All Britain is now open to you," a fellow evangelist exulted, but Booth tasted the bitter truth : soon the chapels of the New Connexion barred their doors to him. Undaunted, he pioneered South Wales; for the first time in religious history he unashamedly hired secular buildings to which the lost and degraded would come. At Cardiff, two wealthy young shipowners, John and Richard Cory, came to his rallies in a circus tent then reached as one for their cheque-books—the beginnings of a patronage which lasted almost fifty years.

"We cannot get at the masses in the chapels," Catherine wrote, for now coming events were casting their shadows. At Walsall, Staffordshire, Booth's United Monster Camp Meeting featured for the first time the kind of men he sought to reclaim—" Converted Pugilists, Horse-Racers, Poachers and Others from Birmingham, Liverpool and Nottingham. . . ."

Then, in March, 1865, Catherine, a Londoner by inclination, eagerly seized the chance to lead revival services in the smoky dockland parishes of Rotherhithe and Bermondsey. But Booth, at first, held back; to him their lodgings in Shaftesbury Road, Hammersmith, were no more than a makeshift base for his new-style provincial campaigns. Then, overnight, an invitation from the East London Special Services Committee changed his mind. Forbidden by the police to hold meetings in parks, they had obtained sanction to erect a tent on the disused Quaker burial ground off Thomas (later Fulbourne) Street, a stone's throw from the slums of Whitechapel Road.

On Sunday, 2nd July, 1865, a few minutes before his first

service, Booth watched a lad threading the naphtha lamps which were to light the tent on to a length of rope. " One of these days," Booth said softly, " they will be stringing lights just like that round the world." The strange prophecy came to pass, for in this week Booth saw Mile End Road and his destiny was at last made plain to him.

If Catherine was for once the doubter, this was pardonable. Close at hand, William was sprawled in a wing chair and as from a long way off, she heard his voice, a visionary's voice, recounting the horrors of Mile End : " Where can you go and find such heathen as these—and where is there so great a need for your labour ? "

But Catherine, staring into the fire, seemed to hear another voice : " This means *another* new departure—*another* start in life." Until now, through collections taken at their meetings, the sale of books and pamphlets, they had somehow, on less than £400 a year, brought up six children. But how could they make a living among poverty-stricken East Enders—and who would go bond for them ? What of William's resolution, only three months old, to pare their joint expenditure to £200 a year ?

An eternity of silence, then Booth heard his wife's decision : " Well, if you feel you ought to stay, stay. We have trusted the Lord once for our support, and we can trust Him again."

It was a valiant resolution—for outside the close-knit Methodist world, Booth had little repute, no renown. Only recently he had assessed his personal debts at £85. Later, as the only family man ever to found a giant religious organisation, he would enlarge it within his lifetime to a £1,000,000 concern. He would become a household name throughout the world, on intimate terms with King Edward VII, William Ewart Gladstone, Winston Churchill, President Theodore Roosevelt and Lord Northcliffe. He would found a religion which some derided as " corybantic Christianity " and others hailed as the Saviour's own way. He would command the attention of millions with methods that Barnum or William Randolph Hearst might well have envied. And he would make himself an international legend. Once, at a great rally in Paris, a senior officer of the French Army would grip him by the hand and say, " General Booth, you are not an Englishman, you belong to mankind ! "

But this was 1865, and Booth had nothing but his deep-seated conviction to sustain him : the conviction that the churches had failed the people. To Booth, all men and women stood equal before God, yet in many churches, where the private pews of the rich stood empty for months at a time, the poor were expected to rise when the service ended and stand curtsying or touching their forelocks as the parson strode through their midst. Aside from Christian Socialists like the Rev. Charles Kingsley, famous author of *Westward Ho !*, few clerics sought to grapple with their problems, but Kingsley, a Professor of Modern History at Cambridge University was not, like Booth, a man of the people.

" Read your Bible," was one parson's reply when a drunken miner sought his help, but the man had to confess it : he could not read. Then, the parson suggested, he should come to church. But when the man explained he had only working clothes, the parson ran out of solutions. God might help him ; his spiritual adviser was powerless.

This was typical of the age in which Booth laboured, an age when Queen Victoria wrote proudly that she could never be the Queen of " a democratic monarchy." As yet only one man in twenty-four had the vote ; almost twenty years would pass before the number whittled down to one in seven. Cut-throat competition had bred a harsh ruthlessness that scorned poverty and idolised success ; the Bible of the day was Samuel Smiles's *Self-Help*, a success handbook which five years back had sold 130,000 copies. And, save on Sundays, few parsons had any faith in the common man ; over six thousand of them owed their livings to wealthy private patrons. Some even warmly approved overcrowding—" it kept the poor snug in cold weather."

London's aristocracy were equally broken reeds : the poor were the servants of their tainted pleasures. At Jimmy Shaw's rat-pit in Windmill Street, Soho, rich and poor crowded the arena to see trained terriers slaughter up to a thousand rats per night : to make the outcome certain, the rats' teeth were first drawn with pincers. Nearby, at the cockpit in Endell Street, grimy costers and titled women screamed their approval as the Duke of Hamilton matched his birds and the white sanded floor grew grained with blood. Slumming parties to the dancing booths and opium dens of East London's Ratcliffe Highway were all the fashion ; their chief organiser, Lord Hastings, had in six years lost over £103,000 on the turf. Men like these saw the poor as a week-night peepshow while the clergy saw them as a race apart—not men and women with souls, to rate compassion.

That was why William Booth set out to save the world.

"Be Like the Irishman's Gun..."

1865-79

Time was, William Booth was wont to say, when his whole organisation was under one hat—his own size 7 Lincoln Bennet topper.

Yet the irony was that Booth's decision to stay on in London through the summer of 1865 was not prompted by any ambitions to found an army or even a new religious society. His sole aim was to convert the outcasts the clergy did not reach—and, having converted them, pass them on to the churches then existing.

But the thousands who flocked that summer to the swings and coconut-shies of Mile End Waste, a mile-long strip of broken ground between the pavement and the main Mile End Road, paid little heed to the tall dark stranger, his Bible beneath his arm, who exhorted them outside The Blind Beggar or The Vine taverns. Years later, his eldest son, Bramwell, would reflect, dryly, on the men he met all over the globe, eager to relate how they had " stood with your father when he was alone on Mile End Waste."

Far from standing alone, Bramwell twinkled, Booth would literally have been hemmed in by hundreds, instead of by the meagre handful of converts he first assembled—Thomas Haywood of Bethnal Green, a twenty-five-year-old alcoholic, Billy Ferris, a Limehouse navvy, " Mother " Moore, a drunken Whitechapel charwoman. Won from alcoholism by Booth's passionate oratory, " Mother " Moore became famous for her classic retort to the next man who offered her a pint : " *I* can drink of the wells of salvation—and so can you ! "

For Booth, in these first years, the winning of East Enders to Christ was a bitter uphill struggle. " The sins of London didn't shock him," one of his family recalled later. " They seemed to tear at his heart with claws that drew blood." The buildings he chose as tabernacles show the depths he sought to plumb : when autumn gales tore their tent on the Quaker burial ground to ribbons, Booth and his little band of followers promptly hired Professor Orson's Dancing Academy, a dance hall in New Road, Whitechapel. At four a.m. on Sundays, when the crash of clogs and the scraping of fiddles subsided, his faithful converts were already lined up to haul in over three hundred seats for that day's services.

For weeknight services there was an old wool warehouse in Three Colts Lane, Bethnal Green, where urchins hurled stones, mud, even fireworks, through the high windows. And Booth hired other buildings too—the Alexandra Hall Skittle-Alley at Bedford Street, Whitechapel ; a carpenter's shop at Old Ford ; the East London Theatre, Whitechapel Road ; a hot little room reeking of ammonia behind a pigeon shop in Shoreditch, where fowls clucked endlessly as Booth orated. For a time he even preached in a hayloft so cramped that his top hat narrowly missed the ceiling.

For a man as highly strung as Booth it was a gruelling life. At this stage of his career he was so poor that his income never topped £3 a week. Until November, 1865, when he moved his wife, six children and their Irish maidservant, Mary Kirkton, to new quarters at No. 1 Cambridge Lodge Villas, Hackney, East London, he trudged the eight miles from Hammersmith to the East End each Sunday and eight miles back. Lunch was bread and cheese, eaten from a paper bag in James Flawn's refreshment rooms in Pudding Lane, where the Great Fire of London began. Afterwards Flawn, an early convert, made him a cup of cocoa and the bone-tired Booth stretched out on a back-room sofa until it was time to return to work.

Afterwards, recalling those years, Catherine would narrate how night after night William stumbled home to the house in Hackney, usually after midnight, always haggard with fatigue.

Often his clothes were torn; bloody bandages swathing his head showed where a stone or a cudgel had struck him, or how he had been hurled against a kerbstone while preaching the love of God. Some nights he did not come home at all.

No man less inspired than Booth could have weathered such discouragement. After twelve months' unflagging work his remaining supporters tallied only sixty; a few had departed to pursue private visions of their own. One, a talkative young medical student from London Hospital, Thomas Barnardo, who helped Booth at many indoor meetings, left the Missioners to devote his life to the rescue of London's homeless boys. Hiring a house off Bull Lane, Stepney, for twelve shillings a week, he began, step by step, to fashion the world-famous organisation which has since cared for almost 164,000 orphan boys.

Again, with uncanny foresight, Booth seemed to divine that, like himself, this sturdy grey-eyed twenty-one-year-old faced an unbounded future. " You look after the children and I'll look after the adults," was his farewell salutation. " Then together we'll convert the world."

But others divorced themselves from Booth because they found the rowdyism of the East London mobs unendurable. At the Three Colts Lane warehouse, roughs even fired a train of gunpowder; one missioner, Mrs. Eliza Totman, narrowly escaped cremation alive when her gown caught fire. And Booth himself was perhaps the only evangelist in the world to need a private bodyguard—Peter Monk, an Irish prize-fighter converted in the Tent, who became famous as " The General's Boxer." At times, when meetings grew tense and ugly, Monk, jacket off, sleeves rolled up to reveal swelling biceps, would stalk ominously down the aisles while Booth spoke up for Christ.

" In two minutes all those blackguards were as quiet as lambs," Monk recalled grimly.

The mission's geographical confines were swift to disappear. The Christian Revival Association, as Booth first styled it, was absorbed in The East London Christian Mission; soon, with suburban stations opening south of London, at

Croydon and Bromley, it became The Christian Mission. For Booth appealed to the public for support, and wealthy philanthropists, fired by the patience with which his little band endured persecution, came staunchly to the rescue. Among the first was Samuel Morley, an austere Nottingham textile manufacturer, but over the years, others quickly followed. Thomas Denny, a wealthy bulldog-jawed bacon merchant with a house on Connaught Place, Hyde Park, subscribed many thousands of pounds. There was Henry Reed, a wealthy Tasmanian landowner, who later settled £5,000 on Booth, the income to be enjoyed by him during his lifetime; Albert Freeman, a successful American merchant from Shanghai; the Cardiff shipowners, John and Richard Cory, and John Melrose, an Edinburgh tea-merchant.

Only Mr. F. A. Bevan, head of the banking firm now known as Barclay's, saw Booth's venture as a leap in the dark. Despite a generous donation of £10, he wrote regretfully: "As I don't want to encourage you in keeping up the extensive machinery you have set afloat, I must decline to help the work."

There were grounds for doubt. Already more than five hundred charitable societies doled out an annual £3,500,000 in alms in East London alone—yet despite their efforts, thirty thousand Londoners were gaoled in the same period. Faced with such dire facts, Booth needed all the valour that Catherine could inspire in him. "If we get tired we had better go and be done with," she rallied him. "Anything is better than a dead church." It was caution and careful organisation that Catherine counselled most, while Booth, now looking eagerly ahead, now despairing, saw only the gaol: somehow these people must be saved. On bad days he grew tense and irritable, and his children, who called these "Bishop's Visitation Days," quickly learned to make themselves scarce. Only with Catherine, did Booth, all his life, preserve a young lover's tenderness. Returning home weary beyond belief, he would take her hand as he entered the hall and say simply: "Kate, let me pray with you." Then he would rise from his knees armed with fresh courage.

But though Booth loved the poor, his years as a Methodist

minister had drawn him insensibly apart from them. He could not overnight divest himself of his black frock coat and umbrella and become again the pawnbroker's boy who led the roughs to Broad Street Chapel. Yet the solution once it dawned on him was simple. Addressing a congregation 1,200 strong one evening in Whitechapel, Booth, despairing of his lackadaisical audience, called upon an old gipsy hawker, converted a few weeks earlier, to speak. As the old man began his simple faltering testimony, an unnatural quiet fell upon the meeting.

Never too proud to learn, Booth now saw the sober truth : ordinary working-men in their corduroys and bowler hats could command an attention which was refused to him point-blank. Courageously, he acknowledged the lesson he had learned to his son Bramwell : " I shall have to burn all those sermons of mine and go in for the gipsy's."

In an era when preachers favoured mellifluous phrases, this was revolutionary. But hard experience was forcing Booth back to interpret literally the tenets of Christ. The Saviour had not commanded His apostles to be preachers of sermons ; He had sent them forth as witnesses of their experience of saving grace. He had made Matthew, the publican, an apostle ; Peter, who had fallen as badly, another. What better support could a convert have than the knowledge that he was an active co-operator in the conversion of others ? From this a man could derive a sense of honour, self-assurance, confidence in his own moral strength.

" Just don't start preaching," Booth implored them, " I've got quite enough broken-down parsons on my hands without that."

At first he had sought to return his converts to the churches but found they would not go. Most saw the old stone shrines like St. Paul's and Westminster Abbey as places apart, the province of the well-to-do. And while many churchwardens looked askance at worshippers without Sunday suits, only one man in thirty at Booth's meetings ever wore a collar : the remainder sported rough twisted scarves. Now Booth decided he would no longer strive to return men and women reclaimed to churches that did not want them. He would marshal them for the redemption of their own kind.

From the first he knew just where to lay hands on his preachers. As a teenager, Bramwell Booth never forgot the first time his father led him into an East End pub : gas-jets playing eerily on men's inflamed faces, drunken dishevelled women openly suckling tiny children, the reek of gin and shag tobacco and acrid bodies.

After a moment, seeing the appalled look on his son's face, William Booth said quietly : " These are our people. These are the people I want you to live for and bring to Christ."

It was a daunting task. London's 100,000 pubs, laid end to end, would have stretched a full thirty miles. In East London alone, the heart of Booth's territory, every fifth shop was a gin-shop ; most kept special steps to help even tiny mites reach the counter. The pubs featured penny glasses of gin for children ; too often child alcoholics needed the stomach pump. Children less than five years old knew the raging agonies of delirium tremens or died from cirrhosis of the liver. Others trudged through the Sunday streets bringing yet more gin to parents who lay drunk and fully clothed in bed, vomiting on the floor. These were the by-products of a £100 million a year trade, whose worst victims slept on heaps of soot beneath the arches of Blackfriars Bridge, living only for the next glass.

But seventy years before Alcoholics Anonymous, Booth saw alcoholism for the sickness that it was. From these pubs he now began to recruit his first shock-troops—men who had known the craving for liquor from infancy, soon, through their frequent use of the Hebrew phrase meaning "Praise the Lord," known as the " Hallelujahs." Typical was Jimmie Glover, an illiterate potboy, reduced through drink to sleeping in pigsties. Whenever Catherine Booth travelled by train, Glover went with her and the coach became a classroom ; on these journeys he learned to spell, read and tell the time. Until his death in 1901, he was for thirty years a loyal follower of Booth. Rodney " Gipsy " Smith, later a world-famous evangelist, was, when Booth found him, more used to washing in dew and sleeping in wheatfields; now, as a 17-year-old preacher, in frock-coat and striped trousers, he plumbed for the first time the mysteries of beds and handbasins. John Allen, a trigger-tempered 16-stone Poplar navvy, converted in a meeting at Millwall Docks, gathered other like-minded navvies about him; he became a Sabbatarian so strict that if the clock struck Saturday midnight while he was cleaning his boots he appeared at Sunday services with one boot dingy and the other gleaming. Yet Allen, appointed by Booth to Cardiff, single-handed converted two hundred seamen. One ship's captain delayed sailing for two days while the ex-navvy helped him to find peace with God.

What such men lacked in education they made up for in pungent native wit that the masses loved; despite their strange wide-brimmed hats and umbrellas, their Methodist titles of " exhorters " and " leaders," they could hold a crowd spellbound. " *They* are going to build a public house called The Bull," Allen would tell his street audiences, then add with mordant humour, " and *we* are going to put a ring through its nose." Rodney " Gipsy " Smith was no whit abashed, arriving at Chatham, Kent, when the converts avowed he was too young to lead them. " If you let me stop here awhile," Smith reasoned, " I shall get older. If I haven't any more whiskers than a gooseberry I have got a wife."

But Booth's most valued aide in this era was a man destined to serve the cause unstintedly for forty-eight years—24-year-old George Scott Railton, a stocky bearded ascetic, who already, to Booth's amusement, had set out on a one-man crusade to convert Morocco bearing a banner inscribed " Repentance—Faith—Holiness." A lovable eccentric, capable of laughing until the tears ran down his face, Railton had quit one well-paid job in an export merchant's because commercial ethics called for twisting the truth. Then, as part-time Methodist Mission worker at Middlesbrough, Yorkshire, holding extempore services in a butcher's shop with the block serving as pulpit, he chanced on Booth's sixpenny pamphlet *How to Reach the Masses with the Gospel*. " These," he exclaimed, eyes afire, " are the people for me."

Joining Booth as his private secretary in March, 1873, he agreed to lodge temporarily with the family. He remained a beloved member of the household for eleven eventful years.

At once in sympathy with Catherine Booth, who shared his belief in hard work and self-denial, Railton was indefatigable from the first. A meagre breakfast of coarse biscuits nourished him for the new day's ventures. Indifferent to hardship, his habit of walking abroad bare-headed, uncommon in those days, caused Catherine such concern that she fashioned him a silk skull-cap. Some evangelists shook their heads over a man who advocated " praying till your knees were petrified and preaching until you were too hoarse to make yourself heard," but Railton's stamina got results. Once, returning late without a key and anxious not to disturb the family, he slept content-edly on top of the scullery copper.

Booth had need of such an organiser. Though the bulk of his stations were still in East London, others had opened farther afield—at Hastings in Sussex and Tunbridge Wells in Kent. Yet the only staff available to deal with the problems arising at Booth's new headquarters, 272 Whitechapel Road, were Henry Edmonds, a teenage sea-captain's son from Portland, Maine, and Mrs. Pamela Shepherd, the cook and caretaker, who later launched a ten-year non-stop revival in the Rhondda Valley. Often debts went unpaid, letters went off incorrectly addressed, and Booth, his patience exhausted, would rail : " I will sweep you all into the street if this sort of thing happens again."

For Booth's movement was growing more quickly than even he had intended. He himself was still tied to the East End, but Catherine, much in demand as a preacher, travelled wherever she was invited. Always her sermons drew converts who needed guidance ; the sole solution was to send evangelists post-haste to open new stations. Within ten years of his first sermon at Mile End Booth's followers had spread the word from Millwall Docks to Manchester, from Hastings to Heck-mondwike, Yorkshire. Postings took place at lightning speed; three posts in six months was routine and no evangelist stayed more than six months at one station. Booth was not aiming for settled communities of virtuous folk sitting under a favourite preacher : he wanted " Godly go-ahead dare-devils."

" Make your will, pack your box, kiss your girl, be ready in a week," were his terse instructions to one volunteer. To another, prospecting the chances of initial training, Booth explained kindly. " You must be like the Irishman's gun— go off, loaded or not ! "

By August, 1877, these selfless endeavours had established twenty-six flourishing stations—and a movement which in 1870 had cost a bare £50 a week to finance, ten years later saw the poor alone contributing £14,580 towards the soaring running costs. *The East London Evangelist*, the lively sixteen-page monthly Booth launched in 1868 packed with sensational sub-headings—" Son of Belial," " A Raging Mob Defied " —had given place to the showmanlike *Christian Mission Magazine*.

From the first, of course, the Booth family were in the thick of the campaign. To Catherine it seemed that from December, 1868, when they left Cambridge Lodge Villas for No. 3 Gore Road, Victoria Park, Hackney, home life was ever after at a premium. Abetted by the ardent Railton, Booth pressed attics, even bedrooms, into service as offices. If Catherine retreated to the kitchen to confer with Honor Fells, the cook, William was soon there beside her, perched on the scrubbed kitchen-table in his shirt-sleeves, talking excitedly of plans and sermons while she mixed whole-wheat bread. Even the nursery was a kind of Christian Mission seminary where the children, with their father's true dramatic instinct, re-enacted the Bible's age-old dramas—David and Goliath or Daniel and the Lions. At times their craving for realism scaled undreamed-of peaks : no French polisher in London could have restored the charred surface of the nursery table, where every beast from the giant Noah's Ark in turn became the burnt offering enjoined by the Book of Leviticus.

Discord was not unknown. Often to the chagrin of Booth's second son, Ballington, a dark lean eleven-year-old who

Bitter, often bloody, opposition marked the Army's early years. While eminent men like zoologist T. H. Huxley (top left) and the Earl of Shaftesbury branded Booth 'anti-Christ', mobs like Worthing's Skeleton Army, 4,000 strong, razed Army barracks, didn't stop short at murder

Undaunted by mobs or magistrates, Booth's shock troops, by the end of the century, fought sin and oppression on three continents. Among them (top left and right) were Bramwell Booth, the Army's second General, his wife Florence, pioneer crusader against the teenage vice traffic, and (bottom left) Evangeline ("Little Eva") Booth, whose

flower-girl disguises were legendary. On the right: Australia's pioneer prison reformer, Major James Barker; George Railton, America's bearded ascetic first leader, and his wife Deborah; W. T. Stead, hard-hitting editor of *The Pall Mall Gazette*, whose Salvationist affiliations cost him a gaol sentence

STARS & STRIPES ARRESTED. WE FIGHT FOR LIBERTY.

"Arrested fifty-seven times for Jesus". Joseph Neshan Garabedban, self-styled "Joe the Turk", won freedom of worship in key American cities from San Francisco to Saratoga. An incorrigible showman, Joe's exploits included seizing the mayoralty of a corrupt township, soliciting Army funds dressed as Santa Claus, playing Salvation songs on a saxophone

already fancied himself as a preacher, Kate, aged ten, and Emma, aged eight, brought fractious dolls to his impromptu services. When Ballington ordered sternly " Take those babies out of the theatre," his sisters, triumphant, pointed a sterner example of endurance : " Papa would not have stopped— Papa would have gone on preaching."

In despair, Ballington would turn his attentions to a convert —usually a pillow—who stood in urgent need of sanctification. " This is a good case," he would enthuse, lugging it towards a makeshift communion-rail. " Give up the drink, brother."

Through all this tumult, Catherine Booth worked serenely on in her sanctum below—her peace ensured by a double ceiling packed with sawdust, installed by a friendly builder.

It wasn't that William and Catherine constantly exhorted the children to follow their example : the pattern was plain to see. Once Catherine did tell Kate : " You are not in this world for yourself. You have been sent for others. The world is waiting for you." But years later red-haired Evangeline, who had been born on Christmas Day, 1865, recalled : " My parents did not have to say a word to me about Christianity. I saw it in action." Even in those days, Evangeline, whom Booth had singled out as an orator after his own heart, had her father's innate sense of showmanship. As a small girl she once attired Jeannie her pet marmoset, as an evangelist. In her teens the dolls' hospital she started on her own initiative for slum children, served to rivet the attention of many local families.

But it was Bramwell, Booth's eldest son, who bore the initial brunt of the crusade ; not for nothing had the family nicknamed him " The Dray Horse." A tall pale refined boy, made solitary and withdrawn by deafness, he early learned hard lessons for a ten-year-old. At preparatory school, where he was derided as " Holy Willie," bullies once seized him by the head and legs, smashing him repeatedly against a tree-trunk " to bang religion out of him." Somehow he had reeled home spitting blood ; long months of pleurisy and rheumatic fever followed. At his next academy, the City of London School, Milk Street, Cheapside, he was the solitary boy who lunched off a pasty in St. Paul's Churchyard, whose only friends were pigeons in quest of crumbs. Bramwell did not complain; it was as if he accepted that his whole life would be a dedication. At twelve, he yearned to be a surgeon, clinically dissecting his sister's dolls, but at Gore Road it was hard to think of anything but the crying need of the poor. In his teens he was already business manager of what was virtually the firm of Booth and Son; from breakfast until ten at night he toiled at what he and his father called always " The Concern."

In theory, he yearned for a ferret; in practice he once, as a thirteen-year-old, worked a seventy-two-hour stretch without sleep to pin down a discrepancy in the mission accounts which had defeated everyone else.

For William Booth was no man to console empty bellies with promises of spiritual bliss; he knew too well Christ's command " Give ye them to eat." By 1872, he had five Food-for-the-Million Shops under way where the poor could buy hot soup night and day and a three-course dinner for sixpence. Until administrative headaches caused Booth to scrap them, the sixteen-year-old Bramwell had sole charge of these lunch rooms, rising soon after three a.m. to push a barrow four miles to Covent Garden Market, begging discarded vegetables, buying a few sacks of bones, then four miles back to Hackney. He kept a sharp eye on the heating, too, remembering Booth's injunction: " No one gets a blessing if they have cold feet, and nobody ever got saved while they had toothache ! "

And there were other random attempts at social work. The Christmas of 1868 was the last the Booths ever spent as a family unit. On Christmas morning, after preaching in White-chapel, Booth returned to Gore Road, pale and haunted by the drunken degradation of the streets. As the day wore on all his efforts to join in the children's frolics proved a dismal failure. At last, striding the room like a caged lion, the cry was wrenched from him: " I'll never spend a Christmas Day like this again. The poor have nothing but the public house, nothing but the public house."

Next Christmas, Bramwell and the others ranged the slums

to distribute 300 Christmas dinners, most of them cooked by Catherine and Honor Fells in the Gore Road kitchen.

Despite the grinding pressures of work, they were a happily united family. Booth loved to play and romp with his children, especially in their favourite game of " Fox and Geese "— with father always the fox. Another prized game was " getting Papa on his feet," when Booth's lank frame, raised almost from the floor with near-miraculous ease, would suddenly relapse into dead-weight and slump heavily back amid squeals of joy. There was Snap, with Papa joining in, shouting as loudly as any of the children, his long white fingers dealing the cards like a croupier. He encouraged his sons to collect stamps as eagerly as he followed the fortunes of their guinea-pigs and white mice. At a pinch he was a deft hand at assembling rabbit hutches.

It was a warm and devoted household where Booth sang loudly as he dressed in the morning or ran swiftly up and down stairs. When Victorian mothers remarked wonderingly that so large a family had never buried a child, Catherine could only answer : " Perhaps because I gave them so fully to God that He did not think it necessary to take them away from me." They were never affluent, but if rice pudding stuffed with raisins featured more often on the menu than butcher's meat, they did not rise hungry from the table. And Catherine, always busy with her needle, could alter a dress or make a shirt in a trice.

In early years, their poverty worried the sensitive Bramwell ; when his mother patched his clothes, he objected, " But the boys will laugh at me. They'll think we are poor." " Well," Catherine replied truthfully, " so we are." In later years, Bramwell put this philosophy in a nutshell : " She not only patched our clothes, but made us proud of the patches."

Already the methods of the amazing Booth were provoking nation-wide comment. The sharp vivid allegories that drove home his message seemed to mesmerise his audience, until the vision he conjured up held them spellbound too. " Look at that man going down the river," he commanded them, " going down in a boat with Niagara beyond. He has got out into the stream . . . the rapids have got hold of the boat . . . he is going, going . . . my God ! he is gone over—and he never pulled at an oar ! That is the way people are damned ; they go on ; they have no time ; they don't *think* ; they neglect Salvation—and they are lost."

The only religion to deal out handbills, " Come drunk or sober," inspired unprecedented scenes. In Bradford, Yorkshire, astonished neighbours watched a man newly-converted return at midnight with Johnny Lawley, mill-hand turned evangelist, to roll a barrel of beer from his house, tip its contents down the gutter. Uninhibited converts, sensing a burden of guilt and lust lifted from their shoulders, would shout, " I *do* believe—He *does* save me ! " half-way through the service. When one, transported with joy, cried, " I must jump," an evangelist urged him, " Then jump ! " Some, following on nine-hour prayer-meetings, fell into near-cataleptic trances and were carried to ante-rooms close by. Though Booth kept doctors standing by, none could find that the converts suffered physical harm.

These were not men and women who would thereafter tread the middle road through life, like thousands of professing Christians. With conversion they renounced the world and took up the cross of Christ. At what Booth now styled the Penitent-form—formerly the communion rail, or mourner's bench—men and women knelt, risking ridicule, to confess their sins, resolved to live the rest of their lives in the blazing light of public service. For Christ they were ready to spend in season and out of season, to press His claims on the willing and unwilling alike.

This system, as Booth knew well, not only forced men to accept their problems whole-heartedly ; it gave little scope to bare-faced hypocrites. No working-man could long profess religion before his mates unless he sincerely enjoyed it.

Since most converts were near-illiterate, early testimonies were unique—yet the short simple exhortations went home to the poor and degraded as no high-flown rhetoric ever could. " I am no scholar, my dear friends," George Railton heard one man lead off in a crowded meeting, " You must just take it rough, as it comes from my heart." And another pleaded : " If you only knew how happy the Lord makes us, you would at once come to Jesus." One chairmender was so moved by conversion he changed his trade-cry ; as his barrow trundled through the streets, astonished clients heard now a lusty cry of " Souls to mend." Always the billing of guest-speakers, as at Booth's first Walsall camp-meeting, punched home that this was a religion for the masses—with " The Converted Pigeon-Flier " supporting " A Milkman Who Has Not Watered His Milk Since He Was Saved."

Often this transformation of souls had genuine pathos : one man, after serving a life-sentence for murdering his wife, knelt at the Penitent-form but could recall no words of prayer. At last, tears streaming down his face, his mind went back over lonely years to an almost-forgotten childhood. " Lord Jesus, forgive me," he whispered. " I have been naughty. . . ."

But this most human of religions had its humorous moments too. One man went so often to the Penitent-form that his sanity was held in question ; pressed, he explained that if nobody got saved, he thought the evangelist would be in trouble. A sailor, amazed at the bargain, went away muttering : " Well ! A teetotaller, converted, and nothing to pay." And one Chatham man, urged to make an instant decision by Rodney " Gipsy " Smith, insisted on giving the Devil a fortnight's notice, As an employer, he said, he would expect the same consideration.

For both savers and saved knew the Devil as a real person, a crafty subtle vicious foe, no less true for being invisible. Matching themselves against their Lord, they saw their own souls shot through with malice and envy—but what held them fast to this higher ideal was the discovery that the men of Booth's mission understood a blunderer's problems. John Allen knew how hard it was to live right ; Railton knew the things hungry hearts needed to be told. Nor were they content to preach the wrath of God from the Olympian fastness of a pulpit. They knelt beside the penitents in the throes of their conviction, battling to save the kindred of Jezebel, Ananias and Cain.

Much might preface a conversion, but when it came it was immediate : in one blinding moment God spoke the word of pardon and the penitent arose, transformed by the spirit of Christ. After this Booth's pioneer techniques came swiftly into play : once-weekly visitations, in Methodist class-leader fashion, kept a check on the convert, to prevent him from stumbling.

If these were militant tactics, they were in keeping with militant Christianity : the year that Booth began work on Mile End Waste—1865—was the very year the Rev. Sabine Baring-Gould gave the world his immortal " Onward, Christian Soldiers." The American Civil War and the Russo-Turkish War loomed largest in men's minds. By 1872, the reports flooding in to Booth's Whitechapel Road headquarters were chock-full of military terminology : Hackney Mission reported " siege operations " against the Devil ; Stoke Newington wrote of a convert being " taken prisoner." Already some evangelists were prefacing their signatures " Yours faithfully, toe to toe with the enemy." George Railton himself closed every letter to Booth : " Your devoted Lieutenant."

Most militant of all these men was " Fiery Elijah " Cadman, from Coventry, Warwickshire, whose life story somehow embodied the forty years that followed Waterloo. Aged six, he answered a chimney-sweep's advertisement : " Wanted— Small Boys for Narrow Flues." At four a.m. each day, when work began, the sweep put a calico mask over Elijah's face and a scraper in his hands and forced him from the fireplace to loosen the soot above. When he fell, grazing his limbs red-raw, his wounds were bathed in a saline solution to heal and harden them. From infancy he was almost never sober. As a teenager he migrated to nearby Rugby, and headed a street gang called " The Rugby Roughs." Later, a doughty bantam-weight, he opened a boxing-saloon in a tavern to stage public exhibitions. Conversion came by chance on 30th December, 1861. when Cadman, and a friend, as a post-

Christmas diversion, attended the last public hanging ever held outside Warwick gaol. As the boom of the drop vibrated and the white caps strapped over the victims' faces grew unbearably tighter, Cadman's friend said positively, " That's what you'll come to, Elijah, one day."

A small sturdy eighteen-year-old, with short legs and a strident metallic voice, Cadman was appalled by the realisation of past sins. Typically impulsive, he smashed his own boxing saloon to matchboard, forswearing tobacco and liquor. Now he would fight as hard for God as ever he had fought for the Devil. As a Methodist lay-preacher, he drew crowds by ringing a mighty hand-bell, billing himself as " The Saved Sweep from Rugby." But if sober conduct brought him a master-sweep's prosperity, he still craved an outlet for his brimming energies. In August, 1876, after hearing Booth preach, he volunteered—and was accepted—as a Christian Mission evangelist.

Booth chose shrewdly. More than any of his early apostles, Cadman could rock a crowd on its heels as surely as ever he had rocked his adversaries in the prize-ring. In the autumn of 1877, *en route* to pioneer Whitby, a small Yorkshire fishing-town, Cadman presaged the shape of things to come to a man in his railway carriage. Whitby had churches and chapels enough, the man sighed, but the people were spiritually dead. Vowed Cadman grimly : " By the help of God, I'm going to wake them up."

These were no empty words. Within weeks, came a stirring call for two thousand men and women to join " The Hallelujah Army " in the fight against the Devil's Kingdom. Mammoth posters, signed by " Captain Cadman," as he already styled himself to win sympathy with local skippers, blazoned

WAR! IN WHITBY!

THE HALLELUJAH ARMY, FIGHTING FOR GOD!

Many timid folk, convinced Whitby's steep cobbled alleys would literally flow with blood, now hastily left town to stay with relatives.

A month later, when Booth visited Whitby, Cadman, on his own initiative, took a daring step. His advance billing announced Booth as " General of the Hallelujah Army." Then, fearful that this might rouse the evangelist's wrath, he hid the poster in his house. By chance, the lynx-eyed Booth not only spotted it but warmly commended the little man's enterprise— it was not far removed, after all, from his correct title : " General Superintendent of The Christian Mission." Cadman, whose Whitby campaign had won 3,000 followers, was told to send a copy to George Railton at Whitechapel Headquarters.

Despite this imposing title, Booth's forces were not, as yet, highly organised. Nor were his powers supreme. The Christian Mission, like the Methodist New Connexion from which he had withdrawn, still had its policy laid down by a thirty-four member committee, which met once yearly. But their methods were slow and tortuous ; ardent field-workers like Railton viewed them with impatient distrust. At last, late in 1876, a deputation waited on Booth with a formidable list of grievances. Apart from Railton and Bramwell Booth, the malcontents numbered James Dowdle, converted railway guard, William Ridsdel, former grocer's assistant, and William Corbridge, onetime Leicestershire labourer.

The time had passed, said Railton flatly, for the longwinded process of government by conference. When they sacrificed worldly interests to follow Booth they believed God had chosen him to give a new meaning to religion. None of them had bargained with handing over their lives to a committee's deliberations.

" We gave up our lives to work under *you* and those you should appoint, rather than under one another," Railton protested.

Ridsdel was equally to the point. " You tell us what to do and we will do it," he said, " I can't see the good of a lot of talk, with one wanting one thing and one another."

Booth was in a quandary. He himself was no lover of committees—" if there had been committee meetings in the days of Moses," he would fume, " the children of Israel would never have got across the Red Sea." Yet now, after eleven years of abiding by a committee's rules and decisions he found his evangelists demanding an autocracy. He saw his movement taking on a new and increasing impetus, but as yet even he had no clear idea as to its direction.

"Where is it all leading?" Catherine would challenge him, "Are we a religious body or are we an appendix to the Churches?" And Booth, his mind perplexed, could only answer: "I don't want to found a new sect."

Yet over the months the idea grew and would not be denied. On Wednesday, 7th August, 1878, the last morning of The Christian Mission's annual Whitechapel conference—now called a War Congress—Booth summoned the determination for what he had to do. Rising he now moved a resolution to scrap the Mission's Deed Poll, and substitute another. Control of all Mission property in Britain or any other country was now vested in him as General Superintendent, or his nominee—as also was the power and duty to appoint his successor. Power to change or modify this deed was withdrawn. No alteration was possible without recourse to Parliament.

Though some older evangelists viewed these changes with suspicion, so great was the radical urge to get things done that the motion was carried by a three-fourths majority. The Christian Mission was now an army in all but name.

Yet even this had been decided. Early one morning in May, 1878—three months before the War Congress met—Bramwell and Railton were summoned to Booth's bedroom for the day's instructions. As Booth, who was recovering from 'flu, paced the floor in a long yellow dressing-gown and felt slippers, Railton scanned the proofs of the pink eight-page folder which was the Mission's annual report.

Its preliminary was bold and succinct:

THE CHRISTIAN MISSION
under the superintendence
of the Rev. William Booth
is

A VOLUNTEER ARMY
Recruited from amongst the multitudes who are without God and without hope in the world. . . .

At this time the Volunteers, a part-time citizens' Army, with grey-green uniforms and shakos (later the Territorials) were a favourite butt of cartoonists. Bramwell, aged twenty-two, was stung by the imputation.

" ' Volunteer ! ' " he exclaimed, leaning excitedly back in his chair as Railton read this out. " Here, I'm not a volunteer. I'm a regular or nothing ! "

Booth stopped dead in his tracks. For a moment his eyes were fixed on his son, expressionless. Abruptly, he crossed to where Railton sat, taking the pen from his hand. He struck decisively through the word " volunteer " and substituted the word " Salvation." Simultaneously, they scarcely knew why, Bramwell and Railton leapt from their chairs, crying " Thank God for that ! "

This " army " was then exactly eighty-eight strong.

"*Terrible, with Banners . . .*"

1879-82

It was predicted of the Church of God that it should go forth
" terrible as an Army, with banners "—and just such an army
was soon massing within the long shadow of William Booth.
By the first weeks of January, 1879, he was in command of
81 stations manned by 127 full-time evangelists—100 of them
converted at meetings—with over 1,900 voluntary speakers
holding 75,000 services a year. In 1878 alone, 51 new stations
had been opened.

Not all Booth's followers were as ready as Elijah Cadman
to adopt military titles but more and more were coining
phrases that Salvationists use even to-day. No Salvation
soldier operated from a mission house ; he served in a local
corps, working from a " citadel " or a " fort." He did not
genuflect in prayer ; he did " knee-drill." When the leader
of a meeting shouted " Fire a volley," it was the signal for a
rousing cry of " Hallelujah " ; to " fix bayonets " you raised
your right hand in public declaration. And since Heaven was
the ultimate goal of every Christian soldier, Salvationists did
not die—they were " promoted to Glory."

Yet still the movement lacked some essential magnetism
that even William Booth could not define.

As it happened, the solution was found by pure chance in
the quiet cathedral city of Salisbury. It was here that Charles
William Fry, a local builder and leader of the Methodist choir
and orchestra, offered Booth the services of himself and his
three sons, Fred, Ernest and Bertram. But the fact that Fry
senior played the cornet and his sons also played brass instru-

ments was at first purely incidental. Troubled by the rough handling which the Salvationists received from local hooligans, the Frys stepped in as a bodyguard—and as an afterthought brought their instruments to accompany the songs in the market place. In this unwitting fashion the first Salvation Army band was born.

Yet Booth's initial decision to hire them, not lightly taken, was destined to project The Salvation Army's image across three continents. The rowdy street-corner fervour of the Salisbury Market musicians foreshadowed the day when a Salvation Army band played in the Hollywood Bowl's Easter morning sunrise service to a listening and viewing audience of 100 million. At the funeral of Edward VII, The Salvation Army provided the first civilian band ever to play in the court-yard of Buckingham Palace. These were the first tentative steps towards to-day's total of 2,300 bands, staffed by 45,500 Salvation Army bandsmen, all of them unpaid, providing their own uniforms, contributing towards the purchase of instruments turned out by The Army's own factory at St. Albans, Hertfordshire.

But none of this seemed remotely feasible in 1878. At first Booth made it plain that the band's job was solely to accompany songs—already he had banned the word " hymn " as " too churchy." Instrumental solos which might detract from the Gospel message were not permitted until 1885. " Mr. Booth ! A brass band ! I don't think I should like it in connection with religious services," was the outraged reaction of Salisbury evangelist Marianne Faulconbridge when Booth made known his decision. Like many Salvationists she hotly opposed this innovation, and with reason. Some of the first cornets and tubas were so defective that only string held them together ; their leakages were plugged with soap. So illiterate were the Corps bandsmen of South Shields, County Durham, that they could read music but not fine print : each tune had to be identified by symbols. " Out on the ocean Sailing " had a boat as headpiece ; " Oh to be over Yonder," showed an armchair with a weary man fumbling his way towards it.

If concertinas were all the rage, harmoniums were out—
they smacked too strongly of the chapels Booth had put
behind him. Tambourines were early in favour; by 1882,
Railton noted, The Army had sold 1,600 in six weeks. But
most men, choosing a likely instrument, just did the best they
could, losing more chords than they found; one captain
headed his corps blowing lustily on a cornet after four-and-a-
half hours' practice. While Bramwell played a flutina, forerunner of to-day's piano-accordion, others rang dustman's
bells, blew hunting-horns or strummed on banjos. George
Railton, always the exception, carried his own set of bones;
if a meeting lacked spark, he shook them with a maraca-
player's fervour.

Whatever the early bandsmen lacked it wasn't stamina;
though all were spare-time musicians, some marched over
1,500 miles a year. Many, more used to swinging sledge-
hammers, beat their drums like men possessed. But night
after night they persevered in practice until they achieved a
semblance of harmony, though the shaken Bramwell confessed : " It sounds as if a brass band's gone out of its mind."

But the new spirit of Booth's Army, freed from the confines
of committee, was infinite ingenuity. Fred, the elder Fry
brother, was a man so versatile he once learned to play an
organ by testing every stop and pedal, then drawing and mem-
orising a diagram. It was he, aided by seventeen-year-old
Herbert Booth, the evangelist's third son, and Richard
Slater, former first violin under Sir Arthur Sullivan, who now
took a revolutionary step in The Army's annals : the adaptation
of the day's hit tunes into Salvation Army songs. Soon The
Army's whitewashed barracks and yellow pitch-pine halls
were as potent a lure as any smoke-filled music hall. If a man
knew the lilt of " The Marseillaise," he could swiftly learn the
words of " Ye sons of God, Awake to Glory." Outfitted with
Christian lyrics, " The Old Folks at Home " was reborn as
" Joy, Freedom, Peace and Ceaseless Blessing." Scots could
rarely resist " Storm the Forts of Darkness, Bring them
Down", simply because they had known it first as " Here's to
Good Old Whisky."

The General next to God

At first Booth was dubious of these tactics ; only four years later, when he heard George " Sailor " Fielder, a converted sea-captain, sing in a Worcester theatre were his reservations overcome. Though Fielder was carolling " Bless His Name, He Sets Me Free," the rhythm was as catchy and infectious as a sea shanty and Booth, intrigued, buttonholed a passing officer : " That's a fine song. What tune is that ? " But the officer, an evangelist of the old school, shook a disapproving head : " Oh, General, that's a dreadful tune. Don't you know what it is ? That's ' Champagne Charlie Is My Name'. "

For a long moment Booth stood silent in the ante-room, rapt by the swelling roar from the auditorium. Then he turned decisively to Bramwell : " That's settled it. Why *should* the Devil have all the best tunes ? "

Critics might lambast Booth for reducing religion to a music-hall level, but his musicians met the Devil on his own ground. Within a year of their Musical Department opening up, there were four hundred Salvation Army bands crashing into a repertoire of eighty-eight hit tunes. Few, for reasons of copyright alone, loom large among the 10,000-odd tunes available to-day ; original works have mostly replaced secular adaptions. But in The Army's first years, it was tunes like these, first tried out on a second-hand pub harmonium, that captured and held the crowds. Before his retirement in 1913, Richard Slater alone had composed over 850 ; the brass and percussion of his favourite Wagner struck exactly the note The Army sought.

It was as if a clarion-call had sounded—for now, after four-teen wilderness years, as motley a squad as ever enlisted under one banner were flocking to join Booth. Mill-girl Martha Chippendale, came from Yeadon, Yorkshire, still dressed in clogs and shawl ; from North Shields, on the Tyne, came Billy Herdman, a drunken escapologist, whose Houdini-style techniques enlivened a new-type sermon, " Trap Doors to Hell." George Fox, the Converted Clown, was another show-business recruit ; in Leicester Sarah McMinnies, the Saved Barmaid, had already, in the new Army phrase, " opened fire." There was Happy Hannah, the Reformed Smoker, along with Hallelujah Fishmongers, Blood-washed Colliers and Saved Dog-Fanciers, all of them sworn to one single indomitable purpose: the redemption of mankind.

Often their lack of book-learning was too manifest to conceal but from their errors stemmed the common touch the people loved. Elijah Cadman inscribed his Bible " Cadman's Sword " but he could not read it; though he memorised whole passages by heart, he held it upside down. " God'll take your wheels off," Suffolk ploughboy Charlie Ward, with memories of Pharaoh's chariots, often told bemused sinners. All were poor, but there were lessons even poverty could not teach. At Barnsley, Yorkshire, twenty-year-old Rose Clapham, a sheltered Kentish country girl, appalled at the sight of an entire population of ex-convicts, offered up a fervent prayer for them. Patiently one of the " sinners " explained: he and hundreds like him were coal-miners who cropped their hair to keep it free from dust.

When superior souls poked sly fun at such gaffes, Catherine Booth defended them hotly: " What matter if the dish be cracked so long as it serves you with a good joint ? "

Yet the movement was destined to lure others beside the poor. Mary Murray, tall handsome daughter of an Indian Army General, heard a street-corner preacher explain how the Salvationists had conquered his craving for liquor and told herself: " A power like that could alter the whole world." A conviction she was powerless to resist seized her at a Society dinner-party; with a hasty excuse she ran headlong from the room, arriving at the Penitent-form of a squalid ill-painted Army barracks bare-headed in an expensive evening cloak. Colonel George Nicholson Pepper of the 31st Foot, a Crimea veteran, now joined a new Army whose shot and shell was faith; in their Salisbury home, his wife opened a registry office for " superior Salvationist servants," designed to aid both sympathetic employers and employees sent packing for their beliefs. And there were others with connexions far from martial—Franz von Tavel, a Professor of Botany from Zurich University, one of the world's leading experts on rare ferns ; Lady Sarah Sladen, eighth daughter of the Earl of Cavan, enrolled as Sergeant-Major of a Kentish Village Corps; the Rev. W. Elwin Oliphant, who resigned the fashionable curacy of St. Paul's Church, Onslow Square, Kensington, when the bitter lot of the poor came home to him.

Another pastor later arrived from three thousand miles across the Atlantic: the tall auburn-bearded Rev. Samuel Logan Brengle, a man who had once dreamed of a bishopric but now turned down the pastorate of the fine Methodist Church built by millionaire Clement Studebaker in South Bend, Indiana, to embrace debt-ridden itinerant evangelism. Though Brengle was later to become The Army's first American-born Commissioner, Booth at first accepted his services grudgingly. " You've been your own boss too long," he declared, and to instil necessary humility set Brengle to work cleaning other trainees' boots.

" Have I followed my own fancy this distance to black boots ? " Brengle asked himself despairingly as he bent to his task in a gloomy cellar. Then, as in a vision, he saw Jesus bending over the feet of rough unlettered fishermen. " Lord," he whispered, his pride abated, " Thou didst wash their feet : I will black their boots."

One recruit, Deputy Commissioner Frederick Tucker, a well-born Indian Civil Servant, came all the way from Dharmsala, India, after reading of Booth's work. When the evangelist urged him to reconsider the fat pension he would forfeit, Tucker, a tall ascetic man, who had first felt drawn to religion by the American revivalists, Moody and Sankey, promptly clinched the issue by resigning from the service. " I am now penniless," he told Booth triumphantly, " you must take me." Booth could only agree.

All these had heard Booth's rallying cry on New Year's Day, 1879, when The Salvation Army was young—" Hold the standard high—let us tell the world of blood and fire "—and their hearts were stirred. Calling above the blare of the cornet, the shiver of the tambourine, they heard the voice of Christ.

" Can't this form be altered ? It looks pretentious," William

Booth scrawled on the very first printer's proof that gave him the title " General." But like it or no, the rank that Elijah Cadman had bestowed on him in Whitby was a fixture : Booth was a General with an army that needed cohesion.

Already their route was mapped out on approved martial lines. Their monthly house-organ, scrapping its *Salvationist* masthead, was from now on a weekly, *The War Cry*, though Booth at first opposed the move : he had all too few staff to edit a four-page halfpenny weekly. It was Bramwell who forced the issue and had his way, though at first the task seemed hopeless. After one nightmare day the second-hand gas-engine printing machine installed in a printing office behind a pub in Fieldgate Street, Whitechapel, was pronounced as useless scrap-iron. At eleven p.m. on 23rd December, 1879, after printing two copies, tearing up three, then printing two more, the machine churned to a halt, oil seeping from every joint.

Even next day, with the machine printing 1,400 copies an hour, the problems were not ended. No one could have envisaged the time when 136 Army periodicals, totalling almost two million copies per week, would be a routine international print. On Boxing Day, 26th December, 1879, with the first issue neatly parcelled, a " London Particular," a wet yellow-grey blanket of fog closed down on the city. Only the pertinacity of Captain William Pearson, the publisher, who stumbled into the fog-bound city to find a stranded hansom cab, saved the day. For three snail-paced hours the cab, loaded with Pearson, Railton, Booth, Bramwell—and 17,000 *War Crys*—groped through the murky shrouded streets seeking the main-line railway stations. Near King's Cross Station, the hansom, rearing on to the pavement, almost overturned; once, with the nearside wheel wedged against a lamp-post and the horse still tugging frantically, it was within an ace of being wrenched apart.

Finally, with every parcel dispatched, the weary quartet asked, How much ? Almost diffidently, the cabby put it to Booth : " What about five shillings, sir ? "

But an Army with an unbroken front needed more than a

War Cry; it needed banners, and corps after corps was now getting them. As far back as 1874, in Christian Mission days, Booth had pondered this device : a crimson flag to typify the blood of Christ, its blue border symbolising purity, with the world transfixed by a flaming sword. But by September, 1878, when Catherine Booth, " The Army Mother," presented Coventry Corps with the first-ever Army flag, the world had given place to a blazing sun, inscribed with the motto " Blood and Fire," to affirm the fiery baptism of the Holy Ghost. Only four years later, when The Army began work in India, was the sun, a sacred symbol of the Parsees, translated to a star, the present-day emblem, to avoid giving offence. To testify that God's love is ever-victorious, never once in its history has The Army flag flown at half-mast. Whether at marriages, funerals or the dedication of children, it breaks high and free.

But Booth, an insatiable perfectionist, had not done yet— " this and better will do," he would say, when things ran smoothest. A fighting force should look distinctive, and in Victorian days uniforms were seen everywhere : the post-man's bright scarlet frock-coat, the bobby's dark-blue bob-tailed coat and varnished pot-hat. Even doctors' page-boys, delivering medicine, wore trim shell jackets with silver buttons. But almost two years would pass before Booth's dream of a standard uniform became reality. The first Sal-vationists wore a brass " S " on either lapel to distinguish themselves, often at the cost of bloody noses ; later they donned blue and red armlets, inscribed " The Salvation Army." Others wore stovepipe hats with tin labels bearing The Army crest ; bandsmen sported second-hand military uniforms. It wasn't until the spring of 1880 that Captains— then the highest Army rank—could apply to headquarters for the new blue serge patrol jackets, worn over crimson guern-seys, or fishermen's jerseys. For women officers there were Princess Robes, akin to Dior's New Look, with seamless waist and gored skirt, a simple elegant style popularised by the Princess of Wales. Their headgear was black straw bonnets—

with broad missile-resistant brims—trimmed with black silk and strings.

Not all Salvationists took kindly to the change. Even George Railton feared that uniforms might set The Army apart from the masses, though typically, once Booth had convinced him, he was the first man to wear full Salvation Army uniform. Others were less amenable. Ex-milliner Annie Lockwood, sent to Belfast away from Booth's eagle eye, promptly decked out her bonnet with snow-white ruching. At Salisbury, Captain Marianne Faulconbridge took one look at the black straw coal-scuttle and put it straight back in the post. Until Booth's voice had made itself felt, it travelled like a shuttlecock between Salisbury and Whitechapel.

Finance posed a problem, too. Then, as now, Salvationists paid for their uniforms out of their own pockets and not all in those pioneer years could afford £1 for Princess Robes or a guinea for a captain's outfit. Ten years would pass before The Army's tailoring department was showing a £12,000 a year profit, a sum promptly ploughed back into the fighting fund.

But if uniforms could not, as yet, be standardised, regulations could—and Booth, a disciple of Wellington and Napoleon, was the man to do it. By October, 1878, the first volume of *Orders and Regulations for The Salvation Army*, based largely on Field Marshal Sir Garnet Wolseley's *Field Pocket Book for the Auxiliary Forces* was required reading in every Salvationist household. Some citizens now charged Booth with being a Jesuit, determined that no soldier could " make a move or drink a cup of tea without leave from headquarters." To this Booth had a short answer : he could no more run The Salvation Army without a system than he could run a railroad.

His system seemed well-nigh foolproof. Many soldiers, like their own General, had made a humble start in life ; if their fervour was never in doubt they needed channelling, organisation. Care of the health was paramount. Field Officers should sleep with the windows open, and like Booth himself, a fanatic over hygiene, take a cold bath every morning, a hot bath each week. Breakfast should be eaten no later than eight a.m. When visiting the sick it was prudent to carry a small lump of camphor in the breast pocket.

Billets came under Booth's scrutiny, too. Lodging houses with young people in the family were forbidden ; if an officer of the opposite sex was living there, The Army's enemies had grounds for malicious gossip. It was a duty to secure lodgings in the toughest quarter of a town, simple rooms furnished with plain rush-bottomed chairs : this was a living example to the people whose trust they sought. Three hours of every day must be given up to visiting converts.

As much as any serving soldier, a Salvationist's private life came under his commanding officer's scrutiny. For serving officers, marriage outside The Army was, and still is, forbidden. To discourage husband-hunters, women officers could not marry until after two years' service. Engagement rings were rated as unnecessary. And once Headquarters were notified of an engagement, they normally followed Booth's prescription : " Put a few hundred miles between them. That'll show whether or not they're in earnest." Booth's officers never married in haste to repent at leisure.

No man or woman submitted to this iron discipline for financial gain. Until 1878, modest salaries were guaranteed, but at the historic August conference which gave Booth supreme power, the General had declared roundly : " Now, let everybody understand this, that everything is to be paid before salary ; putting by weekly enough to pay all rents and other current expenses." Now, before he could accept a penny of his fixed weekly salary—which ranged from sixteen shillings for a single lieutenant to twenty-seven shillings for a married captain, plus a shilling for each child— officers needed weekly collections large enough to foot gas, fuel and water bills, pay the hall's rental and a dozen other items.

If these were hard rules they did guarantee Booth a task force to triumph over all opposition : an army of zealots, determined to win people from the darkness of drink and debauchery and to make their presence felt. " Wherever possible,

paint 'SALVATION ARMY' on the roof of the barracks,"
Booth counselled shrewdly, " so that it can be seen from a great
distance."

For the lean bearded General was swiftly learning an abiding
truth : " it is in the interests of the service to be in the columns
of the newspapers as often as possible." Though legend
would credit him with inventing such eye-catching titles as
" The Hallelujah Lasses," this was not true : Booth learned by
trial and error. The billing was the brainchild of William
Crow, a Newcastle printer, briefed to run off a handbill
announcing the arrival of " Two Lady Preachers," Rachel
and Louise Agar, on Tyneside. Crow, feeling the style lacked
punch, called them instead " The Hallelujah Lasses "—which
shocked Booth to the core.

Yet within days came results as resounding as Elijah
Cadman's. Hour after hour, telegrams flooded in to Whitechapel Headquarters : no building on Tyneside could contain
the crowds flocking to hear " The Hallelujah Lasses." Miners
and dock-workers, used to calling their own wives " lassie,"
were moved to hear more about this strange new religion. In
March 1878, Booth could hardly have guessed that the phrase
would echo round the world, but from now on he was content. Any publicity that kept The Army's purpose before the
public was good publicity.

Whatever their roots, his soldiers took the injunction to
heart. Lieutenant Theodore Kitching, a mild-mannered
Quaker, had begun life as a school-teacher—but to catch the
eye of the masses he cheerfully rode into Scarborough, Yorkshire, perched on a crimson-draped donkey. To advertise his
copies of *The War Cry*, he borrowed the school's dinner-bell
and jangled it through the streets. His watch-face bore the
striking inscription : " Every hour for Jesus." Sometimes he
attended open-air meetings in mufti, disguised as a drunk, his
nose aflame with red ochre, his eyes ringed with lamp-black.
And others were as uninhibited. To illustrate the boundless
sea of God's love and forgiveness, Captain John Lawley once
dived clean from the platform—and continued his exhortation
doing the breast-stroke. Six-foot James Dowdle, billed as The

Saved Railway Guard, kept the spectators guessing from the start; as he slammed his violin case down on a busy pavement, Dowdle bellowed " Stand back! It might go off! " Then, as the crowd backed apprehensively, he whipped out his fiddle and launched into a lively jig.

Their methods were as varied as their garb. One man toured the streets as John the Baptist, barefooted, dressed in a skin hearth-rug. By the Home Secretary's special assent, Envoy " Darkie " Hutton, one-time crony of the murderous Charley Peace, reverted to a convict's fetters and the broad arrows of Dartmoor Prison. At Newcastle-under-Lyme, Staffordshire, Captain Anker Deans addressed all meetings in his crimson guernsey—its front with The Salvation Army crest, its back inscribed " The Devil is a Liar." Hackney, East London, lasses drew record crowds parading the streets—at William Booth's suggestion—wearing their nightgowns over their uniforms.

Another convert, won from the Royal Navy, put over his change of heart by dressing as soldier *and* sailor: one half lobster-red with a half fatigue-cap and blue trouser-leg, the other half bluejacket's rig, half a straw hat and white bell-bottom.

These were no mere sensationalists, wedded to ballyhoo for its own sake. Once circus-barker tactics had drawn a crowd, they became passionate pleaders for righteousness and reconciliation to God—and to this end any means were justified. Bizarre props were commonplace; in Leicester, Captain William Corbridge handed out mock railway-tickets: " HALLELUJAH RAILWAY—LEICESTER TO HEAVEN." To put across the parable of the Prodigal Son, other officers led on a live calf. Some swept through the town beating frying-pans with rolling-pins or used billboards as high as a three-story house. One man, who could command no audience, spent a week of winter evenings in the market place, lying silent in deep snow. By week's end, when half the town had flocked to watch him, he sprang up to give a stirring address.

The Booths were mastering these techniques, too. Even

Bramwell, once he had conquered natural shyness, drew crowds by preaching to his hat in dumb show—or rose from a coffin borne by six men with St. Paul's famous " O Death, where is thy sting ? " As No. 12 on the bill at Plymouth's Palace of Varieties he spoke so movingly on man's need for God that an agent offered him a £250-a-week tour, with free week-ends "for your other work." In the Midlands, following the execution of wife-murderer John H. Starkey, Elijah Cadman billed his General to preach a funeral service that same night. An ugly crowd jam-packed the hall, jeering and thundering with their feet, until Booth's voice sounded like the crack of doom : " John H. Starkey never had a praying mother." In the chill silence that followed, every man there felt his hold on life grow suddenly tenuous.

Most prominent of all the attention-getters was " Happy Eliza " Haynes, a rip-roaring factory girl from Booth's own home-town, Nottingham. Finding all normal publicity methods fell flat, Lieutenant Haynes marched boldly through the city streets with streamers floating from her unbraided hair and jacket, a placard on her back proclaiming " I am Happy Eliza." Soon, to the tune of " Marching through Georgia " she was striding at the head of a whole band of singing ruffians, conducting George Scott Railton's words with a fiddlestick :

Shout aloud Salvation, boys! We'll have another song!
Shout it with a spirit that will start the world along
Sing it as our fathers sang it many million strong,
As they went marching to glory!

From then on, " Happy Eliza," like so many of Booth's officers, was almost a national figure. Posted to the Marylebone district of London she rode through the West End on the box-seat of a four-wheeler, playing a violin while a convert pounded the bass drum ; behind, on a second cab, scraping and tooting lustily, came the first Salvation Army band heard in London. Music-hall ditties, dolls, even sweets were named after Eliza Haynes ; urchins crowded the sweetstuff shops for " an 'aporth of 'Appy Elizas ! " She had taken to heart the words of Catherine Booth : " I would lead Hallelujah

Bands and be a damn' fool in the eyes of the world to save souls."

And not only in Britain were Salvationists ready to court ridicule ; they were ranging countless thousands of miles. As early as 14th February, 1880, the prescient Harry Edmonds of Portland, Maine, confided in his diary : " To-day, Commissioner Railton left England for America. I predict that they will make the work . . . surpass that of England." The first man to hold Commissioner's rank, Railton himself had been the prime mover of this momentous decision to claim America for God. Already, he urged Booth, three English migrants, Amos Shirley and his family, former Coventry Salvationists, had " opened fire " in a disused Philadelphia chair-factory and were begging for reinforcements. No Army could reject the love and zeal of troops who had gone so far as to mobilise themselves.

But Booth wavered, and the canny Railton pressed his claims on Catherine. If he sailed now he could at least see the enterprise through its teething troubles ; as staff, he needed only seven " Hallelujah Lasses " to show what women inspired by God could do. Once on the spot, he would recruit American officers to stimulate national pride. He ended wistfully : " The General seemed almost for it last night, but it is not so to-day. New York, is after all, only nine days farther than Chester. . . ."

Hard-pressed for top organisers like Railton, Booth still agreed—and three seasick weeks later, on 10th March, 1880, the stocky, bearded Railton and his lasses marched bravely down the gangplank of the s.s. *Australia* at Castle Garden, New York. As true Salvationists, they came geared to native customs. One corner of their crimson banner bore a tiny replica of The Stars and Stripes. For their first official American service, held right there on the dockside, they chose songs adapted from " The Old Folks at Home " and " My Old Kentucky Home." The siege of New York had begun.

It was fertile territory. The Flash Age, whose lions were nimble financiers like Jim Fiske, was still a lusty memory : an age when twelve-course banquets were given to honour lap-dogs and naked blondes leaped from papier mâché pies at stag dinners. Before the Civil War, only three men had owned more than a million dollars ; now that hundreds could claim as much, their pleasure was ostentation. The new plutocrats had their teeth set with diamonds or served cigarettes wrapped in hundred-dollar bills. The infamous Tweed Ring dominated the city and vice was unashamed and costly : on Sister's Row, West Twenty-Fifth Street, red lights glowed outside every brothel. But on certain nights the callers had to wear evening dress and bring hothouse bouquets.

Almost all of New York City was crowded then into the lower third of narrow Manhattan Island : Brooklyn was still mostly farmland, the Bronx a waste of garden-patches criss-crossed by dirt roads. Manhattan's towering sky-scrapers were non-existent, though when it came to living the sky, for the rich, was the limit.

But Railton and his lasses were less concerned by the sins of the wealthy. What hit them hardest were the statistics of sorrow the wealthy ignored : 10,000 children adrift on New York's streets, panhandling the drunks outside 8,000 saloons. On the city's East Side, the living conditions dumbfounded them : 290,000 people to the square mile were living in viler conditions than Chinese peasants. A minister who had offered the use of his church for week-nights was appalled to learn that Railton's first service would be held in Harry Hill's Variety Theater, on the corner of Houston and Crosby Streets— where, one year later, prize-fighter John L. Sullivan made his New York début.

" It is the most disreputable den in the United States," the minister said aghast. " Go there and you will lose your reputation at once." " Then that's the place for us," replied Railton gleefully.

Railton had, in any case, inspected the dingy two-story frame house owned by ex-pugilist Harry Hill and seen it for what it was : a human zoo, thick with caporal tobacco fumes, where girls lolled in men's laps sipping wine and screaming with bawdy laughter. To his secret joy one patron pressed its claims as " a most respectable place." A man could drink himself paralytic here and know that his watch and wallet would be secure in the morning.

Sunday, 14th March, 1880, dawned cold and foggy in New York; a thin greasy film of moisture slicked the side-walks. Undeterred Railton split his force of lasses into two, deploying them down each side of Greenwich Street, on the Bowery, to exhort the customers in barber-shops and bar-rooms. Impressed by the party's youthful ardour—for only two were older than twenty-four—New Yorkers proved courteous if bewildered. To Railton's query, " Are all here going to Heaven ? " one man, his chin daubed with lather, agreed : Most surely—but he hoped not right away. After rapid mental arithmetic, the barber had just one query : How much was the fare ?

On the face of it, the first meeting, held in Hill's Theatre that very night, fell woefully flat. No liquor, in deference to The Army, was sold during the performance, though the usual ribald mottoes lined the wall :

> *He who loves not women, wine and song,*
> *Remains a fool his whole life long.*

Even the galleries were crammed three deep with men in pearl-grey derbys and checkered suits, but the audience were puzzled from the start. Few of the lasses had an aspirate between them and their accents fell strangely on American ears. By nine p.m., two-and-a-half hours after the start of the meeting, not a soul had answered the call to the Penitent-form. The Salvation Army gave place to a panorama of *Uncle Tom's Cabin*.

One man didn't see the show because he lacked the twenty-five cents admission fee—yet news of the meeting now took him post-haste to The Army's temporary headquarters, a converted brothel at 44 Baxter Street, in the heart of the Five Points slum. Nicknamed " Ash Barrel Jimmy " because he once tumbled into an ash barrel head first and stuck fast until prised out, this drunken old reprobate, James Kemp, became much more than The Army's first recruit. Because his degradation was legendary, news of his conversion punched home as nothing else could have done the kind of man The Army sought to redeem. Night after night, drunkards, harlots and bums, seeking the same potent prescription, packed out the Baxter Street Mission.

In this district most visitors took their lives in their hands. Its undisputed rulers were the savage Whyo gang, pioneers of the murder-by-contract racket, whose tariff ranged from fifteen dollars for chewing off an ear to a hundred dollars for murder. Cops patrolling the beat topped their helmets with slabs of curving rubber as a precaution against " Irish confetti" —bricks hurtling as lethally as bombs from roofs and high windows. But no finger was ever laid on Railton or his lasses. The cardinal point of their mission was accepted : these people had come because they loved the poor.

One reporter who covered a Baxter Street meeting, never forgot the audience : a motley cynical crew of station-house tramps, young men with canes and eyeglasses, seedy old pensioners with faded hair and stovepipe hats, glossy impudent young negresses. " The floors were as clean as the deck of a man-of-war," the newsman approved, " but in a few minutes they were frescoed with tobacco juice, the stench became overpowering and a yellow-fever pest house could not have been less attractive. . . ."

Yet the lasses, he noted in astonishment, seemed totally unperturbed ; they knelt on the spattered floor to take turns in praying.

Meetings like these irresistibly won sympathisers with The Army's tranquil faith : years later it was found that one Methodist Congress numbered fully sixty ministers whose life-work stemmed from their conversion by The Salvation Army. By April, well-wishers had subscribed enough for Railton to purchase a fine new hall with a porch for open-air meetings on Seventh Avenue. Prominent every night was the living testament that their methods worked : " Ash-Barrel Jimmy " Kemp, who had reached Captain's rank when he died in Boston in 1895.

But one impasse proved insurmountable : soon The Army's Hudson River Mission proved too small to hold the crowds and Railton sought Mayor Edward Cooper's permission to preach on the streets—especially the corner of Ninth Avenue and West 29th Street, outside the Mission. Cooper refused point-blank. Only ministers or licensed clergymen had the right to preach in the streets.

The rebuff unleashed all the crusader in Railton. Next day, to the undisguised joy of the Press, his sturdy figure tramped manfully up the steps of City Hall, clutching an ultimatum written and folded in the form of a legal notice. Over the Mayor's head, Railton was appealing to the people of New York ; unless permission was granted in two days, he would move his headquarters to a township where all citizens, whether ordained or no, enjoyed equal privileges " in the matter of serving the Lord and saving souls." Every newspaper ran his plea in full.

When Cooper again refused, Railton added fuel to the flame : the entire Salvation Army in America, he announced, would pray for him until street services were permitted. Promptly *The Daily Graphic* ran a gleeful cartoon : the Mayor surrounded by kneeling lasses, with the caption " Past praying for."

But when Railton saw Cooper was adamant, he knew the time had come to deploy his forces. Leaving Captains Emma Westbrook and Alice Coleman to take charge in New York, he transferred his own headquarters to Philadelphia. Thanks to the Shirley family, The Salvation Army had for twelve months been a living entity in the " City of Brotherly Love " : fully 200 Salvationists with red hatbands rallied to greet him in the old chair factory on Sixth and Oxford Streets. By May, 1880, Railton could cable Booth that his U.S. forces now totalled 16 officers, 40 cadets, 412 privates.

On the face of it, the cause was prospering—but only a man as ascetic as Railton, who habitually travelled steerage, living out of an old Gladstone bag and subsisting on a shilling a day, could have endured the strain. A huge painted notice, spanning the length of No. 45, South Third Street, Philadelphia, proclaimed it the " Headquarters of The Salvation Army in America "—but few realised that headquarters was the basement cellar where Railton worked, lived and went

dinnerless to rest, a brass " S " on his nightshirt collar proclaiming him always on duty.

The first year alone saw 1,500 converts, but Railton could
never amass enough cash to make the work self-supporting :
overheads soon swallowed up the £500 Booth had allotted the
work. Through the sultry summer of 1880, he travelled west,
always third class because there was no fourth, looking for
fresh cities to conquer. In some halls, working single-handed,
he was Captain, Lieutenant, Sergeant-Major and hall-keeper.
Often, diving from the platform in mid-sentence, he hustled
out an unruly drunk, then strolled back to take up the thread
of his discourse. In forty-nine days he travelled 4,200 miles
delivered eighty addresses. For thirty-one nights he slept on
straw, railroad benches and chairs—" a real soldier's life."

Vowing that he would carry The Army flag single-handed
across the Mississippi, Booth's iron-willed envoy chose St.
Louis, Missouri, as headquarters for his western campaign.
But the *gemütlich* city of catfish and crystal chandeliers, whose
elegant Planter's House Hotel gave the world the Planter's
Punch, had scant sympathy with itinerant evangelists. The rich
plantation families were just then settling in for the " winter
season " ; the talk was all of minuets, Virginia reels and
quilting bees. Street preaching, the authorities told Railton
curtly, was forbidden. When Railton hired a hall the owner
abruptly ended the lease ; the audiences had spat on the floor.
No one was willing to hire him another.

Undaunted, Railton did some hard thinking before coming
up with a solution that has long been classic in Salvation Army
annals. It was now November and a grey, glassy carpet of ice
stretched as far as a man could see from the cobblestoned
levee across the Mississippi. The authorities' writ, Railton
reasoned, could not run over the river, especially on the
Illinois side, where the skaters were enjoying a field-day. That
day, after doling out handbills to the labourers hauling ice, he
moved on, singing, towards the skaters' weaving quick-
silver figures. For the first and last time in Army history, an
evangelist on ice urged a congregation orbiting at full speed
to turn and seek God.

But it needed more than ingenuity to launch The Salvation Army in St. Louis. True, it was from a St. Louis cellar that Railton, in January, 1881, launched the first American *War Cry*—and used the unsold copies in lieu of a bed. But he was now so poor that once, calling on a shoe-store owner for a donation to Army funds, he was given instead a pair of over-shoes. Deep white snow still mantled the earth, and Railton had arrived almost barefoot.

And on New Year's Day, 1881, Railton had faced the bitterest blow of all : an immediate recall to London. A loyal soldier, he still sought desperately to change his General's mind. As yet the organisation was young and struggling ; to leave it to fend for itself this early could prove disastrous. Already the Press were won to their cause : one paper had run photographs of rich and poor kneeling side by side at the Penitent-form. Within five minutes, declared another, The Salvation Army could transform a man steeped in whisky into an angel.

" Must have you here," came Booth's inflexible reply.

Still Railton temporised. " We are paying the price in full," ran his impassioned letter ". . . and if so, God cannot fail to supply all our needs." But Booth was immutable. He now saw clearly the truth of Railton's earliest proposition : if The Army was to flourish in the States it must be as a full-blooded American organism, not as a colonial off-shoot, its every move charted from London. His last cable left no room for doubt : " Come alone."

It was no arbitrary decision ; by now The Army was oper-ating so fast and so far afield that London Headquarters had crucial need of organisers like Railton. Already twenty-three-year-old Kate, Booth's eldest daughter, had " opened fire " in France ; no woman, Booth felt, could cope as effectively with the initial problems as the determined fair-haired Kate. Even at seventeen she had proved a preacher so magnetic that when rowdies threatened to drown out a meeting, Booth, the skilled stage manager, would order : " Put on Kate, she's our last card." But even Kate Booth, sharing a tiny flat with three other lasses on the Avenue Parmentier, Paris, found this new enterprise a grim test of resolution. At their Rue d'Angoulème headquarters, a dusty hall in the slums of Belleville, blasphemous roughs calmly lit their cigars with pages torn from Bibles. In the boulevard cafés, loungers seized the lasses' bonnet strings from behind—then tugged until they were flushed and swooning. In sheer self-defence they learned to pin, not sew, the strings, so that the bonnet would fall free. And the language, despite Kate's fluency, had its pitfalls too ; anxious to launch a French *War Cry*, she felt the masthead *Amour* perfectly summed up The Army's love for the poor. In the nick of time she was dissuaded ; four comely lasses crying " *Amour*, un sou " along the boulevards could give rise to misunderstandings. Hastily they changed the title to *En Avant* (Forward).

But Kate, whose militant spirit won her the family nickname " Blücher," wasn't giving up easily. Night after night, for six months, she stood out against a grimy wine-flushed audience of taunting *ouvriers*. At last, when they sought to convert a prayer meeting into a riotous dance, Kate turned the tide with a clever challenge : " *Mes amis !* I will give you twenty minutes to dance if you will give me twenty minutes to speak ! "

At once a dark handsome workman in a blue blouse leapt to his feet : " Citizens, it is only fair play." Then, standing watch in hand, he timed their capering to the minute, before calling on Kate. Eighty minutes later, with her audience still spellbound, she knew that God had granted her a precious victory. Soon she was preaching nightly to crowds 400 strong; by year's end, only a new hall on the Quai de Valmy, seating 1,200, could contain them. Converts, a meagre hundred in the first year, were next year multiplied by five.

But not only in France did Booth need more officers, more organisation. Far away in Adelaide, Australia, two men unknown to one another, attending a quiet Wesleyan meeting, had simultaneously startled the sedate congregation with bullroars of " Hallelujah ! " Introductions swiftly followed : John Gore, the " Happy Milkman," converted by Booth thirteen years back in a Christian Mission meeting at Stepney, found a kindred spirit in Edward Saunders, a stone-mason from Bradford, England. By September, 1880, without flags, drums or even uniforms, Gore and Saunders were two lone men proclaiming the Gospel under a blue gum tree in Adelaide's Botanic Gardens.

" We need you," they pressed Booth, " as quickly as fire and steam can bring you."

And Canada, where two like-minded pioneers had begun on their own initiative, needed organisers too. From May, 1882, when Jack Addie, an eighteen-year-old dry goods salesman and Joe Ludgate, a clothes presser, paraded the streets of London, Ontario, in blue tunics and helmets like British bobbies, The Army's cause spread like fire under a leaning wind. At Bowmanville, where every leading citizen became a local officer, new ordinances soon forbade men swearing in the streets. At Guelph, one-ninth of the entire population were Salvationists. When Captain " Hallelujah Abbie " Thompson, a vivacious nineteen-year-old brunette, began drawing crowds of 12,000 a night, a sharp-witted Kingston, Ontario, cosmetics manufacturer was quick to cash in. Swiftly he launched a new line in toiletries—" Hallelujah Abbie Soap."

As fast as he could, Booth was training cadets for the field, but it was uphill work. Prior to 1880, when he moved his family from Gore Road, Hackney, to a sixteen-room house in the north-east corner of Clapton Common, East London, no training facilities had even existed. Now the Gore Road house was fitted up to take thirty women cadets, trained under Booth's daughter Emma ; a year later the General's second son, the tall fiery Ballington, had charge of a training home for men at Devonshire House, 259 Mare Street, Hackney.

To-day's Salvation Army cadets, graduating after a two-year in-residence course from one of forty-two training colleges, lead a hard and disciplined life, but even this pales beside the Spartan rigours of the routine at Mare Street. There were no learned tomes to study ; high-flown theology had no part in the curriculum. What they learned was " Scrubology " —rising at crack of dawn to scour the white stone steps, brightening boots and windows, making their beds. Their

seven-week course was practical from first to last : after facing
up to bad eggs and filthy abuse in open-air meetings, they went
on to wash the wasted bodies of the sick and comb their
matted hair. Then they trudged home to peel potatoes for the
evening meal—bread, tea, perhaps a bloater. Often the tea
was watery, the bread sour.

Even in November, 1881, when Booth raised £15,000 to buy
the London Orphan Asylum, Clapton, a vast chilly barracks,
girdled by high brick walls, problems were multiplying. The
foremost was finance : all cadets, in theory, contributed something towards their keep but not one in a hundred could
afford a fraction of the cost. And grants to keep the work
going were at all times dependent on the whims of philanthropists. One wealthy Methodist to whom Booth appealed
for funds, Dr. James Wood, a Lancashire lawyer, wouldn't go
above £100 until he had personally attended a Whitechapel
meeting and sat among the converts. Later he explained why :
a close-up view of these working-men and women revealed
that all had washed their necks and ears.

" General," he enthused. " Yours is a work of practical
godliness. I shall give you £1,000."

To qualify as officers in the 'eighties recruits needed both
stamina and faith. From the second the six-thirty a.m. whistle
shrilled reveille they lived life at the double, scurrying up and
down steep stone stairs, retiring dog-tired to unheated
cubicles. By 1886, when training time was upped to six
months, and cadets were trained in half-yearly batches, life was
so arduous that most wore out a pair of boots before gradu-
ation. Three manuals of war existed to guide their footsteps—
the Bible, Orders and Regulations and the knotty 119-page
" Salvation Army Doctrines "—but there were lessons only
experience could teach. Bearding abusive pubkeepers in their
own saloons was a dreaded initiation, but Booth's teaching
stressed one point : life would be tougher still in the field.
" I sentence you all to hard labour," he jested grimly to one
passing-out parade, " for the rest of your natural lives."

For this reason, Booth rarely asked local Salvationists to
become officers : they must volunteer through the Captain of

their corps. Only men impelled by God could weather a life where salary was not guaranteed for even a day.

For cadets soon found that The Army, as Bramwell put it, was " no agency to foster idle priests." The second three months of their training saw them brigaded into the fields under training-home officers, geared to launch their own campaigns in towns and villages. Now the true hardships of a field officer's life were made plain : a day that began with a three a.m. call to pray with a dying man might end on the last train from town, escorting a runaway girl back to anxious parents. Above all, they saw that if their health cracked up The Army could do little to help. Money was scarce even now: as the work expanded, it would be scarcer yet.

For all, the prayer " Give us this day our daily bread " would soon take on new and urgent meaning. As the visionary Booth reached out to embrace the world for his parish, the problems of salary, even survival, grew hourly more acute.

In the summer of 1882, when word came of a task force soon to leave for India, a circular memo set forth in unsparing detail the life that faced a volunteer. " Remember that you are likely to be absolutely alone—it may be for months together . . . in the villages the men must expect to have no furniture at all, except some mats, and must learn to sit on the ground like a tailor . . . you will have to learn to cook just as Indians do and to wash your clothes at the stream with them. . . .

" You must make up your mind to leave entirely forever and behind you all your English ideas and habits. . . ."

"Kill a Fly and Two will come to the Funeral"

1880-4

Although William Booth had framed no deep-laid plan, his decision to wage Salvation war in India was destined to create an imperishable Army precedent. From now on his soldiers, like true apostles of Christ, would become one with the life of their allotted country.

No man was better fitted to give them the lead than Major Frederick Tucker, the lean ascetic Civil Servant who had renounced all to follow Booth. Not only had his family lived and died in the stormy years of the Indian Mutiny; Tucker had spent eleven of his thirty years in the country. His Urdu, Hindustani and Sanskrit were fluent. Even the bazaar fakirs soon knew him fraternally as the " Get-Saved-While-You-Are-Alive " Preacher.

On 19th September, 1882, his great crusade began; slowly, the mail-boat *Ancona*, 3,000 tons, edged gingerly towards the Apollo Bunder landing stage, Bombay. Sickness had reduced Tucker's original party to four; Captain Henry Bullard, Lieutenants Arthur Norman and Mary Thompson were at first his sole supporters in the work that lay ahead. None of the party spared more than a glance for the posse of policemen, immaculate in white drill, massed on the dockside. There was the offloading of their baggage to superintend—and whoever the police awaited, it could scarcely be them.

Tucker, of course, could not then know that the Governor

of Bombay, Sir James Ferguson, was fanatically opposed to The Army's avowed intention of living like Indians. Almost thirty years after the Indian Mutiny, the British in India still maintained a caste system as insidious as anything a Brahmin could devise ; in the shaded annexes of the haughty Byculla Club, burra sahibs, sipping warm whisky and water, complained angrily that The Army's " invasion," forecast in that day's *Times of India*, would fatally damage the white man's prestige. To a man they approved Sir James Ferguson's vow, made despite the reservations of the police : he would harass Tucker from the city.

But as William Booth saw it, God had entrusted the people of India, over one-sixth of the human race, to Britain's care— yet more than fifty million men and women were racked by physical and spiritual starvation. His last words, as the Major left London headquarters, had been : " Get into their skins, Tucker." Tucker, too, had a vow he was sworn to keep.

Soon, as Tucker's Salvationists, conspicuous in their yellow knee-length coats, pantaloons, turbans, shawls and English boots began piling their baggage on to an ox-wagon—soon christened a " war-chariot "—Police-Superintendent Harry Brewin loomed in view. " When," he asked Tucker point-blank, " will the other members of the party land ? " Puzzled, Tucker replied, " We are the whole of The Army."

For a moment Brewin was speechless. Martial advance billing had claimed The Salvation Army would " storm " India—but how could three men and a girl provoke bloody riots ? " We were expecting you to arrive a thousand strong," he explained sheepishly.

But even one thousand Salvationists could have created no more furore than soon raged round Tucker's party. As they left the dockside, only the constables and a few curious by-standers followed them up—Tucker, the vanguard bearing the " Blood and Fire " banner, Bullard blowing his cornet, Norman, an ex-blacksmith, pounding his drum like an anvil, Mary Thompson in the rear, joyously jingling a tambourine. But when The Army next day, " opened fire " in a large tent in the city's centre, a mighty white-clad throng flocked to see

92

these strange newcomers. " It would be as well not to permit fools to put a torch to gunpowder," agitated one newspaper— and now Sir James goaded his police to act.

Next day, the Commissioner, Sir Frank Soutar, summoning Tucker and Bullard to his office, delivered an embarrassed ultimatum. From now on The Army could conduct no open-air meetings, hold no street processions. Tucker protested bitterly. As versed in Indian law as Sir James, he knew that meetings and marches were entirely legal. Hindus and Moslems paraded the streets with conches and tom-toms, even in the small hours—and Christians held the same right.

The Commissioner was peremptory: his orders were to deny this right. Respectfully but firmly, Tucker replied: " We *shall* go! "

It was no spur-of-the-moment decision. As a former Civil Servant, Tucker knew that to maintain peace between Hindu and Moslem was no easy task. Yet as a believer in justice he must assert the rights of Booth's Army to proclaim their beliefs. That same evening he and his party marched out into the soft blue Indian twilight, singing and playing lustily, but at the junction of Bombay's Obelisk Road, they halted abruptly. From pavement to pavement the road was blocked by a solid phalanx of police, some on foot, others astride groomed, gleaming mounts.

Dismounting, Deputy Commissioner John Godfrey Smith, called dramatically: " In the name of Her Majesty, Queen of England and Queen Empress of India, I order you to disperse."

Tucker, stepping ahead, now raised his hand to command silence. His voice clear and unafraid, he answered: " In the name of His Majesty, the King of Kings and Lord of Lords, I command *you* to stand aside! "

Between The Army and Bombay's Governor a state of war now existed—a war that was to rage intermittently for five long months. Borne off to the lock-up and charged with " forming an assembly likely to lead to a breach of the peace," Tucker's party were at first dismissed with a caution. But when, within days the police hustled them back to gaol on the same charge, the Magistrate, Mr. Dosabhoy Framjee, took a graver view. After a six-hour trial, Tucker heard the verdict. The penalty was a fifty rupee (£5) fine—or a fortnight in gaol.

Tucker, like all pioneer Salvationists, refused the fine on principle and accepted the gaol sentence. When an order was made for distraint on his goods, Superintendent Harry Brewin, a secret sympathiser, promptly bought them at an auction and handed them back.

Sir James Ferguson was smarting at Tucker's temerity. It was unthinkable that this Muktifauj, as Indians called The Army, should parade the native quarter's narrow spice-laden alleys, living like coolies on unleavened bread called chapattis. Already they were peddling *The War Cry* in three different languages ; their propaganda might bring Moslems or Hindus to flashpoint. On 20th October, 1882, Tucker and his officers were arrested for the third time and haled before William Webb the acting Chief Presidency Magistrate. Not a fine but the prospect of six months in gaol now loomed ahead of them.

Only Tucker's unrivalled knowledge of Indian Law won the day. The Queen Empress's post-Mutiny proclamation, he argued, expressly forbade the authorities to interfere with a man's religious beliefs " on pain of our highest displeasure." Wearily the magistrate dismissed the case.

Tucker was playing for time : soon, he sensed, The Army's supporters would outnumber their enemies. Already 3,000 prominent Indians, after a protest meeting in Calcutta's Town Hall, had sent a memorial to the Viceroy, the Marquis of Ripon, deploring the " prosecutions and discriminations shown by the Bombay authorities." Far from inciting Indians to riot, the " Blood and Fire " banner had for months flown unmolested above The Army's tent. And Tucker himself was the only Christian ever invited by the Sikhs to preach to them in their sacred Golden Temple at Amritsar.

In truth, the presence of Booth's Army in India irked no one but Europeans—who saw the notion that Britons and Indians should meet on equal terms as fatal to British dominion. To Indians The Army were oppressed defenders of liberty—and men whose religion made sense. " We will accept Christ," one told Tucker, " when He takes off His hat, trousers and boots."

More arrests followed—and a month's gaol sentence—even though an English barrister, Lewis Ingram, came one thousand miles from Lucknow to defend the Salvationists free of charge. But by February, 1883, the weight of official opinion had swung heavily against Sir James Ferguson. Following the arrest of ten Bombay Salvationists, the chief magistrate seized his chance : Tucker was invited to a private consultation along with Police-Commissioner Soutar.

The upshot was the compromise Tucker had all along proposed ; The Army would hold no processions in Bombay's orthodox Moslem quarters but, save during special emergencies, could sing and pray in non-Moslem streets.

Only later, did Tucker learn that the India Office, London, had stepped in and ordered that the persecution of Salvationists should cease. The Muktifauj had won its first victory.

But Tucker's problems were not ended yet. True, the winning of sympathisers to the cause would ease financial burdens ; the £100 Booth had allotted to the work was long exhausted. In Calcutta alone, well-wishers had raised £400 to buy an Army hall, and Tucker had opened training homes for men and women, plus several thriving stations—Bombay, Calcutta, Madras, Poona, Lahore and Colombo, Ceylon. Yet every recruit Tucker won was already a professing Christian. His efforts to win high-caste Indians were a dismal failure.

The Major knew India too well to condemn its people. In Army training colleges, all castes ate together—but the intricate Hindu caste system forbade any family from taking food with members of a lower caste. A Brahmin turned Salvationist became literally " dead " to his family—his effigy placed on a funeral pyre, the ashes solemnly buried. His parents would pass him on the street without recognition.

One convert, Kumara Singh, was, after urgent pleas, sent to Bombay, 900 miles from his hometown, to escape his family. Yet his angry relatives not only traced, but kidnapped him—and held him prisoner for two long years. His hair was cropped ; his tongue, for fear that he had eaten pork, scored with a hot iron. When he at last escaped to rejoin The Army, his people spoke of him as dead.

Another supporter, Pavistina, a slim and lovely Ceylonese girl, opened her mind to her Buddhist fiancé : unless he embraced her faith marriage was impossible. For answer the man slashed her eleven times with a razor-edged knife. The girl recovered and held fast to her faith, but not all, Tucker knew, could muster courage to sever the ties with their kindred. Among 2,000 who professed conversion most, within months, had turned renegade.

It came home to Tucker that The Army's greatest problem was the rigid stratifications of caste—and the souls he sought were those of India's sixty million outcastes.

Few men were ever subject to such deliberate degradations. At work they had to ring the ground with a wide circle of leaves ; men of higher caste then had proper warning of their unclean presence. They could not drive their cattle across roads used by superior castes. Their dead were carried secretly for burial, like carrion, or lashed to catamarans and floated across rivers.

Tucker now took an epoch-making decision : to win these people, his soldiers, now reinforced from England, must embrace the life the outcastes lived. He pared his party's subsistence allowance down to 3s. 6d. a week. English boots were out-of-place ; from now on they went barefoot, like mendicant friars. Only later, after some had contracted sunstroke through the soles of the feet, did Tucker relent and allow weaker spirits to don sandals. Their clothing was the Indian fakir's saffron robes of renunciation.

Along with English clothing, they sloughed off English names. William Stevens, a former jeweller from Worthing, Sussex, who paid for his training by melting and selling the gold in his shop aptly became Yesu Ratnam (Jewel of Jesus). Clara Case, a wealthy farmer's daughter, was now Nurani (Shining Light); Tucker himself was Fakir Singh, the Lion of God. Others took names translating as Messenger of Truth and Lion of Comfort.

For Tucker's force, soon to total 479 officers, no sacrifice

Bouncers as much as bandsmen, early combinations like the Fry family of Salisbury (left) evolved by degrees into a fervent network of 2,300 bands—among them, The Joystrings, whose pitches range from the steps of St. Paul's Cathedral to London night-clubs

A world known to three million Londoners of the 1880's—the stifling alleys east of Aldgate Pump—spurred Booth and his soldiers to action. (Below) One of scores of British hostels for down-and-outs that sprang from their labours

was too great if it meant winning souls. To reach the Tamils of Southern India, the men shaved their heads Tamil-fashion, leaving only a round patch of hair coiled in a queue, at the crown and back of the head. Their foreheads bore a patented Salvation Army castemark—red, yellow and blue. To win the Bheels, a stocky diminutive warrior tribe in the jungles of Bombay Presidency, Ensign Carl Winge, the Swede assigned to them, adopted the tribal bow and arrow and brass ear-rings. For women officers the brass anklets of Bheel wives became regulation. And the Bheels, who had no elaborate religion like the Hindus, proved worth the winning : four hundred of them enrolled under Booth's banner. In time Winge brought them to love God as an embodiment of perfection, to look on prayer as a communion with all that was ultimate, beautiful and everlasting.

As true Salvationists, Tucker's troops took pride in Indianisation. They cleaned their teeth with charcoal, like all peasants did, washing from a brass bowl ; their simple meals of curry and water were eaten cross-legged on the floor. They came to budget like misers : language lessons were given in the sand to avoid wasting paper. " Hallelujah ! " one new arrival exulted in a letter home, " I haven't been in a bed since coming here but sleep on the ground . . . my feet are swollen and ulcerated with the first week's work and visiting . . . but to see the happy faces of the converts makes up for everything."

So warmly did they welcome this nomad hardness that one group of officers, offered money, refused it point-blank. They still had a spare rupee whose use defeated them until they decided to save it for stamps.

No one found it strange that The Army begged their food from door to door ; to respond to a fakir's appeal in India counts as a deed of high merit. In Ceylon, too, Buddhist priests observe the custom of *pinapati*, standing silently outside a house with a palm-leaf basket, passing on if the owner has no food prepared. One Irish officer, John Lyons, rejoiced in a system inducing true humility ; once, in Angulana, Ceylon, he looked in at sixty-five houses before anyone served him breakfast.

Ex-British Army private William Wilson went still further: to win the outcastes of the Poona district he put himself within their pale, cramped in a straw-roofed mud-hut sixteen feet by twelve. High-caste men moulded their muslin robes tight about them as Wilson approached, cringing from pollution. Shopkeepers drove him from their premises; his food was brought and set on the ground at a gingerly distance. Wilson settled for his provisions by leaving the purchase money on the spot—coins the shopkeeper decontaminated by shuffling them in the sand with his feet.

Wild animals held no terrors for Booth's officers. One, hearing a tiger cough in the midnight jungle, gaily blew his cornet and was troubled no more. But there were deadlier foes than beasts of prey. To worst The Army in their struggle to bring the outcastes dignity and self-respect, high-caste opponents stopped at nothing. One such occasion was when Major William Stevens, threading his way by night through dripping jungle from Keracheri to Nagercoil, near Cape Cormorin, narrowly escaped death. In the lonely darkness, three men leapt from the bushes to work him over savagely with clubs. Painfully Stevens retraced his steps to The Salvation Army's tiny hall, one minute before his ruthless attackers hurtled in after him. A headlong dive through the window saved the Major's life but the hall was wrecked beyond repair.

Other Salvationists fared no better. The high-caste men of one village buried some coconuts near an officer's home, then lodged a complaint at the police station. The coconuts were unearthed and the magistrate passed a heavy sentence for theft. Another lieutenant, buying bananas, was hustled before the police and charged with trespass; a Hindu festival was in full swing and all of contrary faith were at that time banned from the bazaar. Sentenced to three weeks' imprisonment, he lay on the stone floor of a dirty cell in Black Town Gaol. Only Major Stevens's personal appeal to Lord Wenlock, Governor of Madras, quashed the sentence.

How did the Salvationists triumph over such bitter opposition? Much of the answer was through sheer Christian example: what Christians did, not what they said, meant everything. A dark handsome blue-eyed girl from Dundee, Scotland, Elizabeth Geikie, was a matchless example. To her tiny hut in the jungle near Nagercoil—its one touch of home *The War Cry* pictures pasted on mud walls—the villagers brought a man almost crazed with pain. Bending close to the litter Elizabeth Geikie saw a huge thorn driven like a nail through his foot; only the pinpoint was visible. Her medicine chest held only Vaseline, Epsom salts and castor-oil, but if Elizabeth had no forceps she had white firm teeth. Kneeling, she managed to clamp them round the thorn and wrench it free. Then she bathed the wound in coconut oil and wrapped it in clean lint.

Next day, when the pain had gone, the villagers were curious to know more of Elizabeth Geikie's God. Both the wounded man *and* his wife—though they never fully understood her sermons—became Salvationists. But they understood that to save a life a white woman had placed her lips, the most sacred part of the body, upon the most despised member, the foot.

Such primitive beginnings, in the jungle at Nagercoil, led irresistibly to the twenty-six hospitals and dispensaries, the two leper colonies, The Salvation Army now run in India. But they led to spiritual triumphs, too. Some villages, like Manakudi, in Travancore, had already offered up their temples to The Army; the idols were ground to powder, the shrines became officers' quarters. But Elizabeth Geikie had no illusions about her own village of Alady. When the autumn festival of Ganesa-Caturthi came, the same men and women, a drunken howling mob, would bring their offerings to Ganesh, the Elephant-Headed God. The devil dancers, after gulping down bowlfuls of goats' blood, would whirl and scream until they dropped senseless.

Timid villagers warned that attempts to interfere might cost her life. Elizabeth Geikie was undismayed. On the night of the festival she waited hidden in the shelter of the temple—really a small breast-high canopy sheltering the idol. Tom-toms pulsed from the village of Alady; she heard whoops of high-pitched drunken laughter. Presently several score villagers burst into the moonlit clearing, arms piled high with coconuts, lemons and rice, one man with a goat slung round his neck. Suddenly, to their amazement, Elizabeth Geikie stood poised above them at the very apex of the shrine, dramatically clad in a salmon-pink sari, arms outspread.

Her voice was charged with rebuke: "You are now followers of the living God. Put down your offerings; this image cannot use them. Kneel down, for we are all going to pray."

No screams of execration followed, but a long stunned silence. Beneath her, amid the crowd, were men and women she had nursed through cholera and childbirth, needy people she had fed and comforted. Never had they known her to speak other than the truth or to seek anything beside their welfare. Putting aside their bundles they knelt in silent prayer—the first of many to be offered to God on the site that is still Alady's Salvation Army Hall.

The Army's triumph in India was greater than Tucker had envisaged; in time many saw it as a native-born religion. The public testimony of men like Sathanesian, a former devil-priest of the goddess Ammon, helped foster this belief; often, in the market place at Travancore, the tall handsome priest with his iron-grey beard would tell how he had put aside a goddess whose worship demanded orgies between children of eight, for a God who demanded only a cleansed heart and a soul devoted to righteousness. And when Tucker, later promoted Commissioner, arrived at a railway station with his second-in-command, Colonel Arnolis Weerasoriya, a Ceylonese Buddhist who had once deliberately set fire to a Bible, a curious native at first eyed their shaven heads and Army caste-marks in silence. Finally he asked Weerasoriya: "Is this Englishman a convert of yours?"

Indians saw, too, that as Tucker's second-in-command for the whole of India and Ceylon, Weerasoriya took precedence over at least one hundred English Salvationists—the new token of an international force which marched ahead of its day and generation, recognising no barriers of race or colour. "Foreign" was a word erased from their vocabulary; each man was seen for what he was—" a brother for whom Christ died."

The pressures of a vast organisation began to tell on William Booth. From September, 1881, life at his new six-story headquarters, a former billiards-club at 101 Queen Victoria Street, a block away from St. Paul's Cathedral, seemed never-ending. There was little ceremony about the transfer ; converting the building cost less than £600 and most of the Whitechapel Road furnishings came on a rickety handcart steered by " Zulu George," a dark-skinned cadet from Devonshire House Training Home. Amid a routine so arduous, ceremony seemed out of place ; most of the head-quarters staff of eighty soon accepted overtime as the norm. Any man who wouldn't gladly send to Pearce's Coffee Shop for haddock and a mug of tea then toil on till midnight was no soldier of Booth's.

Statistics alone show the measure of his achievement. By 1884, three years after the Queen Victoria Street transfer, his Army was made up of 900 Corps, over 260 of them abroad. Yet of 500 overseas officers, no more than ninety had been posted from Britain ; Railton's concept of evangelisation by agents on the spot was working well. Salvation was now a £30,000 a year, seven-days-a-week concern ; often the hard-pressed headquarters staff received and dispatched 2,000 letters a day.

This year, too, marked the last holiday—a brief retreat to lodgings at Lytham St. Anne's on the Lancashire coast—that Booth and Catherine ever took together. Somehow after that God's business always claimed priority.

Often, his aides noted, Booth grew irritable, even harsh-tempered ; he was now almost never free from the dyspepsia which plagued him. Some men confessed that his presence made them " almost bleed at the pores with nervousness." He breakfasted meagrely on a boiled egg, buttered toast and un-sweetened tea, and he would thunder that he liked his tea as he liked his religion—H-O-T ! Lunch was vegetable soup and cheese, with sometimes an apple or a baked potato, and these were the staple items of afternoon and evening snacks; no headquarters office-boy removing a lunch-tray grew fat on Booth's leavings. For the last forty years of his life he rarely touched butcher's meat. He ate at the famished speed of a man whose stomach is almost always in pain.

But there was still deep comfort to be found in the family life of his Clapton Common home. Young Theodore Kitching, the former Quaker schoolteacher, always recalled an afternoon spent taking tea with Catherine while she placidly darned the General's stockings. But suddenly, as the carriage of Old Balls, the local cabby, ground to a halt outside, Catherine sprang to her feet like a young bride and hastened to the door.

" Oh, William, how good it is to see you, but how tired you look ! " Kitching heard her cry, and at once she was at his side, handing him the woollen slippers that she herself had made, stroking and kissing Booth's hand and smoothing his hair as he took his seat beside her. Deeply touched, Kitching tip-toed from the room. These lovers were now fifty-three years old, and soon they would celebrate their thirtieth wedding anniversary.

And Booth could find comfort, too, in children who had given their lives to God : the sight of them clustered in the kitchen after an evening's meeting, wolfing cheese and spring onions, talking excitedly of new converts and recruits, never failed to stir him. At twenty-eight Bramwell was still his father's devoted Chief of Staff; after initial misgivings about the type of recruit The Army attracted he had come round to Abraham Lincoln's view that God must love the common people because he had made so many of them. The worst of Kate's battles in France were over ; soon Herbert, who had gone to assist her, would succeed Ballington as head of the men's training home. Only Marian, aged twenty, was too delicate to play a warrior's role in the Salvation war. At twenty-four, Emma would soon depart for India as the wife of Major Frederick Tucker ; within the decade, Booth's fifth daughter, sixteen-year-old Lucy, would follow her.

And Evangeline, with her fiery red hair and fierier oratory, promised great things. Some of the credit for this lay at George Railton's door; at mealtimes, if young Eva refused her food, Railton would ply her with tastier portions from his own plate and resist all Catherine's efforts to replenish it. Eva learned to subdue her will: if she was naughty or capricious, someone else would suffer. At first William and Catherine had secretly worried: would Eva, with her inborn sense of drama, leave The Army to become an actress? But Eva had learned to channel histrionic talent; as an eighteen-year-old Army Lieutenant she identified herself instead with the anguish of the poor—" I was the chimney-sweep, the woman selling wilted violets in the square. I did not lead one life, but many. . . ." Street folk called this handsome vibrant girl who once sold flowers in Piccadilly Circus and played Salvation songs on an accordion in public bars " The White Angel of the Slums."

Seventeen years after opening fire on Mile End Waste, Booth could look back proudly on a decision amply justified by time. On one day, challenging a Bishop's criticism of The Army's aggressive methods, at Exeter Hall, in the Strand, he so stirred his audience they subscribed £9,000 to the cause. But other clergy were moved to court him. Early in 1882, the Archbishop of York, Dr. William Thomson, had mooted a radical change: the amalgamation of The Salvation Army with the Church of England. There were people, he confessed, that his Church was powerless to reach; one week-night London survey of this era tallied almost 17,000 worshipping in Army barracks as against 11,000 in ordinary churches. But though Booth sat in on a round-table meeting with such leading ecclesiastics as Dr. Benson, Bishop of Truro, and Randall Davidson, then Dean of Windsor, the plan was soon abandoned. Booth would not relinquish one iota of his control—and George Railton's view confirmed his own. The Army had spanned the globe for the very reason that it was mobile, single-minded and defied convention.

" You see," Booth summed up gently, to one cleric who puzzled over The Army's success, " We have no reputation to lose."

Wherever they laboured, their results were still uncanny. In the Rhondda Valley, once the most drunken and degraded zone in all South Wales, 2,000 souls, professing conversion within six weeks, donned white rosettes to signify their loyalty. One pub, in an entire week, drew only three pints. In Newcastle-on-Tyne, a distraught gin seller offered Rachel and Louise Agar, the original " Hallelujah Lasses," £300 to leave town on the next train ; their fervour was putting him out of business.

But success attracts not only supporters but implacable enemies, and the opposition was fast massing. By 1886, this ominous advice loomed large in " Orders and Regulations," the fruit of bitter experience ; " When the windows of a barracks are broken, the best plan is to barricade them with wood on the outer side. It would be very foolish to replace the glass until the riotous spirit has passed away. . . ."

No idle whim led William Booth to enjoin his soldiers to caution from 1880 on ; for more than four embattled years, the fate of The Salvation Army trembled in the balance. Booth could drive himself and others unmercifully when occasion arose but the need for prudence was plain. If Catherine had taught him that his women helpers didn't expect to be treated like china ornaments the General still wanted living evangelists, not dead martyrs.

Behind the green baize doors of his Queen Victoria Street office, its walls dominated by a huge portrait of Catherine, Booth studied with mounting dismay the reports of riot and carnage flooding in from all over Britain. All too conscious that The Army had driven deep salients into the heart of their territory, publicans and brothel-keepers were launching a savage all-out counter-attack ; the cost, in terms of human lives and injuries, became daily more apparent. The bureaucratic pinpricks of Bombay and New York were seen for what they were. The Army learned the bleak truth of the Spanish proverb : " He who would be a Christ must expect crucifixion."

Methods and missiles might vary but the mob's aim was

avowed : the annihilation of this too-powerful Salvation Army. At Gravesend, on the River Thames, drunken seamen sent ship's rockets searing towards a crowd of singing lasses at point-blank range. In Whitechapel, East London, lasses were first roped together like cattle, then pelted with live coals. On dark nights, hooligans used sprinklers to shower the marching troops with tar and burning sulphur. At Hucknall, Nottinghamshire, one cadet was slugged so savagely with a scaffolding plank he lay unconscious for three days.

Many men who should have known better whipped the mobs to greater frenzy. At Hastings, the town's leading grocer offered rotten eggs free to all comers as anti-Salvation ammunition. At Folkestone, Kent, a clergyman sent a public message to The Army Captain : " Is the peace of this town to be disturbed night after night for a bastard flag that represents nothing and nobody ? " And he went further : a cash prize would go to the first tough capturing The Army's banner and bearing it to his study. Promptly Mayor Edwin Bradman added fuel to the flame : " Drive 'em all into the 'arbour or into 'ell. Take their flags and tie it round their necks and hang 'em." From now on Folkestone Salvationists ran a merciless gauntlet of hooting fishermen. Roads were blocked against them with the masts of fishing-smacks ; fish refuse and rocks burst about them.

No General to hang back and leave his troops to bear the brunt, Booth was often in the thick of it. When a kerbside rough spat at him on one Midlands tour, Booth curbed a solicitous aide : " Don't rub it off—it's a medal ! " At Sheffield in January, 1882, his generalship was tested to the full : a monster procession organised by Elijah Cadman tramped steadily through the grey stone streets towards the city's Albert Hall. Ahead rattled a wagonette, with a brass band playing lustily ; behind them, mounted on a white horse, rode Lieutenant Emmerson Davison, converted champion wrestler of Northumberland. In the rearguard, scores of uniformed Salvationists kept step behind the General's carriage. A sidelong glance showed close on 1,000 cloth-capped ruffians, called " The Sheffield Blades," massed on the winter pavements, jeering and gibing. Suddenly, with a blood-curdling yell, they spilled into the roadway, streaking like furies for The Army's line of march.

Flying clods of soft wet mud hailed about the band; mud choked and blinded them and the music wavered. A stone struck Lieutenant Davison clean between the eyes; as the wrestler swayed in the saddle, half blind with pain, a flying cudgel caught him an agonising welt across the base of his skull. Only the combined efforts of two roughs to unhorse him saved him from toppling headlong to the pavement. As one tugged from the left, the other strained from the right; the harder they wrenched, the more secure was his seat. Somehow fellow-officers drove them off, literally propping Davison on his mount until the hall was reached. "I hope they'll get saved," the wrestler whispered, then the world went dark. Removed to hospital, he lay concussed for weeks upon the brink of death.

Through it all Booth stood bolt upright in his carriage, mud and dead cats hurtling past him, his face a graven mask as he barked crisp orders. "Stay near the carriage, stay near the carriage!" they heard his rallying cry, his arms outstretched to receive cornets and tubas that hard-pressed bandsmen were thrusting on him. At length, when all had reached the Albert Hall, his battered, bleeding cohorts were ordered direct to the platform. At the sight of their buckled instruments, the uniforms smeared with blood and egg-yolk, a low buzz of horror stirred the vast audience, rising to an angry clamour of protest. "Now's the time to get your photographs taken!" Booth told his aides with grim humour.

To survive at all, his soldiers learned defensive tactics. Often Elijah Cadman ended a march loaded down by a whole armful of dead rats and cats; to drop them, he explained, gave the mob fresh ammunition. In theory, no Salvationists resisted physical violence; their refuge was a sunny "God bless you" and a prayer for their assailant. But sometimes Quaker forbearance wore thin. In Manchester, Mrs. Honor Burrell lost all patience with a man who taunted her: "Here's a woman that can work miracles." Taking a stranglehold of his neck-scarf, her retort was pithy : " I can't—but I can cast out devils." With that she pitched him bodily downstairs. And one Salisbury convert, to Marianne Faulconbridge's dismay, armed himself with a novel shield beneath his alpaca jacket— a thin board shaped to his back, studded with projecting tin-tacks. No man who thumped him from behind came back for another dose. When Marianne remonstrated, the convert was guileless : " But *you* preached about being as wise as serpents and harmless as doves."

As the months wore on, one factor was plain : the British police were broken reeds, backed by the peace-at-any-price policy of the Home Secretary, Sir William Harcourt. Pressed by the magistrates of Stamford, Lincolnshire, as to what they should do if The Army opened fire, Harcourt was succinct : Salvationist processions weren't illegal, but when they pro-voked antagonism and endangered the peace of a town, magistrates " should by every means in their power endeavour to prevent them." Each time Booth sought redress he was fobbed off with excuses ; a complaint to Edmund Yeamans Henderson, head of the Metropolitan Police, about the brutal usage of Whitechapel lasses, was passed to East London's Superintendent Arnold. Arnold at first pooh-poohed it : there had been no complaints from constables on their beats.

Only when Booth produced cast-iron proof did the officer let fall the mask. " Why don't you people stop in your build-ings and let the streets alone ? " he burst out furiously.

But molestation wasn't confined to the streets. At Notting Hill, West London, where the crippled Staff-Captain Eliza Drabble preached from a wheel-chair, troublemakers and Army officers often tussled at the rear of the hall while others wept at the Penitent-form. At Plymouth, Devon, forty men armed with brimming chamber pots stormed the hall to drench James Dowdle, " The Saved Railway Guard," with urine. Time and again meetings closed down in wild con-fusion.

In one year alone—1882—669 Salvation Army soldiers were knocked down or brutally assaulted. Sixty buildings were virtually wrecked by the mob. Even 1,500 police doing extra duty every Sunday seemed powerless to protect Booth's troops.

Neither age nor sex proved a barrier for the mobs were out for blood. In Northampton, one blackguard tried to knife a passing lassie ; Wolverhampton thugs flung lime in a Salvationist child's eyes. At Hastings, Mrs. Susannah Beaty, one of Booth's first converts on Mile End Waste, became The Army's first martyr, buried from Clapton's Congress Hall. Reeling under a fire of rocks and putrid fish, she was kicked deliberately in the womb and left for dead in a dark alley of the Old Town. The doctor's prophecy that her injuries could prove fatal came appallingly true.

Often police and magistrates proved as vindictive as the mobs. In Boston, Lincolnshire, Captain Josiah Taylor was arraigned for obstructing the market-place ; his services were distressing the ailing mother-in-law of The Angel Tavern's landlord. The magistrates heard in silence his plea that taproom customers sang twice as loudly—then gaoled him when he refused to pay their fine. One Truro, Cornwall, captain got two months for a street concertina recital. In Scotland fifteen Forfar soldiers went handcuffed to prison ; they had dared to preach in the open air. And at Whitchurch, Hampshire, a tiny market-town, the magistrate, Melville Portal, heartily commended the local police sergeant ; no less than ninety-three charges of obstruction were levelled against the four local soldiers. Beside them in the dock was a tradesman's wife who had not left her house ; her crime was the partisan display of *The War Cry* in her window. The sentence : one month's hard labour without the option of a fine. Only an appeal to the House of Lords got the sentences quashed.

Such blatant injustices stirred many men to protest. The famous Manchester engineer, Frank Crossley, sprang impulsively from the magistrate's bench at Altrincham, Cheshire, to join a lassie in the dock. From that day over £100,000 of his personal fortune financed Army enterprises. The Bishop of Durham, Dr. Joseph Lightfoot, defended The Army hotly : " They have ... recalled us to the lost ideals of the work of the Church—the universal compulsion of the souls of men."

From the House of Commons, the statesman John Bright wrote to Catherine Booth: "The people who mob you would, doubtless, have mobbed the apostles."

But Booth's soldiers had grown used to fighting alone: coercion was closing their ranks. To-day's Salvationists still publicly dedicate, not baptise, their children, but the since-revised dedication of the 'eighties involved stern and binding promises—"You must be willing that the child should spend all its life in The Salvation Army, wherever God should choose to send it, that it should be despised, hated, cursed, beaten, kicked, imprisoned or killed for Christ's sake."

Half an hour after noon each day no Salvationist failed to heed George Railton's inspired command: wherever duty found them then, they knelt to pray for those in the field.

Officers like John Roberts, in the quiet Devon watering-place of Torquay, drew heightened resolution from the knowledge of invisible allies. The local authorities had vetoed all Sunday street processions but Roberts, minded to resist, took counsel with Eva Booth—"Send Eva!" was now the General's unvarying command whenever trouble threatened. With Eva, Roberts evolved a novel strategy: rather than pay fines, converts could freely go to gaol, but Sunday after Sunday the streets were jammed with proxy bandsmen drafted in from nearby towns. To the police, it seemed these implacable Salvationists sprouted like weeds before their eyes. One mortified superintendent spat out: "Kill a fly and two will come to the funeral."

As Britain's police turned the blindest of eyes the mobs' audacity grew. One hundred young toughs in Oldham, Lancashire, who booted the lasses without mercy, were among the first to organise a "Skeleton Army"—but within weeks the sick virus of hatred had infected the nation. When the Skeletons opened subscription-lists, brewers and publicans weighed in generously; at Guildford, Surrey, one saloon-keeper offered £1,000. They took their name from the skull-and-crossbones banners they adopted, inscribed with strange legends—gorillas, rats, even Satan himself. Their weapons were flour, ordure, red ochre, and jagged death-dealing brick-bats.

Others showed more ingenuity. At Weston-super-Mare, 2,000 Skeletons let loose a flock of live pigeons through The Army Hall's shattered windows. Swooping and blundering in terror, the birds dislodged acrid clouds of red pepper secreted beneath their wings ; eyes and nostrils on fire, The audience stumbled out to face the fury of the mob. But their plight and that of many like them, won scant sympathy from the powers-that-be.

In fact, despite the Church's proposed merger, Booth was truly hated by many in high places. A man whose soldiers stood at street-corners like vendors, proclaiming Christ's power to save, was rated an indecent charlatan ; even the great reformer, Lord Shaftesbury, branded him " anti-Christ." Clerics disliked his Quaker tactics of publicly declaring the truth ; they resented his contempt for religious controversy, his dispensation with baptism and the sacraments. But Booth, a shrewd psychologist, took radical steps for radical reasons. Too easily, he knew, fresh, often weak-willed converts came to lean on external forms ; a true Salvationist's strength must come from within. And many in his ranks were reformed alcoholics ; one sip of sacramental wine could plunge them back into the abyss.

Hotly resented, too, was the General's elevation of women to man's status : a Victorian woman's place was in the home. But as early as 1878, when The Christian Mission died, Booth had seen the force of Catherine's argument : where women preachers were given their heads, the cause made giant strides. " The best men in my Army are the women," he avowed then. From this time on, a woman officer enjoyed equal rights with a man ; then, as now, when lasses outnumber male officers by five to one, " Orders and Regulations " ceased to distinguish between " he " or " she." A Salvation Army lassie can be General, doctor, editor, chaplain—and officiate at marriages and funerals.

One lassie set out to worst a Skeleton Army almost single-handed—and the upshot was a bitter bloody battle. Early in

1884, twenty-three-year-old Captain Ada Smith, pretty and deceptively demure, took over the newly-formed Worthing Corps, a quiet summer resort on the Sussex coast. To her amazement she found all street processions, of The Army's own volition, had been suspended. Only a narrow brick alley, eighty yards long, gave access to their meeting-place, the upper story of an old warehouse on Prospect Place ; half-way up was the side-door of a gin-shop. Stung by The Army's attacks on liquor, the gin-seller had barricaded the passage.

Following one spirited Army protest, the landlord tore it down, but from then on opposition was massing. Whoever daubed the alley's walls each week with a black sticky curtain of tar, the Salvationists never knew—but they knew the havoc it played with their uniforms each time they marched out in procession. Promptly The Army's Captain Frances Kirkby, suspended all street meetings.

Then Ada Smith took over to find a situation that made no sense : a congregation of well-to-do tradesmen picking their way up the alley each Sunday in cautious Indian file while the street-corners teemed with the very roughnecks The Army sought to reach.

By 1884, The Army held thousands of open-air meetings each year in Great Britain alone—and Ada Smith saw no cause why Worthing should lag behind. " If the Devil doesn't attack us, we ought to attack him," she vowed. From now on her Sunday meetings would be held in the slums of the town, or along the four-mile stretch of sandy beach.

It was the signal the enemy had awaited. Within days the ringleaders of a gang of bullies almost 4,000 strong, potboy Jimmy Medhurst and labourer Edward Elridge, met at The George tavern to swear in recruits for Worthing's Skeleton Army. Each man would recognise his fellows through a distinctive flash : a small piece of yellow ribbon with the motto " Excelsior " tagged to his cloth cap. Those who fancied them sported king-size sunflowers in their button-holes or walking sticks with skull-and-crossbones handles. But all knew the flag they followed, for its device would stop a man short at thirty paces—a human skeleton topped by a grinning skull, stark white against a jet-black background.

From the first the townsfolk were solidly behind them. *The Worthing Gazette* sneered openly at the Salvationists—" excitable young men and hysterical young women who mistake a quasi-religious revelry for godliness." A wealthy boarding-house keeper was strident : " One of the finest seasons ever known at Worthing has been utterly ruined by the noisy parades." The drunken gangs of Skeletons who harried Captain Ada's little band of twenty through the streets, lobbing egg-shells charged with blue paint, met with full approval. Prominent on their subscription list were Police-Surgeon Augustus Collett and Worthing Hospital Committee's Henry Tribe, who offered a £20 reward to any man pitching a lassie into the sea.

At Queen Victoria Street, Booth, hearing that trouble threatened, acted swiftly : until further notice, Ada Smith and her band were confined to barracks. Before he committed his troops to the streets, Booth wanted written assurance that the West Sussex County Constabulary would keep a fatherly eye on them. But the Chief Constable, Captain George Robinson Drummond, sat securely on the fence. He would treat both Salvationists and Skeletons " with impartiality."

By July, 1884, Booth was beside himself : a blistering memo to the Home Office charged that Worthing magistrates simply refused to summon riff-raff molesting The Salvation Army. Sir William Harcourt stood by the letter of the law : the Secretary of State had no power over local authorities. Three days later, Booth followed up with a telegram : he wanted steps taken to protect his Salvationists, and now. But Sir William remained adamant.

A month later, on 15th August, Booth sent Sir William " the most remarkable declaration that has ever come into our hands from a police authority " ; a letter from Captain George Drummond that at first glance seemed barely credible. Begging The Salvation Army not to be " provocative," the Chief Constable explained : " The persons who form the Skeleton

From a naphtha-lit tent on a Whitechapel burial-ground Booth moved on to take the world for his parish—travelling by liner, 'motorcade' (below), even bullock cart. In sixty years he travelled five million miles, preached 60,000 sermons

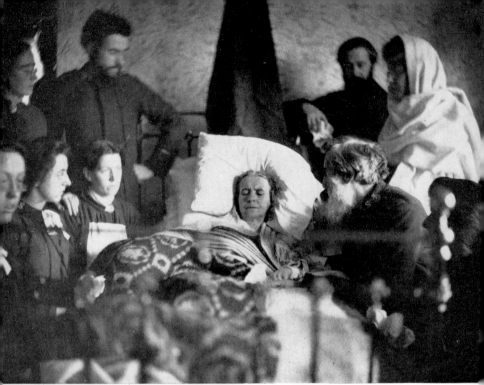

(Above) The General and his children gathered round the bed on which Catherine lay dying of cancer. She died on October 4th 1890. (Left) May 23rd, 1912. Booth posed with his dog Pat for his last photograph, as he waited for the surgeon to decide on an operation which was to cost him his sight

Army have received and do receive considerable encouragement from those in a higher social position."

As Booth wavered, the intrepid Captain Ada, one of the smallest lasses ever to pass out from training-college, made her own decision. " This," she wrote grimly to her General, " must be fought out," and Booth could only agree. " I have now," he warned Sir William, " ordered our people to march on Sundays."

The Worthing police saw the red light. By 2 p.m. on Sunday, 17th August, as Captain Ada marshalled her troops outside the rented Montague Hall, watched by a hooting rabble of Skeletons, reserve constables were trooping in by train and carriage from outlying districts. The Deputy Chief Constable had himself travelled from Chichester, twenty-one miles away, to take over.

Through Worthing's graceful Regency streets, the procession wound at a snail's pace, sweating under a brassy sun, a hell's chorus of sound rending the air—the cornets, tubas and bass-drum of the Salvationists, the shrill wolf-howls of the Skeletons marching ahead. Along the route, blue-clad police packed the pavements, gripping black polished truncheons, alert for signs of trouble.

For almost an hour, uneasy calm prevailed—but as the Salvationists, their itinerary completed, again drew near Montague Hall, the Skeletons struck. As if on cue, they exchanged their measured step for a steady double. Running, they soon outdistanced Captain Ada's band by thirty yards. Halting, they turned, faces flushed and contemptuous ; their cocky smiles did not reach their eyes. There was a shocked momentary stillness, a frozen tableau. Then, with a wild bull-roar, they charged.

The placid stretch of Bath Place was suddenly a sea of screaming men, battling amid brick-dust and broken glass. The crimson-and-blue " Blood and Fire " banner swayed, then toppled like a sapling. Truncheons flailing, the police burst through ; with bottles and boots, the Skeletons fought back, intent on retaining their own banner. Nimbly, clutching their instruments, the Salvationists ducked from the mêlée, escaping to the barricaded sanctuary of Montague Hall. Reluctantly Ada Smith cancelled that evening's procession.

But the Skeletons had tasted blood. At dusk on Monday, 18th August, they were strutting the streets in force—black banner flying, chanting "Wait Till the Clouds Roll By," defiantly brandishing their "blisters," cant phrase for a police-court summons. At Montague Hall, the Salvationists, holding a peaceful weeknight service, heard with trepidation the war-song of the advancing army. Within seconds they had sought hasty refuge beneath the seats; boulders crashed like meteorites through the high windows and broken glass showered about them as they prayed.

Within the hour, the police learned a chastening lesson: even they were not immune. As they bore off Skeleton leader William Medhurst for assaulting a constable, the mob followed them up: outside the police station in Ann Street they cut loose with a barrage of rocks, then defied the police to come out. Not a constable was seen again that night.

It was the chance the Skeletons had awaited. Soon, 4,000 strong, they were roistering through the twilit streets bound for the Montague Street shop of George Head, Salvationist plumber and painter, and owner of Montague Hall. A man of property, Head was deemed fair game; as the shop's glass doors shivered into fragments, ten Skeletons, piling through, went to work with the fierce energy of vandals. Hastening from the cellar, Head, a quiet bearded resolute man, saw that he was outnumbered ten to one—and already one thug was flicking lighted lucifers towards his oil-measurer.

Outside in the street, a curious crowd made no move to intervene; Head saw just one course of action. Seconds later, the incredulous raiders stared down the narrow gleaming barrel of a revolver. "If you don't leave this shop," promised Head, his hand rock-steady, "I'll fire."

Abruptly, a revolver cracked; alarmed, the watching crowd saw two of the Skeletons, blood pouring from their faces and hands, stagger blindly from the shop. As their mates clawed frantically after them, the bystanders turned and ran.

By Wednesday, when the first Skeletons came before the

magistrates, the police meant business: they saw imprisonment, not fines, as the sole deterrent. Without demur, the
magistrates awarded Medhurst and two other ringleaders a
month's hard labour.

It was the spark that lit the fuse. At late afternoon the little
seaside town trembled on the brink of mob law; straggling
bands of men prowled the streets in an ugly mood of violence.
Medhurst, they swore, would never leave Worthing to serve
his sentence. The alarmed Lieut.-Colonel Thomas Wisden,
the presiding magistrate, sent a post-haste message to Preston
Barracks, Brighton. At nine p.m., for the first time in Worthing's uneventful history, a squadron of forty Dragoon Guards,
in scarlet tunics with blue facings, came clattering into the
town.

But their impassive show of strength, as they swept through
the streets, inflamed the mob still further. At eleven-twenty
p.m., after repeatedly exhorting the crowds to break up,
Colonel Wisden mounted the town hall's gas-lit steps to read
the Riot Act—an unrepealed decree of George I empowering
any Justice faced with a dozen or more rioters to clear the
streets.

His voice clear and resonant, Wisden ordered firmly:
" Our Sovereign Lady the Queen chargeth and commandeth
all persons being assembled immediately to disperse themselves, and peaceably to depart to their habitations . . . God
save the Queen! "

Now as his voice died, the cavalry, tight-packed and
formidable, rode steadily towards the massed roughs, white
leather gauntlets clamped tight over steel sword hilts. But at
once the angry cries redoubled; a rain of bricks burst about
the dragoons' brass helmets. Horses reared and bucked;
with long staves drawn, the police hurtled forward, flailing a
purposeful path through the Skeletons' ranks. Not until one
a.m., still gibing and grumbling, were the last trouble-
makers straggling homeward.

But the police remained vigilant. Beneath Montague Hall,
George Head, The Army's landlord, stored vats of oil and
spirits; the Skeletons had boasted that if the chance came

they would burn Captain Ada and her troops alive. Now four constables did dusk-to-dawn duty outside Montague Hall, with six Salvation sentries posted within.

Almost seventy years later one of them, Rank-Sergeant Harry Standing, still recalled that on those incredible all-night watches he and his fellows were the first and only soldiers ever to guard a Salvation barracks armed with loaded six-chamber police revolvers.

Within the next three weeks, Captain Drummond, taking no chances, enrolled almost 230 special constables.

It was a timely action. On Sunday, 7th September, Ada Smith prudently confined her afternoon service to Montague Hall—but to her alarm the Skeletons invaded the balcony, groaning and booing, calling for " Three cheers for Old Booth's baa-lambs." Six of them, perching precariously on the Penitent-form, conducted an ear-splitting cacophony of groans and hisses ; in vain Captain Ada called for order, blowing shrilly on a small whistle. Suddenly, alerted to trouble, a posse of constables swept in ; one of them, near-berserk, smashed an innocent bystander to his knees.

Now a jungle-screech of execration burst from the balcony ; the narrow stairs to the main hall were choked with savage clawing men bent on destruction. A seething trampling mass of bonnets, helmets and cloth caps battled amid a blizzard of torn song books, toppling across overturned forms.

Incredibly, events now followed the identical pattern of violence that the town had earlier witnessed. As the police hauled the ringleaders to the station, they were followed by a running fire of rocks and soot. Powerless to disperse the mob, they bolted their doors. Rampaging back to Montague Hall, the Skeletons found barred doors resisting them. Only one building remained as target for their fury—George Head's shop.

It was an amazing scene for a peaceful seaside Sunday—the hot white sand, the Channel sparkling like a blue-grey brooch and 4,000 hate-crazed men massing before Head's solid bow-fronted Montague Street shop.

With sudden shocking impact the drawing-room windows

seemed to split apart; an ominous row of white stars leaped into relief across the pane. One Skeleton leader, Edward Olliver, a Worthing cabby, crumpled and fell, blood gouting from a wound in his lower jaw. Pressed against the window-glass, the wreckers glimpsed Head's face, pale with anger as he fired and fired again. On a sudden the grey expanse of the street was a stampede of shabby men fighting to get away.

Symbolically, those shots marked the close of Worthing's Salvation war. Though Head was arrested and tried at the Kent and Sussex Assizes, charged with maliciously wounding Olliver, the jury's verdict was unanimous: Not Guilty. And the Judge added a rider of approval: Head had been fully justified in protecting his life and property. Emboldened, Worthing's police resolved to do their duty by The Salvation Army: at each Sunday parade, special constables lined the streets as for a Royal procession. Walls and hoardings were loud with black-lettered police notices: from now on Skeleton Army subscribers would be treated as criminals, liable to three months' hard labour without the option of a fine.

But to Captain Ada and her warriors, the most heartening sequel was the vindication of their faith in man's essential goodness. Ashamed that they had often stood by and condoned the Salvationists' ill-usage, many leading tradesmen now donned white armbands and formed a voluntary body-guard at their open-air meetings.

Fully seven years would pass before magistrates and police at Eastbourne, Sussex, came down so heavily on The Salvation Army's side that persecution began to dwindle. The first onslaught saw fifty roughs fined £5 ; fourteen of them, in default of payment, served a month in gaol. All over Britain authorities paid belated heed to the earlier ruling of the Lord Chief Justice, Lord Coleridge: "Walking through the streets in order and in procession, even if accompanied by music and the singing of hymns, is absolutely lawful, in the doing of which every subject has a right to be protected." A staunch supporter of Booth, Lord Coleridge mused on an earlier parallel: had John Wesley created a disturbance at Lincoln College, Oxford, simply because the undergraduates had pelted him with mud? Singing hymns and shouting " Hallelujah " was not " brawling " within the meaning of the law. The Salvation Army, like all citizens, had their inalienable legal rights.

All this lay in the future. For William Booth in the early 'eighties there was one problem almost greater than sustained opposition : his Army was fast outstripping its resources.

For by 1883, one year before the riots erupted bloodily at Worthing, Booth's Army was in possession of over 400 buildings seating over half a million people—£64,000 worth of property, with the building fund £12,000 in deficit. Local prejudice decreed that buildings were rented, not borrowed ; chapels and schoolrooms that were free to other denominations were closed to The Army. Often this proved a blessing in disguise ; men and women who would attend no other place of worship flocked to The Army's tabernacles—auction rooms, pawnshops, old sawmills, skating rinks, even disused brewery yards.

But many were so cold and damp that to work in them was an ordeal. At Heckmondwike, Yorkshire, flurries of rain drove through the hall's shattered windows ; sparrows twittered in the high rafters. In Durham city, headquarters was the cellar of a riverside chemist's shop, untenable each time the river burst its banks. Only the fiery fervour of Salvationism could warm the blood of the 4,000 converts who weekly packed out Hull's Icehouse, once used for storing meat. At Bradninch, near Exeter, even bricks and mortar were lacking ; the officers worked from a carthouse loft, flanked by a cesspit and a slaughterhouse. Those who claimed salvation knelt on the dirt floor, fighting to drown with their songs the screams of butchered animals.

More and more Booth worried about the strain on his officers' health. As early as 1878 he had been forced to issue a " General Order Against Starvation " : to meet the rentals of their halls and keep their places in the battle-line, officers were undergoing appalling privations. They lived in dingy rooms where unsold copies of *The War Cry* served for sofa-cushions and table-cloths ; if a haunted house was on the market they lived *there*, for the rents were lower. They ate meagrely by the wavering light of a candle jammed in a bottle, sometimes with five sharing the one plate the quarters possessed. Some did not eat at all. The frequent insinuation that Salvation Army officers feathered their own nests so angered Captain Mary Jane Casley, a fiery redhead of Kendal, Westmorland, that she refused to accept a penny salary until her Corps' debt was wiped out. Often, fainting from hunger, she toppled bodily from the platform.

And others fared as leanly. John Lawley, one of Booth's earliest aides, for a time lived solely on cucumbers and bread and butter. Henry Edmonds, a young American officer who pioneered Scotland, subsisted for more than six years on five shillings a week. Salvationists coined a wry jest : " As poor as church mice—or as Salvation Army mice, which would be poorer still."

It was the same all over the globe. In Paris, Booth's pioneers trod such a tightrope of debt that young Herbert Booth lived for five weeks on spoiled grapes and French fried potatoes. Just in time Kate, his sister, stopped an eager volunteer selling her luxuriant golden hair : a wig-maker had offered £20. Captain John Milsaps, commanding a fledgeling corps in Sacramento, California, survived for days on crusts left over from a picnic-party, found in a discarded steel drum. The crusts were as hard as sea-biscuits and the drum had once held kerosene ; thirty years later Milsaps could still shudder at the memory.

It was small wonder that Napa City, California, officers with only fifteen cents between them, rejoiced when hoodlums pelted them with onions and potatoes ; these, with a dime's worth of steak made a memorable breakfast. A Melbourne cadet who acquired the quaint skill of buttering bread with a paint-brush in lieu of a knife held the job for the duration of training.

Despite these punishing hardships, they achieved results better-nourished men might have envied. Travelling through a snowstorm to Sunderland, William Booth, after straining his ankle, continued his journey on a man's shoulders, transferred to the straw at the bottom of a milk-cart, finally reached his Middlesbrough lodgings being trundled in a wheelbarrow. Bramwell, as frugal an eater as his father, reached Wellingborough, Northamptonshire, on one typical Sunday, conducted two meetings, walked ten miles, preached again and was back at his desk early on Monday morning. Yet for years, following his childhood bout of rheumatic fever, his heart had pained him so acutely he could scarcely sleep lying down. At all levels, their stamina seemed limitless; evicted from a hall in Marylebone, West London, Booth's officers carried on their work on the rain-soaked grass of nearby Regent's Park, spreading their own overcoats for sinners to kneel and seek God.

Undaunted by persecution or poverty, these warriors, between 1881 and 1885, brought 250,000 men and women to The Army's Penitent-forms.

It was at this critical period, when Booth's enterprise seemed close to equipoise, that a scandal of megaton proportions leaped into the world's headlines. " This," one illwisher declared, with what seemed like reason, " will *smash* The Salvation Army."

"It Doesn't Even Raise the Neighbours"

1885

Pale morning sunlight flooded the grey stone canyon of Queen Victoria Street, City of London, as caretaker Major William Fenny, promptly at seven a.m., sleepily unbolted the main entrance-door of Salvation Army Headquarters. But the sight that met Fenny's eyes at this spring dawn in 1885 banished all thoughts of sleep. Crouched on the doorstep, clad in a vivid dress of scarlet silk, was a teenage girl, incongruously clutching a Salvation Army song book—and demanding " to see the General."

Within the hour, Bramwell Booth, as his father's chief of staff, listened impassively while the girl, gulping nervously at a cup of tea, told a halting story he could scarcely credit. The Salvation Army had unwittingly saved seventeen-year-old Annie Swan from a life of degradation. A village girl from Shoreham, Sussex, she had come to London to work in private service—and walked into a cleverly-laid trap. The private service called not for cap and ribbons but for the red silk dress. The house in Gloucester Street, Pimlico, South London, was a brothel, whose inmates were captive teenagers.

But Annie Swan, as a youngster, had attended Salvation Army meetings ; her Army song-book was still a cherished possession. If she stole from the cellar where she had barricaded herself for refuge, would the small maroon-covered book yield up the General's address ? By a miracle it did. At four a.m., when the house was silent, she crept through the side-door used by departing clients and hiked three miles to Queen Victoria Street to await William Booth.

Pacing his low-roofed second-floor office, Bramwell thought furiously. The staff officer he had despatched to Pimlico at first drew a blank—until the brothel-keeper, unwilling to tangle with The Salvation Army, yielded up Annie Swan's trunk and confirmed her story. But this was not the first Bramwell had heard of a brutal traffic in country girls who answered newspaper advertisements. Much of it had come from his bride of almost three years, Florence Soper, a blonde, blue-eyed doctor's daughter, whom he had married under The Army's articles of marriage at Clapton's Congress Hall. Like thousands of Army officers after them, they publicly prayed that this union " will enable us better to please and serve God, and more earnestly and successfully to fight and work in The Salvation Army."

Sentimental enough to treasure a coat button Florence had fingered during their courtship, Bramwell was still a cool logician ; secretly he felt her stories of teenage prostitutes were highly-coloured. Yet Florence, if anyone, should know the truth. A dedicated officer who had soldiered in Paris with Kate Booth, she now had sole charge of a pioneer Army enterprise : a refuge for reformed street-girls in Hanbury Street, Whitechapel.

The work had begun only four years back—and, like many Army ventures, almost by chance. A local sergeant, Mrs. Elizabeth Cottrill, had made a lone effort to shelter girls in her own home, until her husband, a non-Salvationist, resented the tawdry guests. Next, with Bramwell's help, Mrs. Cottrill rented the tiny Hanbury Street cottage but soon, like most Army ventures, it had assumed inconceivable proportions. In the first year, eighty-six girls passed through ; before three years were up Florence and her helpers had redeemed 800.

It was laborious work. Running costs were a bare £8 a week, but money was always scarce ; even fresh cups and saucers were a strain on the budget. Often the girls' black silk skirts and red satin blouses masked underwear so filthy it had to be burned. Until Florence found a public laundry, linen was washed and dried in the living-room; afterwards, looking back to those days, she could still feel the droplets of water plashing down her neck, as a dozen girls stitched red Salvation Army guernseys and talked about the cards that Fate had dealt them.

But only under cover of night, when both had retired, could Florence find strength to tell her husband of the betrayal and brute force these girls had endured.

At twenty-nine Bramwell Booth was a fitting knight-errant. A silent introspective man, so deaf he used an accousticon hearing-aid, his steady brown eyes missed nothing. Deeply compassionate, he was a man who wept readily, and here he saw cause for tears.

The case of Annie Swan confirmed what Florence had told him. A great iceberg of vice lay submerged beneath the placid waters of London society and The Salvation Army was due to meet it in headlong collision.

Within days Bramwell had sought his first ally—in the first-floor offices of the influential *Pall Mall Gazette* in Northumberland Street, off the Strand. Many people rated its crusading editor, 36-year-old William T. Stead, as the most powerful man in Britain. Pale and sparely-built with penetrating steel-blue eyes, Stead had edited this hard-hitting evening news-sheet for just two years—but his fealty to The Salvation Army went back as far as 1879.

Then two Hallelujah lasses had hit Darlington, County Durham, with cyclone-impact and Stead, as editor of the local *Northern Echo* had marvelled at their feats. On Saturday nights the police cells stood empty of drunks. Fully 1,000 men and women answered the call to the Penitent-form—among them "Knacker Jack" Spence, a drunken cat's-meat dealer and chief of Darlington's "Skeleton Army." Cabbies awaiting fares outside the station blissfully hummed Salvation Army songs. Soon Stead was proud to style himself "Honorary Trumpeter in Ordinary of The Salvation Army."

But despite this, Stead still wavered. His influence *was*

great—but would he imperil it by embarking on a forlorn crusade? Others had urged him to probe this traffic in teenagers to the regulated brothels of the Continent—among them Benjamin Scott, 75-year-old Chamberlain of the City of London, head of a committee to expose white-slavers and Benjamin Waugh, founder of the Society for the Prevention of Cruelty to Children. After talks with Scott, Bramwell had felt Stead was the one man in England to help him.

By the time Bramwell had left Northumberland Street, he had at least wrung one concession from the dubious editor. Stead would visit Army headquarters and hear from Florence's charges something of how pimps and their decoys worked.

It was a masterly gambit. As Stead, blue eyes blazing, fingers eternally fiddling with paper and pencil, sat beneath the monster portrait of William Booth which dominated Bramwell's office, three pale-faced girls, all under sixteen, told of the anguish and remorse of their lives as street-walkers. The fourth witness, 45-year-old Rebecca Jarrett, set an expert's seal on their stories. A tall fair-haired woman with a dragging limp—the result of a drunken fall—she herself had run a brothel and trapped scores of trusting girls. Only the selfless care of The Army's Captain Susan Jones, who found her at breaking-point in a Northampton hotel, had saved her from an alcoholic's death.

From Hanbury Street, where Florence had befriended her, Rebecca Jarrett moved on to aid Mrs. Josephine Butler: a pioneer reformer and wife of an Anglican canon, her rescue home for prostitutes in Winchester City was akin to The Army's own. From twice-weekly sorties to reclaim teenagers from Southampton and Portsmouth brothels Rebecca knew vice was still a buyer's market.

Stead waited in silence until Rebecca had left the room then, raising his fist, he smashed it so violently on Bramwell's desk that the inkpots seemed to tremble. " Damn ! " he ground out, his face working, and then could say no more.

" Yes," said Bramwell sensibly, " that is all very well but it will not help us. The first thing to do is to get the facts in such a form that we can publish them."

It Doesn't Even Raise the Neighbours

Few men without Bramwell's inner faith would have essayed such a mission. As far back as 1882, a Select Committee of the House of Lords had issued an alarming report : juvenile prostitutes were increasing every year. Only then was the age of consent raised reluctantly from twelve to thirteen years, but a new bill unifying the committee's proposals—among them, fixing the age at sixteen—was rejected out of hand. Days earlier, on 20th May, the House of Commons had thrown out this Criminal Law Amendment Bill for the third contemptuous time. It was the eve of the Whitsun recess ; only twenty hostile M.P.s had even bothered to attend.

" Oh my God, are we come to this ? " raged Catherine Booth when she heard. " I did not think we were as low as this ! One member suggested that it should be reduced to ten, and oh my God, that it was hard for a man having a charge brought against him not to be able to plead the consent of a child like that."

But Bramwell was less surprised. Ten days before the Bill came up, he and Stead had witnessed a travesty of justice : the cynical hushing-up of the case against Mary Jeffries. A handsome widow in her forties, she was proven owner of twelve brothels—including four in Church Street, Chelsea, a Hampstead cottage for flagellants, and a house for perverts in Holborn's Gray's Inn Road. But her clients were men in high places : not only Members of Parliament but Queen Victoria's cousin, the King of the Belgians, who spent £1,800 a year debauching English girls. Playing the cards her solicitor dealt her, Mrs. Jeffries rode to court in a brougham and demurely pleaded guilty. She paid her £200 fine in cash and left the court still in business.

Since 1865, the year Booth declared Salvation war, twenty such procurers had been known to the police and all of them had gone scot-free.

Even now Stead could scarcely credit it. He sought independent confirmation from his old friend, Howard Vincent. As former Director of Scotland Yard's Criminal Investigation Department, Vincent had two years earlier testified before the House of Lords Committee : as the law now stood, girls over thirteen lacked any protection. Even younger girls could be drawn into the vicious racket; without a writ of Habeas Corpus, no policeman could enter a brothel to search for them. And writs took time to procure; a drugged and helpless girl could be spirited elsewhere. Nor was abduction in itself an offence unless the girl was in her father's custody at the time. A profligate who seduced a fourteen-year-old could laugh in the face of the law—and the police knew it.

" But do you mean these things are going on *now*? " Stead asked incredulously.

Vincent was impassive. " Yes, now—every night."

" The very thought is enough to raise hell," said Stead, appalled, but Vincent knew the bitter truth. " It doesn't even raise the neighbours."

" Then," said Stead, in white-hot passion, " *I* will raise hell."

Events now moved swiftly. On Whit Monday, 25th May, a secret commission, headed by Stead, began a six-week non-stop probe into teenage vice. Though most were *Pall Mall Gazette* staffers, one young Salvationist, Jenny Turner (a pseudonym), valiantly offered to work her way into a brothel and report her findings. The procuress who chanced on her in Hyde Park was overjoyed, for Jenny, though a newcomer, had one regular client; a pale man with ice-blue eyes who came almost nightly to the house in Wanstead, on the fringe of East London. Stead had clinched his first inside contact.

It was a perilous move—and one which cost Stead and Bramwell precious hours of sleep. The intelligence that Stead bore away nightly was frightening enough: thousands of innocent girls, most of them under sixteen, were shipped as regularly as cattle to the state-regulated brothels of Brussels and Antwerp. A world-wide trade was geared to please specific buyers: Glasgow brothels had been alerted because Herr Hagedorn of Frankfurt craved a thirteen-year-old Scottish redhead. Before shipment, recalcitrant girls were doped, then ferried in nailed-down coffins vented with air-holes. Sometimes a victim awoke during the voyage, to die in terror clawing at unyielding wood.

Yet despite her link with the outside world Jenny was a prisoner in the Wanstead house, which stood in a garden, shut in behind high walls. She had now lived ten days in the brothel. Soon, she warned Stead, she would be shipped to the Continent, in charge of a party of teenagers.

Stead alerted his investigators—among them Sampson Jacques, a Greek free-lance writer and an expert on international white-slavery—to stand by for zero hour. If need be the girl must be rescued by force at Charing Cross Station, main London terminal for the port of Ostend.

Then, abruptly, the plan recoiled like a boomerang. At the outset of her perilous mission, Jenny had slipped her Army badge, like a talisman, inside the lining of her jacket—and the procuress chanced across it. From then on Jenny was locked away from the other girls ; there were plans to ship her to the Continent by another route. Only the eleventh-hour intervention of Captain Frank Carpenter, Jenny's Salvationist fiancé, delivered her from jeopardy. All unaware of Stead's plan for a railway station coup, he stormed the house with a band of officers in true cavalry-charge tradition. They found Jenny lying unconscious in the garden ; in a desperate leap from a high window she had wrenched her ankle and fainted clean away. Despite an attack of pneumonia she once more took her place in the ranks.

For every investigator, these six weeks proved a nightmare assignment. Within days one fear was paramount in the minds of Bramwell and Mrs. Josephine Butler : that Stead's sanity would crack before the evidence was ever collated. To Mrs. Butler, his eyes seemed " like burning coals." His faith in justice, even in God, trembled in the balance. " It is a sham, a horrible sham, the whole of our professed Christianity and civilisation," he cried in torment.

For Stead, happily married family-man who listed " playing with children " as his recreation in *Who's Who*, the ultimate horror was to loll sipping champagne in West End brothels, dandling small girls on his knee. Sometimes, to win a white-slaver's confidence, he rouged his cheeks, masquerading as an old debauchee. But once clear of the premises, savage reaction set in. Never would Josephine Butler forget one awful midnight cry as Stead fell forward on his desk: " Oh, Mrs. Butler, let me weep, let me weep, or my heart will break."

Often, for an hour at a time, Bramwell and Stead knelt together, praying for strength to go on. Many times Stead's prayers broke up in uncontrolled weeping until Bramwell revived him with strong coffee.

This was no mere emotionalism. What Stead and The Army were plumbing between them was the vilest side of a traffic netting £8 million a year. From the Hanbury Street cottage, Florence fed them telling statistics: out of one hundred consecutive cases she had handled, a third had been seduced, often through incest, before they were sixteen. London alone held 80,000 prostitutes; the tight square mile round Charing Cross harboured over 2,000 pimps. One in every fifty Englishwomen was a street-walker.

Each night as Stead's four-wheeler rattled through gaslit streets, he saw sights to pierce the heart: in Islington High Street, called " The Devil's Mile," in Regent Street and the Haymarket, pathetic hordes of painted teenagers wearing pork-pie hats with battered blue or red feathers patrolled as regularly as policemen on a beat. Most were country girls; few set a higher price than ten shillings on their bodies.

These were the cast-offs of the trade. In the quiet curtained chambers of St. John's Wood and Maida Vale, the brothel madams were frank with Stead: the real profit came from virgins, in trade parlance " fresh girls." To seduce a virgin, a roué might pay up to £100: the signal was a guarded note to his club, announcing " a new importation from the country." Often money-minded prostitutes became deliberately pregnant; at thirteen a daughter commanded a market-value of £40. Most common bait for virgins was the method that came close to trapping Annie Swan: advertisements seeking country girls for London domestic service.

Charwomen were good enticers; they had unique chances to tell glowing tales of better billets to young maidservants. Nursemaids, well-paid for their treachery, toured Hyde Park as early as eight a.m., seeking lonely girls who were swift to trust. Irish girls arriving at Liverpool were ready prey for sweet-faced women dressed as nuns : the prospect of help from a kindly Mother Superior was too tempting to resist.

Decoy systems varied—but never the girl's ultimate fate. Pressed to a harmless glass of beer or gin, she shortly slumped to the floor, stupefied by a knockout dose of snuff or laudanum. Once a brothel man-servant had callously raped her, the die was cast. The girl's trunk was seized and the doors bolted day and night—while her debt for board and lodging mounted daily. If she held out she was turned penniless into the world —whose rigid moral code decreed that all except virgins were " bad girls " fit only for the gutter.

Not all got off so lightly. To some clients the shrieks of a virgin being raped or flogged were the essence of delight. Behind locked doors and windows secured by heavy shutters, they took their pleasure unchecked, even in fashionable Half Moon Street, a stone's throw from Piccadilly. A girl who fought off her attackers was bound down with padded straps. But once violation was accomplished, the victim's sobs proved galling. " Child," one roué rebuffed a weeping fourteen year-old, " don't dirty my shirtsleeves."

These were not chance customers but professional libertines. One clergyman overtly visited brothels to distribute tracts ; here he could pay up to £20 for the girls he coveted. A Harley Street physician despoiled one hundred virgins a year, at a cost of £7 a girl. Another lecher boasted proudly that he had ruined 2,000 women.

Nor were they confined to London alone. Anna Rosenberg's in Liverpool did a trade as thriving as " The Infant School " in Hull, the bulk of whose inmates were twelve years old. The house was closed up only for selling liquor without a licence. But most brothels styled themselves " temperance hotels " to escape police supervision—or paid the piper. One famous East London house doled out £500 a year in bribes, with free quarters for detectives and constables.

Already Stead was compiling a damning dossier of evidence. Accepting him as a womaniser with money to burn, two flourishing West End traders had offered him nine girls under sixteen—four of them armed with midwives' certificates of virginity. But Stead, a shrewd newsman, saw these investigations lacked a crowning touch of authenticity.

The one sure way to bring Bramwell Booth's point home was for Stead himself, posing as a vicious pervert, to enter the slave market, buy a girl aged over thirteen, and enact the whole macabre charade short of actual violation. Thus decided he went post-haste to Bramwell.

Bramwell, impressed, hit on a solution : why not ask Mrs. Butler to send Rebecca Jarrett, the converted procuress, back to London from Winchester ? They needed now the adept skill of the fowler who had set the snares.

Next day, clad in a brown ulster and a dark shady straw hat, Rebecca sat nervously in Stead's office, listening with mounting horror as the editor outlined his plan. It was all so unreal she could scarcely believe it was happening : these people who had saved her from the soul-shattering degradation of the alcoholic were urging her once again to turn her coat.

Vehemently she shook her head. If she returned to her old haunts, even for one day, she would be forced to drink—it would be like pulling up a blind on a forgotten life. But Stead was inexorable.

" You've told me you've procured and ruined scores of innocent girls," he said brutally. " If you're *really* penitent, make amends for your crime by procuring one, not for ruin but for rescue, whose purchase will save more girls being sold in future than all those you've ruined in the past."

After an eternity of silence Rebecca bowed her head in assent.

Stead now moved fast. A hasty visit to his solicitor, William Shaen proved reassuring ; there could be no crime, the lawyer said, without criminal intent. Next he outlined his plan to three unimpeachable witnesses : Dr. Edward White Benson, Archbishop of Canterbury, Cardinal Manning, head of the Roman Catholic Church in Britain and the Bishop of London, Dr. Frederick Temple. Though Temple and the Cardinal warmly approved, the Archbishop was appalled at the risk ; he was certain Stead would be knifed in a brothel. But the editor was adamant. If he backed down, no other man could carry it through—and the Criminal Law Amendment Bill would remain a dead letter.

The hawks were poised and hovering. Now they lacked only the pigeon.

Towards noon on Tuesday, 2nd June, thirteen-year-old Eliza Armstrong, a Marylebone, West London, chimney-sweep's daughter, was summoned to No. 37 Charles Street, a few doors away from her home. Eliza knew Mrs. Nancy Broughton, a burglar's wife, who lived there, as a casual drinking companion of her mother's, but Mrs. Broughton's friend, who wore an old brown ulster and a straw hat, was a total stranger. This, Mrs. Broughton explained, was " Mrs. Sullivan " whose " slice of luck " had been to marry a commercial traveller and set up home at Wimbledon, outside London. Now she needed a little girl to help with housework. Would Eliza care to go ?

A dark-eyed sturdy child, Eliza guessed that life in service would offer more than life at home—a cramped one-room pigsty at 32 Charles Street, where all eight Armstrongs lived, cooked and slept. Already her sister was living out, earning five shillings a week ; Eliza, too, wanted to help out the family budget. As she agreed eagerly she could not, of course, know that " Mrs. Sullivan " was the ex-procuress, Rebecca Jarrett, that Rebecca and Nancy Broughton, as one time linen-maids at Claridge's Hotel, had often worked together to procure children, or that she, like all the others, was now a pawn in Stead's game.

That night, the eve of Derby Day, Rebecca reported back to Stead's office. Naming no names, she said that the deal was almost clinched : an old drinking-crony in Marylebone had arranged to provide " a pure girl " just turned thirteen for the client of a Wimbledon brothel. The fee would be £5—£1 to the mother, £2 down for the friend, plus a further £2 when a midwife had confirmed the child's virginity. According to Rebecca, the mother was jubilant about the offer.

Stead, counting out five gold sovereigns, gave one final caution. For the case to be foolproof, the child's parents must fully understand she was wanted for immoral purposes. Rebecca reassured him. Except to the child herself, the facts were brutally plain.

Later Mrs. Nancy Broughton told a conflicting tale. No mention had been made of " pure girls " for " gay houses " ; to the best of her belief, Rebecca had married a man named Sullivan and wanted a girl for workaday domestic duties. Nor had she ever received four gold sovereigns ; on the morning of 3rd June, Derby Day, Rebecca had handed her just one sovereign to redeem a shawl from pawn. And it was Mrs. Armstrong herself who had hailed Rebecca from a window, claiming that Eliza was " a nice little scrubber and suchlike."

Though she vehemently denied all complicity, hard-drinking Mrs. Elizabeth Armstrong behaved strangely from the first. No mention was ever made of Eliza's wages—nor did she query that " Mrs. Sullivan," pleading her husband's fastidiousness, bore her daughter off to nearby Edgware Road and outfitted her from head to foot : maroon frock, grey-brown cape, heavily-trimmed Duchess of Devonshire hat.

Was Eliza going for a week's trial or a month's—and, in any case, to what address ? Why was she taking no bundle of working clothes ? These questions Mrs. Armstrong did not think fit to pose, for, as Rebecca testified, " she had her money and I could take the child where I liked."

Nor could Mrs. Armstrong explain why she failed to mention the bargain to her husband. Not until seven p.m. on 3rd June did chimney-sweep Charles Armstrong return for supper to find that his daughter had vanished into service with some-one known only as " Rebecca." The sweep was so angry he had not been consulted he lashed out and sent his wife spinning. Mrs. Armstrong's reaction was typical ; she left the house to get so drunk the police took her in charge.

By ten p.m., when she was bailed out, Stead's morality play approached its final curtain. Anxious to give Mrs. Armstrong the benefit of the doubt, Rebecca had even returned to exhibit Eliza in her new outfit : surely the enormity of her action would come home now ? This was on the early afternoon of 3rd June, but Mrs. Armstrong had already retired to The Black Boy nearby. She did not see her daughter leave Charles Street.

At three p.m., Eliza, shepherded by Rebecca, had arrived at Marble Arch to board a bus for No. 16 Albany Street, an apartment house by Regent's Park. A shade bewildered, she still warmed to the new-found friends she met over tea, though neither were introduced by name : the pale red-bearded Stead and Major Caroline Reynolds, one of Florence Booth's staunchest lieutenants. So they had settled down to chat—as strange a tea-party as existed anywhere in Britain that day. Had Eliza been to school ? Yes, she could read and write quite well, and sometimes wrote poetry. No, she had only been to the country twice in her life, on school trips to Epping Forest and Richmond—the only time she ever saw the Thames.

Though Eliza presently left the room, Stead kept his voice pitched low : "Are you quite sure that the child's mother consented to her being violated ? "

Rebecca was positive. " I said to her and Mrs. Broughton that if Eliza had been too familiar with boys she wouldn't suit."

A mile away, at No. 3 Milton Street, Dorset Square, one of Stead's ablest investigators, Sampson Jacques, the Greek free-lance, was just then in close conversation with Madame Louise Mourez, a French midwife. Speaking French, Jacques explained carefully that he was agent for a wealthy man who had laid plans to rape a small girl—but first he must be satisfied of her virginity. Was Madame Mourez willing to oblige ? The midwife shrugged ; this was commonplace. She had certified many virgins, even tended them afterwards for the appalling injuries inflicted on them.

Around 9.30 p.m. cabby Henry Smith was perched on the box of his four-wheeler on the Great Quebec Street rank by Marble Arch. A heavily-moustached man he later identified as Jacques approached him. " Drive to No. 3 Milton Street," Jacques ordered, "but stop this side of the door." As the four-wheeler rolled to a halt, the cabby watched a lame woman descending the steps hand in hand with a small girl.

" Drive to No. 32 Poland Street," the woman told him as they climbed aboard.

Still Eliza felt no premonition. At Milton Street she accepted without question that a physical check-up was a routine prelude to her job; the examination, conducted on a bed behind a screened-off partition, had lasted less than a minute. Unhurt, she was still shocked and confided in Rebecca that Madame Mourez was " a dirty woman."

As she re-arranged her clothes she did not hear the midwife's low aside to Jacques : " Poor little thing, she'll suffer a great deal." Pity prompted her to press a shilling phial of chloroform on the Greek to deaden the pain—though she retained sufficient money-sense to charge him thirty shillings.

Through the thickening shadows of Derby Day night, the cab, bearing Eliza, Jacques and Rebecca Jarrett clattered on through stifling alleys. Drunken laughter and the hoarse cries of newsboys came through the dusk ; at Epsom that afternoon Lord Hastings's Melton had romped home at 7s to 40. Outside 32 Poland Street, Soho, where a ham-and-beef shop stood, cabby Henry Smith saw a man's spare form loom from the shadows. Stead was on time for the rendezvous.

Above the shop, Stead knew, was a house of assignation. In single file the party now trod delicately up narrow stairs smelling of gas and stale perfume. Bespeaking two first-floor rooms, Stead paid in advance : 7s. 6d. a room. " Bring whisky," he ordered the brothel-keeper, then, as a deliberate after-thought, " and some lemonade too." Would the woman demur, he wondered, at this palpable hint that a child was with them ? But drinks were brought without comment to the room which Eliza and Rebecca occupied. Shortly, Stead and Jacques helped themselves to whisky, then withdrew.

Alone for a while, Eliza felt the strangeness of it all sweep over. To Rebecca, who reappeared suddenly beside her, she confessed she felt too excited to sleep. Was this already Wimbledon ? Eliza wondered, but Rebecca said No. Next day, they would go to Wimbledon ; meantime the child must undress and rest.

Eliza did not notice Rebecca had a small phial in her hand,

until the woman urged " Take a sniff of this," shaking a few sickly-sweet drops on to a handkerchief. For a moment Eliza inhaled submissively then, nauseated by the smell, flung the handkerchief from her. Rebecca crept quietly from the room.

Outside the door Stead waited motionless, tasting triumph. His case was all but proven now—and to the hilt. He had bought Eliza Armstrong to save not one child but a thousand —and if he, a novice, armed with £5, could spirit a teenager into a brothel selected at random, what horrors could a seasoned debauchee accomplish ?

This was proof infallible beyond his wildest dreams. He had shown that you could procure an innocent child with its mother's full consent. You could persuade a midwife not only to examine the girl but abet the seduction with drugs and medical aftercare. A brothel-keeper would tolerate the girl under her roof for immoral purposes and, lacking a licence, still supply the party with drinks.

Cautiously Stead tested the tarnished door-knob. Eliza would be sleeping fitfully now ; he would stand one moment beside her bed and reflect on all the things a man bent on evil could have done in his place. But Stead was wrong ; the chloroform had only rendered Eliza drowsy and now the sound of a footfall brought her bolt upright in the darkness. A sudden terrified scream rent the Soho night : " There's a man in the room ! Take me home ; oh, take me home."

Stead stole noiselessly away.

Towards sunset on Wednesday, 8th July, 1885, Scotland Yard abandoned all attempts to control the mightiest traffic jam Central London had ever seen. For more than two hours the Strand and the long defile of Northumberland Street had been blocked by a milling throng of men and boys, faces purple from pressure, struggling to reach the offices of *The Pall Mall Gazette*. Earlier that day William T. Stead had published the third in his series of horrifying revelations of Britain's white-slave market. Now the crowds outside the building were so great, the circulation department had lost all contact with its news-vendors.

Two days earlier, Stead's first fearless article—" A maiden tribute to modern Babylon "—had struck the London public like a lightning bolt. Even the " maiden tribute " that Athenians of legend paid to King Minos of Crete—seven youths and seven maidens wandering blindly in a labyrinth until the Minotaur, half-man, half-beast, devoured them—paled, Stead claimed, beside nineteenth-century London's nightly sacrifice of virgins.

The testimonies of brothel-keepers and " fresh girls " . . . Howard Vincent's dramatic statement . . . the working of the decoy system and the locked and shuttered rooms . . . all these Stead had blazoned before the public, capping them dramatically with the story of Eliza Armstrong, for anonymity's sake known as " Lily."

Reactions were unequivocal—and unbridled. Stead was a public saviour—or a pornographer bent on boosting circulation. The newsagents W. H. Smith banned the *Gazette* from their railway bookstalls ; Stead, it was rumoured, would soon be gaoled for publishing obscene matter. But when the City of London Solicitor clapped twelve *Gazette* newsboys under arrest, the Lord Mayor, presiding at Mansion House, dismissed the summons. Stead, he thought, had been influenced by " high and honourable views." Among other well-wishers were Lord Dalhousie, who had headed the House of Lords Committee, the famous reformer, Lord Shaftesbury, and the editor of *The British Medical Journal*. Another was twenty-nine-year-old red-bearded George Bernard Shaw, who as one of Stead's reviewers, took a quire of *Gazettes* into the Strand and sold every one.

By the evening of the first day of publication, with the edition sold out, black-market copies of Eliza's story were changing hands at half a crown apiece.

Meanwhile, the cause of all the furore was lodged safely 400 miles away in L'Oriol, France. Already the memory of Stead's stealthy invasion of her room was fast fading from Eliza Armstrong's memory ; the month that followed had been too crammed with incident. As early as 8 a.m. on 4th June, Rebecca Jarrett had escorted her from their night's

resting-place, a surgeon's house in Nottingham Place, to
Charing Cross Station. On the platform, in full Salvationist
uniform, was Madame Elizabeth Combe, wife of a soldier in
the Army's Geneva Corps. " You belong to The Salvation
Army now," Madame Combe greeted Eliza.

By 6 p.m. that day Eliza was a cherished charge of The Army's
French headquarters on the Quai de Valmy, Paris. After care-
free weeks selling *The War Cry* on the boulevards, along with
Evangeline Booth, The Army placed her in the care of French
Salvationists at L'Oriol.

Stead and The Army had hence killed two birds with one
stone. They had proved that a teenager could be spirited
across the Channel with no one any the wiser—and they had
saved Eliza from the dangers of being sold a second time to a
genuine exploiter.

By Tuesday, 7th July, the Home Secretary in the newly-
formed Salisbury government, Sir Richard Cross, was beside
himself. He called Stead to a private interview and begged him
to stop the presses. The editor refused, but offered Sir Richard
an honourable way out. " Say in the House that *The Pall Mall
Gazette* has covered itself with everlasting glory."

The Home Secretary was shocked. " Of course I cannot say
that."

" Then," replied Stead blandly, " I wish you would say that
The Pall Mall Gazette has committed an abominable outrage
on public morals and that you have instructed the Law Officers
of the Crown to prosecute me at once."

But by Wednesday, the success of Stead's crusade trembled
in the balance. To meet his deadline at all, he had dictated,
sometimes for forty-eight hours at a stretch, to a relay of three
shorthand clerks, wet towels coiled round his head as he lay
prone on the office-boy's couch. But the crowd massing outside his office late that afternoon were not men thirsting for
justice but an army of thugs, recruited by slave-traders, bent
on storming the building. Stones and bricks came hurtling ;
the dusty windows rained long daggers of glass. Straining
and heaving, Stead's reporters manhandled desks and cabinets
against the outer doors, prepared for a siege if need be.

Stead saw the situation as desperate. That very afternoon there had been a motion in the House of Commons to resume the adjourned debate on the Criminal Law Amendment Bill : the next issue *must* reach the public. Now he decided : " I'll send a message to General Booth. He may be able to help us."

At Queen Victoria Street, the messenger who had slipped from a side door of the *Gazette* was swiftly ushered into the General's presence by doorman Fred Sherwood. Booth listened in silence, slumped in his swivel-chair, then declared : " Tell Mr. Stead that we'll throw open *this* building for the sake of his paper. We'll do everything in our power to help him."

And in his own hand he wrote urging Stead : " Go on ! Every blow tells . . . multitudes are filled with horror and . . . cry out with agonising entreaty for the Bill. Others refuse to look at the black iniquity on the plea that a mistake has been made. . . . Anyhow, we shall get the loathsome malady looked at now. . . . Yours in the war with all iniquity, William Booth."

This decision turned the tide. All over Britain Booth's Army worked to keep public indignation at boiling point ; the General himself led mass meetings at Manchester, Leeds, Sheffield and Newcastle-on-Tyne. At one monster rally in London's Hyde Park Stead was borne on a chariot through the crowds ; even top-hatted merchants promenading with their own daughters were mobbed in the belief they were abductors. And at Exeter Hall, London, Catherine Booth jolted thousands with a true story culled from Army files : a pharisaic merchant paid a brothel-keeper cash in advance to obtain a small girl for next Sunday. Proud of his skills the keeper lured a child away from Sunday School—then watched the merchant recoil in horror, entering a padded room to confront his own daughter.

In seventeen non-stop days of protest meetings Booth's soldiers netted an unprecedented 393,000 signatures to a petition for raising the age of consent—a monster scroll, which, unfolded, measured over two-and-a-half miles. On Thursday, 30th July, a grim-faced legion of Salvation soldiers marched out from Clapton's Congress Hall to lay their petition before Parliament : mounted officers ; a brass band, fifty strong, striding eight abreast ; a hundred and fifty Life Guards, a newly-formed Army contingent in red jerseys and white helmets, among them Wong Ock, a Clapton cadet, in training to invade China ; the mammoth petition, swathed in Army banners, reposing in a canopied car drawn by four white horses. At Trafalgar Square, one mile from the Palace of Westminster, where all processions must halt, the petition was manœuvred from the car and borne on the shoulders of eight Life Guards to the House of Commons. There Professor James Stuart, M.P. for Hackney, formally presented it to Parliament.

Within days, a five-man committee whose members included the Archbishop of Canterbury, Cardinal Manning and the Bishop of London, after carefully cross-checking Stead's findings, reported them " substantially true." The Government could do nothing but act.

At Westminster, excitement was at fever-pitch now ; the Attorney-General, Sir Richard Webster, and his legal experts were toiling day and night to make the Bill a masterpiece of social legislation. Both Stead and Bramwell spent long hours with the Home Secretary, Sir Richard Cross, making proposals to strengthen the Bill—paramount among them the police's right to raid suspected brothels, the stamping out of the inter-continental traffic in girls. By Friday, 14th August, the Bill, carried by 179 votes to 71, became law. From that time on the age of consent has remained sixteen.

There seemed good reason for Booth to exult in *The War Cry* : " We thank God for the success he has given to the first effort of The Salvation Army to improve the laws of the nation."

Now a shameful thing happened—shameful because the police, rankling at The Army's exposures, seized a swift opportunity for revenge. By the second week in July, Charles and Elizabeth Armstrong could no longer bear the neighbours' taunts that they had sold their daughter to pimps ; if the Armstrongs chose to turn a blind eye to " Lily's " probable identity the people of Charles Street, Marylebone, did not. Angrily Armstrong blustered into Marylebone Police Court and demanded Eliza's return.

The police lost no time. Through an intricate chain of witnesses, they found that both Bramwell Booth and Rebecca Jarrett were deeply implicated; their calls at Salvation Army Headquarters became a matter of implacable routine. At first Bramwell stubbornly resisted all pressures, but gradually doubts assailed him. If Mrs. Armstrong spoke truth, she hadn't knowingly sold her daughter into slavery; for this they had all along relied on Rebecca's word. Reluctantly he gave the police the addresses of Eliza and Rebecca.

It was enough. Along with Inspector Charles von Tornow of Scotland Yard, Armstrong, an uncouth bleary-eyed man, went hot foot to Paris to collect his daughter from Salvation Army Headquarters. Though the child had begged to stay on, von Tornow's extradition warrant could not be denied. By 24th August, Eliza had been returned to her parents in England. Five days later, knowing a warrant was out for her arrest, Rebecca Jarrett surrendered to the police at Bow Street Police Station, London.

From Grindelwald, Switzerland, where he was holidaying with his family, Stead cabled the *Gazette* indignantly: " I alone am responsible. Rebecca Jarrett was only my willing agent. I am returning by the first express to claim sole responsibility for the alleged abduction."

But Stead was denied this privilege. On Monday, 7th September, he stood in the dock at Bow Street Police Court—but ranged alongside him was almost every protagonist in this strange drama: Rebecca, Bramwell, Sampson Jacques, the midwife Madame Mourez, even Madame Combe, who had escorted Eliza to Paris. And the preliminary hearing, which dragged on until 26th September, became classic as one of the stormiest ever staged at Bow Street. Outside a power-drunk mob drummed up by the traffickers bayed for blood; at times a wailing like an arctic blizzard drowned out both counsel and witness.

It was Bramwell who suffered as much as any; until the

police laid on transport by " Black Maria " he was four times torn from his cab and mauled by toughs. From then on the family noted, his deafness increased yearly. " Darling one came home with a very bad blow on the nose," wrote Florence on her twenty-fourth birthday. " Had been wretchedly mobbed coming out of court by the Magistrate's door." Prime instigator of the troublemakers was Mrs. Mary Jeffries, who three times arrived in her brougham to dole out rotten eggs.

Hysteria swept the city. Wax effigies of Rebecca Jarrett surged like banners through the streets; on one evening a torchlit horde trampled through the grounds of Stead's Wimbledon residence, flourishing the waxworks at his windows, caterwauling and hallooing. But the bitterest blow was the decision of magistrate James Vaughan to commit the defenders for trial at London's Central Criminal Court, the Old Bailey. Stead's motive, he sniffed, might have been lofty and pure—but couldn't it equally have been to garner material for the " deplorable and nauseous " account of Eliza's detention which had " greatly lowered the English people in the eyes of foreign nations " ?

Yet other nations, as a direct result of Stead's articles, were busy putting their houses in order. Already, Australia had raised the age of consent; in America, many States had followed suit. *The New York Sun* was moved to praise : " *The Pall Mall Gazette* has wrung the heart and electrified the conscience of the British nation."

Yet by strange paradox Lord Salisbury's Government, whose twenty-clause Criminal Law Amendment Act was based fifty per cent on Bramwell's and Stead's suggestions was bent on proving their accusations groundless. International prestige, trade and diplomatic relations—all were at stake, and in the last resort Stead and his fellow crusaders must be thrown to the wolves.

The charge was that, " feloniously, by force and fraud," they had taken away Eliza Armstrong, a child under fourteen, with intent to deprive her parents of her possession, and that they had unlawfully and indecently assaulted the child.

From its outset, 23rd October, the thirteen-day Old Bailey trial was a travesty of justice. The Attorney-General, Sir Richard Webster, aggressive and square-jawed, hectored witnesses without mercy. Mr. Justice Lopes, a tall thin man with prominent eyes and an untidy beard, was hostile to the Salvationists from the first. Despite repeated attempts by Stead—who conducted his own defence—to prove that Mrs. Armstrong could never have identified " Lily " without guilty knowledge of the transaction the Judge checked him time and again. The entire case, he stressed to the jury, hinged on rock-ribbed interpretation of law: if Eliza was taken away from home without her father's consent, the accused were guilty. Motives, good or ill, were beside the point. When Stead called the Archbishop of Canterbury as witness, Lopes ruled it as inadmissible. The Archbishop could have no possible know-ledge of whether Charles Armstrong had consented or not.

Now the jury fidgeted uneasily on the hard wooden benches for evidence had at least made plain that Rebecca, far from seeking the chimney sweep's consent, had never even met him.

No one fared worse in this sad farrago of lies and prejudice than Rebecca herself. All through her initial detention she had been cheered by the songs Eva Booth and two cadets sang each morning outside the cell, but as the Attorney-General, Sir Richard Webster, rose to cross-examine she crumpled visibly.

The first question cut like a whip. " Prior to being em-ployed at Claridges, had you kept gay houses ? "

" Please, sir," Rebecca blurted piteously, " Don't go back on my past life ! "

But Webster was moving in for the kill. Within minutes, under a running fire of questions, Rebecca, tears streaming down her face, was cowering in the dock. Panic-stricken at the Attorney-General's attempts to probe her past life and associates she told lie after palpable lie. Bramwell could only stare at her in mingled pity and horror. Stead, visibly shaken, had buried his face in his hands.

Next day, when Webster returned to the attack, Rebecca withdrew into a shell of cold indifference. " If you want to know about that, you have got to find it out for yourself," was her sole retort.

In vain, her counsel, Dr. Charles Russell, Q.C. (later Lord Russell of Killowen) argued that Rebecca's evasions were excusable. How could she in honour supply the names and addresses of criminals from whom she had severed all connexion ? A devout Roman Catholic, Russell had been so moved by Rebecca's plight that he had broken a rule of twenty-five years' standing to study his briefs on Sunday—but even his stirring two-hour plea was of small help now.

As the watchers in the public gallery sat electrified, the same tension was fast spreading all over Britain. Could The Salvation Army's status survive a scandal which was now headline news across the globe ? If Madame Combe had early been dismissed from the case, a proved Salvation Army convert had been discredited before the world—and The Army's own chief of staff was still in the dock. An antagonist's prophecy that this would " smash " The Salvation Army seemed all too likely.

His most peaceful moments, Bramwell reflected wryly, were spent in the death-cell, where the warders, as a formality, briefly locked him each morning before he entered the dock. Vainly Catherine Booth sent telegrams almost daily to Queen Victoria, begging her to intercede. But the Queen proved unhelpful : " It is well understood that Her Majesty cannot interfere in the proceedings of any trial while it is going on."

And the Judge's summing-up, lasting all of five hours, left the jury in dire confusion. After a three-hour war of words, they filed uneasily back to hear foreman James Branch plead for a directive : if Rebecca had obtained Eliza by false pretences this, they felt, was contrary to Stead's intent. The sudden thunderclap of applause from the public gallery so incensed Lopes he threatened to clear the court. Only one point at law concerned the jury, he rapped out : was Eliza taken from her father's possession against his will ?

As the jurors shuffled out, Bramwell's wife Florence, sitting with Josephine Butler in an Old Bailey corridor nursing her four-month-old daughter Catherine, summed up the pitiless essence of nineteenth-century law: "Oh, Mrs. Butler, how little do these men know of the lives of the *very poor*."

Three hours later, when the jury filed back, foreman Branch urged a rider; Stead, if guilty, had been misled by Rebecca. The Judge waved it aside. Now even one of the Attorney-General's team leapt up to lodge a protest. At once Lopes snapped: "I will tell you at once that it is a verdict of 'Guilty' against Stead and Jarrett."

Though Bramwell was favourably acquitted, his co-defendants were not only judged guilty but bitterly reviled. Stead, sentenced to three months without hard labour, was labelled "a disgrace to journalism." Rebecca, "a disgusting and abominable woman," served six months in Millbank prison. An ardent Salvationist until her death in 1928, she swore that the cordial letters of Commissioner George Railton, who even sought to take her place on Christmas Day, kept her faith intact. Eliza, who grew up in Salvation Army care, married happily and bore six children. The lightest sentence—one month—was served by Sampson Jacques. Madame Mourez, who got six months' hard labour, died in gaol.

And there were ironic postscripts. Within days of leaving gaol, Stead, on an inspiration, went to the Registrar of Births and Deaths department at Somerset House to learn a truth which would have toppled the whole case for the Crown: Eliza Armstrong was her mother's illegitimate child by another man. Charles Armstrong had never had the right to decide where Eliza went or with whom.

Yet the greatest irony was that the trial did not harm The Salvation Army; it sent their prestige soaring to the highest peak in its stormy twenty-year saga. Their longtime benefactor, Samuel Morley, pressed £2,000 on Catherine Booth that the rescue of fallen girls might continue undiminished. In Cardiff, Manchester and Liverpool, newly-formed vigilance societies worked hand in hand with police and Salvationists to wipe out the vice-traffickers. Even as the trial drew to a close, the poor were realising as never before that The Army were

From lonely beginnings on Mile End Waste, East London, in July 1865, with a scant handful of converts, Booth became a legend in his lifetime. On August 28, 1912, 10,000 Salvationists marched in his funeral procession past London's Mansion House

Marching as to war, Booth's Christian soldiers, operating in 71 countries, campaign as needs dictate. In pre-prohibition New York, annual "Boozer's Days" featured walking whisky bottles 10 feet high; in Tokyo, the Army's target was the red-light district of Yoshiwara

their friends. " 'Ere, old cove, I'll tell you what'll cheer yer heart," a cockney newsvendor hailed one astonished Salvationist, " Bramwell ain't guilty ! "

From this moment on the work gained in vigour; within five years Booth had thirteen homes, housing over 300 girls, in the United Kingdom alone, a further seventeen abroad—foreshadowing the mid-twentieth-century total of 119 homes, caring for 4,000 girls a year. A few, William Booth would recount dryly, were always a shade confused as to the identity of their benefactors. " I know who we've to thank for this place," shouted one girl who first arrived at Hanbury Street during the notorious Whitechapel murders. " We'd never have had it but for old Jack. God bless Jack the Ripper, I say ! "

"How Wide is the World?"

1885-7

Months before the Old Bailey Trial which proved such a turning point in The Salvation Army's fortunes, William Booth, his eyes twinkling, challenged a mass rally of London Salvationists: "How wide is the girth of the world?" From the serried ranks came the full-throated response "Twenty-five thousand miles." "Then," roared Booth arms outspread, "We must grow till our arms get right round about it."

It was an ambition worthy of Booth's stormy spirit, yet there were stumbling blocks in plenty—not the least being the ever-present lack of funds. By December, 1884, Corps debts totalled £10,000; even Booth's nation-wide appeal netted only a third of this sum. Soon, with The Army operating in eleven countries, the foreign fund was £1,300 overdrawn. Each month saw William and Catherine racked by the aching responsibility: thousands were offering their unstinted allegiance, throwing up well-paid jobs, even severing family connexions. To train them and provide working quarters, The Army was accumulating property at a terrifying rate, and the Booths, unversed in finance, learned to balance their ledgers through bitter trial and error.

"We had to build the ship while we were at sea," Bramwell disclosed, "and not only build the ship but master the laws of navigation."

Worse, Booth, strong in independence, really hated asking for money, though for Christ's sake, he did it bravely all his life. "It is not wise for a money-grabbing operation to be gone through whenever I appear," he once cautioned Bramwell sternly. " General Booth ought to be seen elsewhere than at Madame Tussaud's *not* asking for money." But Bramwell, as Chief of Staff, lived face to face with the truth : often, after writing a cheque, he could only sigh and prop it against the inkpot. Until God had provided, The Army's bankers, the National Provincial Bank, would look askance at extending credit further.

Over the evening meal, which might be taken at any hour up to midnight, Florence Booth too often heard : " Darling, I am very burdened about money. I don't know where to turn. Surely the Lord will help us." Their eldest children, Mary aged four, and Catherine aged two, early learned to finish evening prayers : " Dear Lord, send The Army a lot of money to make Papa happy."

Often the money that did tide them over came for unpredictable reasons. One man donated £100 every time the Press attacked The Army, pinning the clipping to the cheque ; a truly vitriolic outburst rated £500. On another occasion, passing down Aldersgate Street, City of London, Booth saw a costermonger loading sacks of scrap-iron on to a barrow. When one sack proved too heavy, the General's reaction was instinctive ; doffing his tall silk hat, he stepped in to lend a hand. Told by a passing bobby that this was General Booth, a bystander vowed promptly : " If that's the spirit of The Salvation Army, I shall help it as I have opportunity." Next day he walked in on Bramwell unannounced with a cheque for £1,000.

One inspired campaign which helped stay the gap was Self-Denial Week, main source of The Army's income, which between 1886 and to-day, has raised untold millions for Army funds. Like many Salvation ventures, it came fresh and new from the mint of one officer's mind ; as one of the vast congregation jamming Exeter Hall, London, in mid-August, 1886, Major John Carleton, one-time Irish textile executive, was stirred by his General's dream of becoming almoner to the world. All round him sat wealthy civilians, jotting lavish sums on their " canaries "—Army slang for the yellow forms on which donors promised gifts—but Carleton, like his colleagues, had no salary margin to juggle with.

Then the logical solution came home to him and in an instant he too was scribbling his own unique " canary " : " By going without pudding every day for a year, I calculate I can save 50s. This I will do, and will remit the amount named as quickly as possible."

. This offer touched Booth more deeply than any lavish endowment—yet the thought of a man skimping his meals for an entire year went much against the grain. To keep their places in the battle-line, officers needed all the food they could get. Next morning, bursting into the office where Carleton and Bramwell were working, Booth came up with a novel plan of his own. No Salvationist should eschew anything for a calendar year—but why shouldn't all unite to deny themselves each day for a week, with the money saved swelling Army funds ?

The first Self-Denial Week, confined to the United Kingdom alone, raised £4,820—and the bulk of it, to Booth's delight, came in pennies and halfpennies. Though his aides were dismayed by the paucity of gold, the General enthused : " Never mind ! There is plenty of copper." Often, he knew, this spoke of a greater sacrifice than more precious metals.

Initially Booth had seen the campaign—then one autumn week of Self-Denial, now held in the spring—as an effort made by his own soldiers on behalf of the needy : an unvarying £10 was his own annual contribution. To every province, division and corps went the same yearly message—" Smash the target " —before the officers set out manfully to beat last year's results. No diet was too unpalatable : Bramwell and his family lived on bread and water for a week. No task was too demeaning : one captain, pressing a fishmonger for a contribution, was contemptuously bidden to go and hawk a barrel of herrings in the gutter—"then I'll believe there's something in your religion." Promptly the officer donned a blue apron and stood hands on hips bawling like a pierhead barker ; within the hour the Self-Denial fund was £1 9s. richer.

Infinite ingenuity was the keynote. To save a sixpenny

barber's fee, some officers trimmed each other's hair : even Booth, despite his grinding schedule, found time to keep bees and market their honey for the fund. One convert, advised to bypass the direst slums in the east coast port of Yarmouth, still went doggedly on to collect £2 in the shape of 1,920 farthings.

But soon the idea fired the hearts of non-Salvationists, too. A retired Indian Army General currycombed a gipsy's horse and donated his fee. A draper's shop, opening half an hour earlier, turned over the extra trading profits *en bloc*. Miners worked an extra stint at the coal-face ; on Scottish fishing boats, one line in six was consecrated to God. Even the old and infirm weighed in ; one woman hatched a saleable brood of chickens in her invalid couch.

In Colenso, Zululand, once The Army opened fire, old Maria, a half-blind Zulu widow in her eighties, crawled from her hut and begged a local farmer for just one week's work hoeing mealies. Self-Denial Week drew near, and there was precedent for a widow offering up her mite. Touched by her faith, the farmer at length assented. Maria could work for a week in the fields for the same pay as the village girls—sixpence a day and her food. Seven days later, on Sunday morning, a small girl led the old blind woman by the hand to the Self-Denial altar in The Army's hall. Softly the congregation sang, " When I survey the Wondrous Cross " before The Army's Major Johannes Andersen called for the envelopes that held the offerings to be laid on the altar. Kneeling, her eyes lifted to an invisible Heaven, Maria prayed : " Lord Jesus, take my gift. I wish it were more, but it is all I have. May this help You to send light to people who are in greater darkness than I am."

Afterwards, looking back to this era William Booth saw one thing as plain. Wherever a country's rulers gave his soldiers freedom to act, they swiftly proved their worth to the hilt—and soon the authorities would step in to subsidise their work.

Nowhere was this truer than in Australia, where The Army's joyous religion harmonised with day-long sunshine and the broad blue savannahs of the outback. On the face of it, Booth's man in Melbourne, Victoria, Major James Barker, had been one of his least promising officers ; a twenty-seven-year-old compositor from Bethnal Green, East London, he had often found the work too much for him, vanishing for days at a time. But Barker's self-knowledge was to prove a passport to the irresolute souls he sought. After a year's work with his wife Alice in the Bendigo goldfields—where converted miners were known as " Salvation nuggets "—a transfer to Melbourne brought him in contact with Dr. John Singleton, the city's best-known philanthropist. Through Singleton, Barker became the first Salvation Army officer ever to act as official prison visitor.

Soon the impetuous young Major was spending more time in Melbourne Gaol than in his Collingwood Flats office, amid a malodorous mile of cheap billiard-saloons and brothels. He conducted weekly meetings in the prison chapel ; he sat beside pale wasted men in the hospital. He roamed the labour yard, pausing for a word with sweat-soaked men as they toiled at stone-breaking. At other times, with the full secrecy of a confessional, he was closeted with prisoners in their cells.

But Barker saw further scope for his talents. At the Police Court, he readily went bond for men who would otherwise have gone to gaol. Soon he had more converts than he could readily cope with : Jack Moody, a battered pugilist who became janitor at Melbourne headquarters, Maggie O'Donohue, reprieved from a life sentence for murder and appointed Corps Sergeant. Without precedent to guide him, Barker set them all to work selling *The War Cry* on the streets of Melbourne. Understandably, sales were phenomenal : lacking uniforms, Barker had dressed his vendors in vivid red military tunics donated by Victoria's Government Stores.

Now Barker's ears were attuned all day to a sound like an advancing army : the steady tramp of purposeful feet ascending the hundred wooden stairs that led to his office. " Give me a chance," pleaded one sixty-year-old, discharged from Pentridge Stockade, Victoria's Sing Sing. " I don't want to die in gaol." Despairing, Barker's chief-of-staff, John Horsley, took him home, fed him and found him work. A month later, when the old miner died, his last recorded words were: " The Army was like home."

The solution that had eluded Barker until now came as a blinding reality. " It's a *home* these men need," he told Alice. " A home where everyone is happy and friendly."

It was an act of profound faith. Funds were so low they could afford only a tiny four-room cottage close to the gaol, at 37 Argyle Place South in the suburb of Carlton—but on Saturday, 8th December, 1883, it opened as the first Salvation Army Prison Gate Home the world had seen.

Within weeks, the house proved too small and two others were rented, but Barker hadn't done yet. Men fresh from gaol needed time to come to terms with themselves but not all who stood in greatest need would know where to go.

From then on, Barker set a Prison Gate officer to keep daily vigil outside the gaol, and urge men to accompany him to the home. Often the ex-prisoner was the centre of a lively tug-of-war—between Salvationists anxious to redeem him and larrikins out to reclaim a drinking-crony.

British staff officers, arriving a year later on an inspection tour, were flabbergasted at the respect Barker commanded. As seasoned Salvationists they saw his results as a satisfying norm; of the first fifteen inmates of Argyle Place, eleven went on to lead lives of dignity and purpose, though most had served more than a dozen years in gaol. In England this year— 1884—was the strife-torn year of the Worthing riots, yet in Australia, with the prison home one year old, the visitors found the first country to hold The Army in something approaching awe.

" The child," reported one officer wryly, " has outgrown its father."

Impressed by Barker's fighting spirit, the Government of Victoria went further. To give him greater authority with criminals they made him an honorary magistrate and chaplain of the lunatic asylum. A sharp rise in unemployment proved a fresh challenge. The Government made an initial grant of £400 and virtually passed the problem to The Army. Undaunted, Barker found work for almost 1,800 men; even six years later, in 1890, his Melbourne staff were dispensing 700 cut-price meals a day. First offenders were now remanded to The Army as a matter of course. The Executive Council gave them authority to take charge of any child found in a brothel.

For the Government's chief secretary, Graham Berry, saw that The Army had passed the acid test: their methods might break the cake of custom but they worked. By May, 1885, one of their miracles was the talking point of the Antipodes: Poll Cott had renounced her infamous life and the police from Darwin to Ballarat heaved a sigh of relief. Transported for life from County Cork as a hell-raising Irish sixteen-year-old, she had for sixty years left a swathe of broken heads and broken bar-rooms across the continent. Her first conviction was for wrecking the surgery of the doctor she held responsible for her first-born's death, flooring him with an ether bottle; it took eight policemen to carry her to the gaol. After that, whisky was a potent factor in transforming the lovely raven-haired hellion into the vicious old harridan who notched up 257 gaol sentences—one of them for trying to exhume the doctor years after his death.

Anyone who stood in her path—grocers refusing free food, constables who tried to move her on—felt the full fury of a skull-shattering blow from a lemonade bottle cased in a stocking. Intent on mutilating a railway porter who had ousted her from a first-class carriage she stormed into a hardware store in West Maitland, New South Wales, to buy a pair of scissors—and ran full tilt into The Army's Captain William Rundle.

Rundle's greeting involved words no one had used to Poll Cott since she stumbled aboard the hulk in Cork Harbour: " Good morning, mother. What about coming home for a bite of dinner ? "

But no pious exhortations to mend her ways won Poll Cott over. What moved her was the Rundles' simple unaffected conviction that she was a human being whose fate troubled them profoundly. For the first time in seventy years, someone had put her to bed and tucked her in. The turning point came when she unexpectedly entered the living-room to find Mary Rundle kneeling and weeping as she prayed. " O God, save her ! " was Mary's heartfelt plea. Looking closer Poll Cott saw, with a strange sense of unworthiness, that a pool of tears puddled the polished floorboards.

Twenty years after the solemn moment of conversion Poll Cott's testimony was still a compulsive call to the Penitent-form all over the Antipodes.

So great was Barker's success that Booth, to his chagrin, swiftly haled him back to Britain to oversee London's first Prison Gate Home—sited, curiously, at Argyle Square, King's Cross. It was deeply frustrating work. The British Home Office, unlike the Government of Victoria, were still distrustful of Booth and his methods. Despite the " Red Maria "—Salvation counterpart of the " Black Maria "— which rode daily to London's prison gates, drawn by a pair of spanking greys, prejudice blocked Barker's progress like a gaol's granite walls.

At Pentonville Prison he was shocked to conduct his first interview in a cage crammed with convicts and visitors : at other gaols, iron bars separated him from men who sought Christ, while warders sat tight-lipped, monitoring every word. Almost ten years would pass before the Home Office accepted a prisoner's inalienable right to choose the organisation which should help him on release and to have its representative visit him in gaol.

Yet converts as notable as Poll Cott went a long way to press The Army's claims. At sixty-four, Glasgow-born Archie Sloss had spent forty wasteful years of his life in gaol ; at six he was a boy thief as adept as any trained by Fagin. In his 'teens, raiding a wine shop via the skylight, he fought a horrifying battle to the death with a large black retriever. Later, as a cash-customer he heard the proprietor tell countless times of the heroic fight put up by the dog—now stuffed and preserved in a glass case in the bar. No one saw the knife in Sloss's pocket, which dovetailed with the tell-tale gash in its throat, or the raw blue scar of teeth-marks, livid beneath his choker.

And Sloss bore other scars. Eight floggings of fifty lashes

had left his back " like a ploughed field " ; they could not break his will. Transported to Western Australia, he scaled the walls of Fremantle Prison, escaping with the flag that flew from the turret as trophy. Twelve long years of his life were passed in Sing Sing. Portland Prison, Dorset, knew him so well old-timers christened him " The Duke of Portland." Between prison terms he and a gang of desperadoes whose members included " Glue Pocket," " Cock Robin " and " Tommy Horrible " brought off savage coups, sometimes netting £10,000.

At sixty-four, time had caught up with Archie Sloss. His cat-like agility, his muscles, his nerve—all had gone. He was reduced to sleeping in parks and under stone arches and only hatred had power to stir him ; in a square face, as pale as wax, fringed by a stubbly white beard, his cold cruel eyes burned like small black flames. Then a passing philanthropist's suggestion changed his life : wouldn't The Salvation Army's Clerkenwell, North London shelter, offer a snugger billet than a doorstep ? And he backed his advice with a florin. Sloss was surprised to find threepence bought a bed, a pint of cocoa and a hunk of bread—and dumbfounded to see, proclaiming Salvation from the platform, his friend, " Old Appleblossom." When last seen the ex-convict had been strapped to the triangle at Portland, writhing under the cat o' nine tails.

It was " Appleblossom," as Sloss was for eleven years to testify all over Britain, who coaxed him to the Penitent-form and pointed him to a peace that passed all understanding. " What more than forty years in prison could not do, Jesus Christ did in a moment." Soon the sight of Sloss in Army uniform posted each morning outside Pentonville Prison, was persuading others to tread in their Saviour's footsteps ; these in turn became the backbone of Prison Gate Homes still spanning the world from Oslo, Norway, to Brisbane, Australia.

With mordant humour, William Booth would avow that no other religious organisation was better fitted for the task. The Army, he explained, was " the only religious body which has always some of its members in gaol for conscience' sake."

How Wide is the World?

Much the same problem faced Booth's soldiers in Sweden : once the sterling value of their work became realised, sudden distrust gave place to unstinted backing. As early as 1878, Bramwell, vacationing in Värnamo, south of Jönköping, to stave off a total breakdown in health, typically found relaxation in a non-stop chain of meetings, aided by an interpreter. One meeting place was a large room behind Värnamo's post office ; the postmistress, Hanna Ouchterlony, blonde handsome daughter of an old military family, became Sweden's first Salvation Army Officer. But many well-to-do Swedes were alarmed by the bleary-eyed mobs that gathered to hear The Army's message ; for twelve lonely years Hanna Ouchterlony's officers faced only stiff-necked opposition. Fearing riots, the police forbade all open-air meetings after dusk. Canny Salvationists retaliated by carrying newspapers to the meetings; as long as it was light enough to read the headlines out of doors, how could it be dusk?

Then, as so often in Army annals, came a brainwave from the ranks. As a one-time teacher in a school for the deaf, Captain Oktavia Wilkens realised that many of Stockholm's converts were not only deaf ; they were incapable of clear speech. To aid them a headquarters waiting-room was set aside for Oktavia to hold special meetings : The Army's first thriving deaf-and-dumb corps was born.

News of this strange Army's work for the deaf and dumb struck a chord with liberal-minded Swedes. Most remarkable of all their converts was Fritiof Pousette, a blind deaf-mute from Norrtälje, near Stockholm. As a cruelly handicapped ten-year-old, Pousette had been taught carpentry at school ; in the sound-proofed darkness of his world he persevered until he had made his own bench and tools—including a fixed plane over which he moved the wood. In his teens he set up in business as a carpenter. No timber-dealer could cheat him for he could determine any wood by biting, smelling, even licking it.

By strange paradox, this man whom life disqualified was to play a major role in The Army's struggle to win acceptance in Sweden. A chance visit from Oktavia Wilkens spurred him on to read the Bible in Braille; thereafter an open Bible was never absent from his bench. But Pousette, a convinced Salvationist, sought to do more than bask in the love of God; he must impart it to others, too. Those who witnessed it still recall that Army history offers no more heart-stirring picture than the cathedral-hush of the meetings in which Pousette testified—right hand scanning his Braille Bible, left hand gripping the fingers of another deaf-mute, the message passing in sign language, from hand to hand, word by word, through a packed and silent room.

It was Sweden's King Oscar II, a tall blue-eyed humanitarian, who summarily broke down the barriers. This concern for men entombed while living so moved him that despite Court officials' misgivings he donated 500 kröner (then worth roughly £27) to the Self Denial Fund. His next gift set the Royal Seal on their work : land that became an Army wood-yard employing 10,000 men a year. Taking their tone from the King, officers of the Swedish Army now cracked into parade-ground salutes each time Booth's warriors passed on the street. To-day thirty officers operate from Stockholm and seven provincial cities, in year-long dedication to the needs of Sweden's 6,000 deaf-mutes and 8,000 blind.

But in other countries, where The Army was given no chance, it was a bitter uphill battle all the way. The first Salvationist to peddle *The War Cry* on the streets of Stuttgart, Germany, was clapped into gaol, his " seditious " papers confiscated. Egged on by the Protestant Church, the police worked doggedly to make The Army's task insuperable. All public meetings, they impressed on Staff Captain Fritz Schaaff, a New York trainee, were forbidden after eight p.m.

Next, incensed that crowds still flocked to the hall despite the early hour, they forbade public meetings at all. From now on, Schaaff could hold meetings only for which tickets of admission had been issued.

Nothing loath, Schaaff and his aides tramped manfully through Stuttgart's beer-gardens, doling out tickets with such marked success the police countermanded the order. Henceforth, the tickets must be " personal "—inscribed with the name of the guest.

All Schaaff and his successors could do, then and for fifteen years thereafter, was arrive at the hall early enough to scrawl the names on upwards of five hundred tickets—but attendance slumped once police officers ranged the aisles, noting every visitor's name and address.

From every German city came the same story. In Worms, an innkeeper contrived his own off-limits sign : " Pedlars and members of The Salvation Army not admitted." A shopkeeper, fearing a local boycott, took newspaper space to quash a rumour : neither he *nor* his relations were Salvation Army converts. When Commissioner George Railton arrived to sort out the tangle, the police chief of Berlin was blunt : he personally would do everything in his power to impede Die Heilsarmee, as the Salvationists were known. At one gathering Railton's entire audience was made up of two men, two women and two boys—though the Chief of Police, an official from the Ministry of the Interior and a detective were along to maintain law and order.

Even William Booth, no stranger to persecution, was amazed at the atmosphere prevailing. Arriving to address a crowded meeting at Berlin's Athenæum, Booth stepped from his cab to hear a voice from the ranks let fly with a rousing " Hallelujah." At once Railton, his eyes flashing, shouted : " Silence ! " When Booth called sternly for an explanation, Railton defended himself : " Highly dangerous, General—it might have been used as a pretext for the police to close the meeting."

" Stop a meeting for a Berliner praising God ? " replied Booth outraged. " Then, if that had happened, it would have been the best thing for The Army in Germany and I should have considered I had done a good day's work in being the cause of it. Let the Salvationists shout ' Hallelujah ' wherever they are and whatever be the consequence."

The ultimate consequence was that though Territorial Headquarters remained on Berlin's Blücherplatz, Railton himself was expelled from Prussia, carrying on by remote control from Hamburg, a Hanseatic Free Port. His successor, Commissioner Thomas McKie, took nominal charge of an Army 1,500 strong, recruited from fifty-six million people. Often, when a new building was rented, McKie offered a private prayer that the audience would be just so-so on the opening night—lest the police closed them down for overcrowding.

In Paris, too, despite her personal magnetism, Kate Booth had found the going hard. When the police forbade handbills advertising meetings, her officers were driven to parade the boulevards wearing heavy home-made sandwich boards, while the crowds complacently sipped Pernod, deriding them as " English freaks." Her lasses might take pride in visiting almost a thousand cafés a week but often they returned to the Avenue Parmentier flat with their faces a mask of blood. Angry cries of " Take that for your Jesus " haunted their dreams. Time and again local prejudice was implacable : a Dunkirk hospital evicted a woman dying of cancer when her Salvationist beliefs became known.

Now Booth made a rare but fatal error of misjudgment. His initial policy for France had followed the American pattern : a small cadre of Britons whose prime concern was to recruit native-born officers on the spot. But few of Kate's band were as fluent as their leader ; not many French citizens had offered themselves for commissioning. Then, Booth argued, why not open fire in French-Switzerland, a largely Protestant country, with the accent on an all-out recruiting drive ?

Booth, in his enthusiasm, had overlooked the fact that the cold proud city of Geneva was the birthplace of John Calvin, whose religion taught pre-election. The destiny of every soul, Calvinists argued, was determined before it ever entered the body : if some were irrevocably chosen, others were irredeemably damned.

It was a disastrous decision—for in no country outside Britain was The Army subjected to such bitter persecution. From the moment that Kate and her new chief of staff, Major Arthur Clibborn, a towering six-foot Irish Quaker, opened fire in Geneva's Casino de St. Pierre on 22nd December, 1882, a chill wind of disaster blew down the Rhône Valley. At their third meeting, in the Salle de la Reformation, ugly brawls broke out among the 3,000 strong audience, many of them students wearing coloured woollen caps. At once Kate applied to the Canton of Geneva's Grand Council for extra police protection.

The President of the Department of Justice, Monsieur Marc Héridier, fought this for all he was worth. Rising before the Council his indignation knew no bounds : " We have been petitioned to call out a company of gendarmerie, sword in hand, to protect these foreigners." Suddenly, his self-control snapping, he shouted : " *I will never consent to such a step!* Do you wish that our military department should enter on a campaign to defend The Salvation Army ? " He ended ominously : " For my part I would never have signed the passports of these foreigners."

Daily police and press grew increasingly hostile. In one village outside Geneva, " Les Salutistes " as they were styled, were fined for interfering with a drunkard ; their joyful singing had drowned out his own maudlin tones. The newspaper *Le Reveil* took Kate and her lieutenant, seventeen-year-old Maud Charlesworth to task : " These women would be better employed knitting stockings or studying a cookery book." Opponents spread the scurrilous untruth that every convert was sweetened with a four-franc bribe. On 2nd February, 1883, after holding just over seventy meetings, the Canton of Geneva proscribed The Salvation Army.

From now on it was an offence to wear Army uniform on the streets or conduct public services. Ten days later Kate was expelled from Geneva. She sought refuge in Berne where the giant Clibborn was already busy with appeals to the President of the Republic.

No child of William Booth ever shirked a challenge and Kate was no exception now. A striking figure with her golden curls and close-fitting blue serge uniform, she rose like an English Portia before the Grand Council in Geneva's Hôtel de Ville to plead for The Army's rights. From the start the Senior Councillor set the uncompromising tone of the hearing : " You are a young woman ; it is not in accordance with our ideas and customs that young women should appear in public. We find it offensive."

Kate Booth would not be cowed. If she and Maud Charlesworth had come as actresses, she challenged the Council, even Héridier himself would have paid good money to watch them. No matter how flashy their costumes, wives and daughters would have been brought in to applaud. Yet two women seeking the welfare of 40,000 Genevans who never entered a church, were to be expelled like criminals.

" Are they not a danger ? " was her stirring climax. " Does not their lost condition cry out against you ? " But the Council were unbending : their decree now stood as law.

Across the frontier, in the Canton of Neuchâtel, things were little better. As unfriendly as Geneva's Grand Council, the authorities at first merely forbade afternoon meetings, but as early as six a.m. town rowdies armed with scythes and pitchforks picketed The Army's hall to boo and barrack. Once, moved to anger, Kate strode out to confront them and a crowd of ruffians boiled round her. When one man shouted that they had their own pastors, Kate was icy : " My friend, you don't do them much credit."

" It's our money you want ! " shouted another vindictively, but at this Kate lost all patience. " You say that again ! Say it ! You daren't : you know it's a lie." And taking the man by his shirt collar, she lugged him unceremoniously into the hall, dumped him in the front seat and launched into a non-stop meeting. At the close she saw that many, like men in shock, were moving towards the Penitent-form.

This was but a local victory. In September, 1883, during Kate's brief absence in France, the Cantonal Government of Neuchâtel took a leaf from Geneva's book : all public meetings of Salvationists were henceforth forbidden. Kate's reaction was automatic : she would test the power of the decree by disobeying it.

On Sunday, 9th September, the afternoon was still and golden. Amongst the pine trees of the Jura mountains, 500 Salvationists in crimson-and-blue waited in quiet defiance— five miles above the steel-blue waters of the Lake of Neuchâtel.

Twenty-five years marked the span of The Army's last great crusade: the 1952 shutdown of the infamous Devil's Island. Through the fighting faith of Ensign (now Commissioner) Charles Pean (left), thousands of prisoners like these above gained repatriation, new clothing, fresh hope

As "The Army of the Helping Hand" two million Salvationists may serve in any major theatre of war—from the trenches of World War 1, where 'doughnut-girls' changed the Army's U.S. image overnight, to the soup-kitchens of Seoul, Korea

Soon a sentinel came doubling : the prefect of police, Charles Gerster, escorted by a posse, was fast approaching in his carriage. Until Gerster trod quietly across the thick carpet of needles, Kate waited in silence. Then she began to pray.

Still Gerster made no move. For two hours he stood quietly at her elbow while testimonies followed songs on the mellow pine-scented air. He heard at least one convert, pointing to a member of his posse, avow : " That policeman over there knows me ; he took me to gaol, but now I am a changed man." Only when the service drew to a close did the prefect fumblingly produce his warrant. Kate was direct : why had he not served it earlier ?

Gerster admitted it : some power had seemed to hold him back. His voice tight with emotion he added : " This is a magnificent work. You do nothing but good. I beseech you not to hold me responsible for this act."

In Neuchâtel, the man who *was* responsible, Monsieur Robert Comtesse, President of the Council of State, was apologetic—but the law must take its course. For twelve days Kate remained a prisoner in Neuchâtel's cold medieval gaol. Mice scurried on the damp stone floor ; the metallic odour of bad plumbing tainted the air. Afflicted like Catherine, her mother, with spinal trouble, she was often in pain ; one lieutenant, Kate Patrick, had voluntarily shared the gaol sentence to care for her. From London, William Booth wrote anxiously : " If you do not suffer in your health, I don't care. It will all work out for good. But your health is of more importance to me than all Switzerland."

But it took more than gaol to daunt the fighting Booths. At her trial in the old court-house at Boudrey, the needle-witted Kate, with her mother's shrewd logic, cleverly identified The Army's cause with that of law and order. " What are we to do with the masses ? " she challenged the jury at the climax of a two-hour speech. " If they are not reached by the power of the Gospel, a day will come when they will turn round against you, and awful will be the consequences." And she went further : " If these disturbers are capable of manifesting such hatred, such rage against citizens who pray to God, they will also be capable of manifesting the same rebellious spirit against any other opinions or any other law which may not please them."

The seven-strong jury, appalled by the prospect, found the prisoners guilty of violating the decree but added that they had acted with no culpable intent.

" The accused are acquitted," the judge announced dryly.

From the Salvationists who packed the court, a wild volley of " Amens " and " Hallelujahs " now rent the air. But Kate's triumph was short-lived. Furious that victory had eluded him, the Minister of Police and Justice, Monsieur Cornaz, now refused the defendants all police protection once they left the court-house. Under a stinging hail of flints and accurately thrown bottles, Kate and her lieutenants stumbled back to their lodgings. On 8th October, the Canton of Neuchâtel went further than Geneva : they expelled all foreign-born Salvationists from their soil.

These were the first rounds in a war which, incredibly, was to rage on at white-heat for six years longer. Where loyal Swiss soldiers carried on the fight, they did so in secret, like old-time Covenanters, gathering in pine-forests or black-smith's forges, often to frustrate the police as early as five a.m. One early convert, Captain Susanne Küpfer, a pretty vivacious ex-chambermaid, never forgot her pioneer work in Biel, Berne Canton : benches were manhandled from The Army's hall and smashed to matchboard in the streets by mobs shrieking " Crucify ! Crucify ! " Traders organised a total boycott : bread, milk and potatoes were unobtainable at any price. Hundreds of cockchafers, a regular pest of Swiss summers, were let loose from paper bags at the meetings ; the air was thick and dark with their wings, their buzzing drowned all conscious thought.

Soon Berne clamped down the now familiar ban on all Army meetings. At Neuveville, a village above Bienne, Colonel Arthur Clibborn, two women officers, Captains Susanne Wyssa and Anna Furrer and ten soldiers were gaoled for holding an all-night meeting of prayer in a private house. For five hours their home was bombarded with mighty rocks weighing upwards of five pounds. Canton after canton succumbed to the same fever of hatred. At Nyon, in the Canton of Vaux, smiling police stood by while a thousand-strong mob stoned the Salvationists through the streets. At Bienne, one officer, Lieutenant Alfred Kuntz, was drenched in sticky black train-oil by roughs who cornered him in the station waiting-room.

As late as October, 1888, Captain Charlotte Stirling, a young Scots officer, served a one hundred day gaol sentence in the Castle of Chillon, on the Lake of Geneva. Her sole crime: she had invited some schoolchildren in the village of Orbe to an afternoon meeting, providing their parents didn't object. By an Act of 1834, tampering with a child's faith was an act punishable by imprisonment.

A year later, on 1st November, 1889, the State Council, without warning, closed all Salvation Army halls; election time was approaching and they feared riots. Clibborn protested bitterly: already he had complied with an earlier demand that meetings must be by invitation. Next day's invitations had gone out; the meetings must continue as scheduled.

On the evening of 2nd November, Geneva's police broke violently into three Army halls. One girl cadet, kneeling in prayer on the platform, was booted into the auditorium. Three others were thrown headlong down a flight of stairs for the mob to trample and worry. Clibborn, dragged from his own hall, spent a memorable night in Geneva gaol along with a thief and a prostitute; outside Clibborn's cell gendarmes kept up a ribald non-stop chorus of Hallelujahs. Next morning a handsome gendarme, twirling his moustache, looked wantonly at the girl and remarked: " How well you go together, you three—a thief, a prostitute and Clibborn. *Ah, c'est tout à fait ça.*" To Clibborn it was as if William Booth had pinned a medal on his tunic.

Not until March, 1890, did the State Council of Geneva formally accede The Salvation Army's right to wear their navy-blue coats and gowns in the street, with caps and bonnets trimmed after their own taste. Promptly fashion-writers warned women-readers: for this season navy was out.

A dark-blue bonnet was the signal for a shower of stones or spittle.

It was left to a Swiss official of another century to write the ironic epilogue : Giuseppi Lepori, who as Minister of Posts, Telegrams and Railways in 1958 was pondering designs for the year's new stamp issues. By that date The Army had over 400 officers operating 120 corps in twenty-two self-governing cantons and was as highly esteemed as any church in the land.

Without more ado, it was decided that one stamp among the new issues should commemorate The Army's seventy-fifth anniversary—and the design, in dark blue and crimson on a pale-blue background, was the once-despised " Hallelujah Bonnet."

The battle for freedom of worship was still raging in Switzerland when William Booth paid his first—and most urgent—visit to America. Just six years after Railton and his lasses had " opened fire," The Army's future in the United States lay in the lap of the gods.

At first, Railton's successor, Major Thomas Moore, a tall, bearded cockney, had forged ahead with unquenchable zeal ; as virtual leader of a nation-wide youth movement, he commanded an army of up-and-doing teenagers living on a pittance of $5 a week. As in England, they opened new stations in pairs, hiring halls-cum-living quarters christened " Fort Salvation," posting bills that proclaimed The Army creed : " Don't Despair ! ! However POOR you may be, however WRETCHED you may be, However BAD you may be, You have Two Friends ! One is Jesus Christ and the other is The Salvation Army."

Often the blazing of new trails had proved a sore test of faith. Seventeen-year-old Captain Eddie Parker, appointed to command a new corps in Mobile, Alabama, found funds so low that The Army could pay his fare only for the thirty-seven miles between Chicago and Joliet. With true Army resource, Parker adopted a troubadour's tactics ; as a trio of concertina, guitar and cornet, he, his lieutenant and a young cadet, sang for their suppers across 895 miles of the United States. They arrived in Mobile with exactly a dollar between them.

But Major Moore, though strong in zeal, was short on business acumen; by the summer of 1884, Booth's travelling auditors reported his accounts in such a tangle that the General decided to replace him, ordering him to transfer to the command of South Africa. Booth, of course, could not know that Moore, a naturalised American in whose name all American Army property was deeded, would declare his own war of independence. Taking umbrage, he now proclaimed himself General of America's Salvation Army.

And most of Moore's scattered cohorts—300 officers, 5,010 enlisted converts—saw his action as Simon-Pure logic. Who was this William Booth but an unknown figurehead, based 3,000 miles away in London? When Booth's new nominee, Major Frank Smith, a lean pinched thirty-year-old, arrived to take charge in November, 1884, he found a daunting situation. Out of 100 Salvation Army Corps, only seventeen still acknowledged Booth as General.

Dismayed, Booth sent sixty British officers to reinforce Smith, but numbers were the least of the Major's problems. Flags, meeting-halls, hymn-books—Moore had impounded them all. To design a crest which didn't infringe Moore's copyright, Smith hit on the device that to this day singles out The Army's U.S. crest—with the crown, symbolising the Crown of Life, replaced by eagle's wings.

Soon a bizarre situation arose. Before long, the trustees of Moore's army were sharing Booth's view of their leader; deposing him for mismanagement, they appointed Colonel Richard Holz in his stead. Even now, Moore wouldn't admit defeat; doggedly he claimed the right to publish a *War Cry* of his own. On 23rd September, 1886, Booth, in full Salvation Army uniform and black silk topper, stepped off the s.s. *Aurania* at New York's Cunard Pier to restore order in the one country in the world boasting three Salvation Armies.

It was the stimulus his soldiers needed. No man to spare himself, the fifty-seven-year-old General launched on a whirlwind eleven-week campaign from New York to Kansas

City. Though he spoke for almost 200 hours, the 180,000 Americans who heard him were impressed by more than volume of words: they heard phrases which made the evils of the world a matter for passionate concern. Town after town listened spellbound, as Booth's long thin body swayed to and fro on the platform, his hair and flowing beard rumpled, arms clasped behind him, right hand over left wrist, his eyes like glowing coals.

"Sin," he would charge them, his whole frame vibrating as he neared his climax, "*Sin is a real thing*, a damnable thing. I don't care what the scientists call it, or what some of the pulpits are calling it. I know what it is. Sin is devilish. It is sin and sin only which prevents the world being happy. Sin! Go into the slums of the great cities, pick up little girls six years of age, sold into infamy by their own parents. Look at the drunken mother murdering her own child. Look at the father, strapping his crippled boy. Sin! That's what I call sin . . . something beastly and filthy and devilish!"

But if Booth could throw words like fiery darts his speech was salted with humour too. "1865?" he quipped to the Mayor of one town, "Ah, yes, that's the year *your* war ended and *my* war began." Not always, he liked to tell his audiences, were The Army's ministrations welcome; only recently a drunken Irishwoman, found unconscious in a Toronto gutter, was carried to The Army's first home for women on Albert Street. Next morning, awakening to a spotless unfamiliar room, she groped through a haze of hangover to ask where she was. "At The Salvation Army," explained the officer in charge, Captain Susan Florence. But at this the woman's agitation knew no bounds: "For Pete's sake get me out of here before I lose my reputation."

Three years would pass before Colonel Richard Holz finally merged the "Army" he commanded with the international Salvation Army—but it was Booth's vivid fresh approach to his audiences that convinced many waverers: this was the leader for them. When Booth elected to replace Major Frank Smith, now haggard and ailing, by twenty-seven-year-old Ballington Booth, the General's second son, recently married to Kate's lieutenant, Maud Charlesworth, took over a force of 654 officers now operating in 312 cities and towns.

Yet still The Army's standing in the United States was a paradox in itself. As early as March, 1886, six years after Railton's advent, President Grover Cleveland became the first U.S. President to receive Frank Smith and a group of Salvationists at the White House—the forerunner of a dozen Presidents who have since endorsed their work. Yet still in many American towns the police, as unfriendly as Switzerland's own, waged a bitter war of attrition against The Army. Boston, governed by Irish liquor-dealers, allowed only Sunday marches conducted in total silence. New York officers had to attend daily on the city's officials to receive a permit for the day's march. Permits were not granted a day in advance or a week, or even sent courteously through the mail. They had to be fetched, daily, cap in hand.

Strong-arm tactics were commonplace. Fresh from her battles against Worthing's "Skeletons," petite Captain Ada Smith was dragged from a Hazleton, Pennsylvania, sidewalk by a cop who slugged her mercilessly with his night stick. In Springfield, Illinois, the corps' drummer was fined for saving himself when a truck-driver tried to run him down. In aptly-named Leadville, Colorado, bullets whined like hornets past the officers' heads as they preached the love of God. An Iowa officer, convicted for open-air preaching, was sentenced, despite failing health, to break rocks in a chain-gang. He finished his sentence a chronic invalid, near-senile at twenty-eight.

But slowly, all over the States, the sheer Christian example of Booth's soldiers saw the turn of the tide. When the Salvationists of Saco, Maine, turned out to visit the sick and needy in snow three feet deep, the *Police News* paid tribute to their "soldier-like disregard for the weather." At Omaha, Nebraska, all opposition was stifled when Adjutant Frank Aspinall found an alcoholic on the verge of delirium tremens in the street outside the barracks. A Lancashire publican's son, once so degraded by drink he slept with a knife under his pillow to terrorise his wife, Aspinall saw the man trembling on the brink of damnation : he did the only thing a Salvationist could. He took the verminous whisky-sodden wreck home, shared his bed with him and converted him in the morning.

Often the soldiers' joy and buoyancy of spirit drew converts like a lodestar. No one could help but admire the spirit of the Scranton, Pennsylvania, officer who cheerfully took a job well-digging to help with expenses : " the souls here " he reported, " are like the drainage—uncared for." Another young zealot, repairing the wires atop a telegraph pole, saw a group of hard-drinking women living it up in a fourth-story window. His top-of-the-pole sermon had soon drawn traffic-stalling crowds. At Elgin, Illinois, gaoled Salvationists, happily carolling Army songs, weren't even put off their stroke by the gaoler turning the hose on them. Promptly they launched into " Where streams of living water flow."

Soon the police of forty-eight states recognised the bitter truth : to clap Salvationists in prison was to create custom-built martyrs. One was Brooklyn's Captain Henry Stillwell, who packed out the old Lyceum Theatre on Washington Street by billing himself " The Hallelujah Gaol Bird."

And the Salvation spirit, defence attorneys saw, could melt juries too. In Connecticut, New Haven, officers and soldiers, summoned for " making a disturbance in violation of the city ordinance " were invited by their Jewish attorney to show judge and jury that their singing was neither irreverent, blasphemous or disorderly. Promptly, to a background of rhythmic hand-claps, the Salvationists took the witness-stand and burst into song :

> " *I'm a soldier bound for glory,*
> *I'm a soldier marching on,*
> *Come and hear me tell my story,*
> *All who long in sin have gone,*
> *I love Jesus, Hallelujah, I love Jesus, Yes! I do*
> *I love Jesus, He's my Saviour, Jesus smiles and loves me too.*"

Wryly the Judge dismissed the case. The Army's object was a good one and he could see no breach of the law.

How Wide is the World?

The Army's sunny demeanour could disarm even their foes; men like Andrew Mohrant, a handsome rum-steeped no-good from Baltimore, Maryland. Offered 50 cents by a saloon-keeper to break up an Army meeting, Mohrant was too mellow to oblige; he awoke next morning to find an unfamiliar song-book in his pocket. " My God," he cried, with the appalled guilt of a man plucking a blonde hair from his lapel, " I have been in The Salvation Army." But soon, wholly convinced of sin, he himself became a corporal. On New York's Bowery, Captain Carrie Joy Lovett, a husky dark-haired lassie from Trenton, New Jersey, found valued partisans in her rescue work for girls: conscience-smitten saloon and dance-hall keepers. " There's a new one, Carrie," one would brief her covertly. " See what you can do for her." Once, her face bloodied, Carrie Joy skirmished for more than a block with a squad of procurers—but thanks to her allies' diversionary tactics she reached the safety of the elevated station with her charge intact.

Stranger allies still were the " Jonahs," a self-exiled herd of rogues male who were The Army's staunchest bodyguards in Kansas City. " If there's no hope for us," one of them told Maud Ballington Booth, " why not for others ? " Teetotallers to a man, though they smoked and gambled, all the " Jonahs," private meetings opened with prayer; they closed with a generous donation to the treasury, money which helped the gentle warriors of the Lord make ends meet. If a major's wife found her new-born child getting heavy, a spanking new perambulator appeared magically outside her door. At open-air meetings a cordon of " Jonahs " kept a leary eye on trouble-makers. If a lassie's way home led through skid row, a block ahead and a block behind tailed a detachment of " Jonahs " —each man sporting the sparkling horseshoe which was the fraternity's badge.

Saloon-keepers, too, became allies despite themselves: One Bowery landlord not only welcomed lassies with *The War Cry* but introduced them all round to the boys in the back-room. A Pueblo, Colorado, saloon-keeper, stung by police persecution, offered The Army his saloon free for prayer-meetings. A San Francisco tavern-owner approached head-quarters with a riddle : these people were a force for good, but how come he could never hire a Salvationist bar-keep ?

These formidable changes of heart led a Northfield saloon-keeper to make formal and unsuccessful application to the State of Minnesota : would they please grant him official protection against The Salvation Army ?

But there were still hard cores of local opposition—and in the closing years of this decade, one valiant man set out to crush them single-handed.

No soldier of Booth's made a more shattering impact on the American scene than Joseph Neshan Garabedban, a barrel-chested 6 ft. 2 ins. giant known as " Joe the Turk." Actually a drunken Armenian cobbler, operating from 48 Sacramento Street, in the heart of San Francisco's infamous Barbary Coast, " Joe " was probably the most colourful convert The Army's Captain John Milsaps ever made—and a man who did nothing by halves. Before Joe's change of heart, Finnegan's saloon next door knew no better customer ; a conveyor belt of beer-cans passed all day long through a hole bored in the wall. Now, to his fury, Finnegan found the hole plugged—and with a Salvation Army almanac.

Clad in a fez, with bloomer-like pants of firehouse scarlet and a matching jacket trimmed with gold braid, " Joe the Turk " had one stop-at-nothing resolve : to make his own and The Army's presence felt. Irate customers, storming into his shop, were soon demanding the import of the brass " S " hammered into the soles of their shoes. Joe was seraphic : they could take four choices—" Saved from Sin," " Saved and Satisfied," " Salvation Soldier " or " Solid Soles." But Joe used better leather than any shoemaker in San Francisco ; the gesture cost him few customers.

In 1887, now a full-time officer, " Joe the Turk " began his trouble-shooting campaign for The Army's freedom to worship. Armed with a bugle and a yellow, red and blue umbrella, bearing Booth's likeness and the Statue of Liberty, he paraded the streets of Los Angeles until the cops obliged by clapping him in gaol. At the trial, Judge O'Meliny, an overt sympathiser, tongue-lashed the police and told Joe warmly : " Go out and blow your horn louder than ever to the glory of God."

Three days later the entire police force of Los Angeles was discharged and new cops drafted in. Joe had won his first victory—but ahead loomed fifty-six more.

A hundred-carat extrovert with a guttural booming voice like the Bull of Bashan, " Joe " was soon a byword across the length and breadth of America. He was the first Army officer to solicit funds dressed as Santa Claus, the first to play Salvation songs on a saxophone. At East Portland, Oregon, the slogans he painted in his gaol cell—" Remember Mother's Prayer," " Jesus is the Drunkard's Friend "—were such a tourist trap that the local railroad company allowed stop-over tickets. But the street crowds who came to gawk at Joe stayed to listen—to a man the *Boston Transcript* styled " a human circus poster garbed in flaming red." Hotelkeepers— and private householders—viewed his descent with mixed feelings : the Turk was soon busy with ink pad and rubber stamp, franking walls, furniture, even linen with the motto " Jesus Saves." Even 6,200 miles away, in the Vatican City, Pope Leo XIII was puzzled to find himself on Joe's weekly mailing list of *The War Cry*.

But William Booth, a keen admirer of Joe's—" one of the most courageous men in the organisation "—saw method in the Turk's madness : a fundamental belief in democracy. Wherever Salvationists were arrested for holding open-air meetings, Joe was there too, demanding a trial. " Arrested fifty-seven times for Jesus," he would, if convicted, appeal— and keep on appealing till he won his case. With every victory came a decision to protect Salvationists who stayed behind.

Despite his mighty physique, the Turk did not go unscathed. Once his nose was broken. He was stabbed in the right eye with a sharp iron rod. But nothing deflected his simple faith— " There's hope for the whosoever " —or his iron-willed purpose. Arriving in Chicago, his baggage labelled " Salvation or Damnation " in letters of gold, he was arrested for holding an open-air meeting and invited to leave the city. When Joe, as always, demanded a trial, the desk sergeant was flabbergasted : " We don't *give* trials in Chicago ! "

But Joe held out. He hired a prominent Chicago lawyer. By the time the trial was through, ten cops had been suspended for two months and fined $60 apiece for molesting The Salvation Army. As orders went out, Handle Salvationists like egg-shells, Joe, notching up another victory, hit out for Macomb, Illinois.

No drum-beat of welcome greeted him in this small mid-Western town and " Joe the Turk " knew why : the Mayor of Macomb, A. B. Lightner, a Texan desperado whose band had taken over the town, had awarded a fourteen-day suspended gaol sentence to any officer who beat a drum. Promptly, the officers had sought Joe's aid. They were due to leave for Sandalie, Missouri, on a revival tour but a suspended sentence meant they dared not quit the town.

When Joe headed straight for the court house, Lightner, who had seen him coming, promptly slipped through a side-door. Pounding after him across the square, the barrel-chested Turk blocked his way, dark eyes glowing, twirling his magnificent moustachios : " Either imprison these men," he boomed, " or release them from their sentence." Promptly Lightner clapped the corps officers in gaol.

This was what Joe had hoped for. He now took over the Macomb corps. Each day he led them to the gaol to cheer the prisoners with songs and testimonies. Angrily Mayor Lightner ran from the court house, struck Corps Sergeant Ed Coffman a savage blow then drew a revolver on the Salvationists. Mercifully the gun jammed.

By now Macomb's citizens were taking a lively interest in The Salvation Army's future—an interest fanned by the Turk's announcement that in defiance of the Mayor he would hold a special parade on the day his officers were released. A sympathetic editor accorded him a daily forum in the local paper to denounce Lightner's corrupt régime. At this point the Mayor saw the writing on the wall. On the day the Salvationists left gaol, Lightner spurred hurriedly out of town, not to be seen again. His henchman, the Chief of Police, wasn't slow to follow.

Joe the Turk now made Salvation Army history. He declared himself Mayor of Macomb. The Army's Captain Ivings became Chief of Police. Their first act, watched by a cheering multitude, was to close the town's one saloon. For six weeks, until a new Mayor was appointed, Macomb enjoyed the unique distinction of being the one town in the world whose civic affairs were run by The Salvation Army.

Macomb's acceptance of The Army was now complete— and soon Joe was on the road again, tilting at fresh windmills. At Green Bay, Wisconsin, he bulldozed his way through a crowd of toughs, intent on lynching The Army's Lieutenant Stevenson, bellowing " Open up in the name of the Lord ! " Before the mesmerised crowd had caught up with the situation he had hustled Stevenson through their midst and on to the first train out of town. Next on Joe's list came Saratoga, where the street commissioners had solemnly passed a byelaw to prevent Joe and The Army parading the streets. Joe retaliated by appending his party to the tail of Barnum's circus procession, mounted on a donkey draped in the Stars and Stripes. One more trial, one successful appeal, won freedom in Saratoga.

By the century's end, thirty-seven years before his death, there were no more worlds for Joe the Turk to conquer. Armed with decisions from superior courts in a dozen states he could reel off the gist of them within seconds of entering a court-room—and by now local Salvationists knew the law too. " I'll take this to the Supreme Court of the United States if I have to," Joe vowed time and again— and while he never had to, his adversaries knew he meant it. Of Joe's arrest at Portage, Wisconsin, the State Supreme Court's ruling spoke for all : " The (Portage) ordinance . . . is entirely un-American and in conflict with the principles of our institutions and all modern ideas and civil liberties."

But if Joe the Turk won The Army's liberty, others worked as inspiredly to win them love. Half a century later the

negroes of Harlem still recalled small friendly Colonel Joseph
Pugmire from Penrith, Cumberland, as " the curly-headed
white man," who cut himself off from his fellows to eat and live
with them for months on end. " I have to thank God for ever
being sent down here," was Pugmire's sincere testimony, " it
has drawn me nearer to His blessed Self." And America's
polyglot population, swelled by twenty-one million immigrants, proved fertile territory ; on New York's East Side,
alone, only one in seven adults spoke English. Under Commander Ballington and Maud Booth, the first Scandinavian
Corps, led by " The Singing Pilgrims," Annie and Mary
Hartelius, opened for Swedish immigrants. Next German-
speaking officers formed their own corps, with *Der Kriegsruf*, a
German *War Cry*, helping to spread the message. Soon work
began for Italian Americans. A Chinese corps, still active to-
day, sprang up in San Francisco's Chinatown.

And just as in Britain, drastic problems prompted far-
reaching remedies. In New York, a slum officer's discovery of
a baby girl lying dead in dirt and rags revealed an appalling
history : the mother, on a five day drinking bout, had forgotten the child even existed. She had left her baby quite
alone to starve and die. Ballington and Maud swore a bitter
vow : they would work on in the slums of New York until all
such cases were wiped out. Soon, in the first Salvation Army
U.S. crèche, 800 cradles rocked incessantly day and night,
caring for babies whose parents worked on till dawn to scrape
fifty more cents towards the rent.

Taking a leaf from James Barker's book they began work
for gaol prisoners—but the foundation of all their prison
work was, and still is, within the prison walls. An entrée into
Sing Sing won Maud Ballington Booth membership of the
regular visiting committee. Soon the first corps of converted
prisoners was holding meetings in San Quentin. Many
American Courts appointed Salvationists as probation officers
to whom first offenders were paroled. In one city, a prisoner's
sentence was unique : to report every day for a month to The
Army's corps officer and attend each meeting.

" This is the way it grew," William Booth would correct

those who saw it all as a planned campaign. " We saw the need. We saw the people starving, we saw people going about half-naked, people doing sweated labour ; and we set about bringing a remedy for these things. We were obliged—there was a compulsion. How could you do anything else ? "

Until now, Booth had believed that his one concern was the salvation of souls : if the Prodigal Son was returned to his father, all would be well with him. Yet now, after more than forty years as a professing Christian, doubts assailed him.

He had had time to ponder the pioneer work of men like James Barker, women like his daughter-in-law, Florence— and the doubts gnawed him keenly. How *could* a man like Archie Sloss re-establish himself spiritually, lacking friends, shelter, even food ? How could a prodigal like Rebecca Jarrett believe that God was her Father if the Father showed no love for her ?

The climax was the historic morning of 1st December, 1887 —the year of Queen Victoria's Golden Jubilee. A few hours earlier, returning at midnight from opening a corps hall at Whitstable, Kent, the General's cab had rattled across the Thames at London Bridge. Craning from the window an appalling sight met his eyes : scores of homeless men, cringing and blue with cold, were huddled in the niches of the bridge, shielded only by torn scraps of newspaper.

An early caller at the Clapton house, Bramwell was greeted with scant ceremony. His father was completing an agitated toilet before his old upright shaving stand, hair brushes whisking, " braces flying like the wings of Pegasus." " Did you know that men slept out all night on the bridges ? " he threw at his son.

Bramwell admitted this came as no surprise to him but was stung by the General's vehement predication that he ought to be ashamed of himself for doing nothing. The Salvation Army couldn't tackle every social evil. And there was the whole complex question of the Victorian poor law to consider, with its distinction between the deserving and the undeserving poor.

But Booth, with one angry sweep of the hair brushes, silenced his arguments. His command was a finality destined to alter The Salvation Army's entire future : " Go and do something ! We *must* do something. . . . Get hold of a warehouse and warm it and find something to cover them. But mind, Bramwell, no coddling ! "

"When the Sky Falls, We shall catch Larks"

1890

On Saturday, 8th September, 1888, British Salvationists, leafing through *The War Cry* over an early breakfast, were shocked to see this pathetic appeal at the foot of page 10:

> CANCER CURE
>
> The General invites communication, describing any real cures of the above named disease, by any readers of *The War Cry*. . . .

For the Booths, the first intimation of tragedy had come as far back as Thursday, 15th February. Between intervals of a two-day revival meeting at Bristol, Catherine—whose closeness to Bramwell was paralleled by William's kinship with Eva—told her son of a small painful swelling in her left breast. Startled, Bramwell had urged the best medical advice must be obtained without delay, but his mother, he later recalled, had not seemed unduly alarmed. Once back in London, she promised, she would consult an able doctor.

That night, in Bristol's Colston Hall, her sermon was underscored as ever with the faith that never left her : " If God is calling you to become a Salvation Army officer, you will never find any peace or power till you become one. Never ! . . . ' Oh but,' you say, ' I don't know what He will want next.' No, we none of us know that, but we know that we shall be safe in His hands. He wants all we are, all we acquire and all we can do to the end of our days. . . ."

Six days later, at dusk on 21st February, a four-wheeler rattled away from the door of No. 1 Harewood Place, Hanover Square, the consulting rooms of Sir James Paget, the fashionable surgeon, bound for Rookstone, the Booths' new home at Hadley Wood, twelve miles north on the Hertfordshire border. From within, Catherine Booth stared out unseeing at a world on which God had just pronounced sentence of death. Abruptly, the grief quickening inside her, she sank to the jolting floor to pray for courage.

At the window of his Hadley Wood study, Booth fidgeted anxiously; within the hour he was due to leave on a whirlwind tour of Holland. It seemed an eternity before he glimpsed the cab swing into the gravelled drive. Still agile at fifty-eight, he ran as fleetly down the steps to greet her as ever he had hastened up the Brixton Road thirty-six years ago. Then, he saw that Catherine had been crying bitterly. But as she led him into the drawing-room she was trying with everything she knew to smile through the tears.

Sir James Paget had spoken unrelieved truth: the swelling was a malignant cancer and only immediate surgery could prevail. But Catherine had wavered. In recent years her heart-action had grown faulty—and the primitive surgery of the day often only prolonged the suffering. What was her expectation of life if the growth went unchecked? Sir James could not dissemble: two years at the most.

The memory of this scene seemed to burn into Booth's brain: Catherine kneeling beside him, smiling frantically through tears and confessing her secret worry. "Do you know what was my first thought? That I should not be there to nurse you at your last hour." Firelight from the grate wavered on a picture of Christ crucified and the thought flashed into Booth's mind: I never understood His agony until now.

He sat there stunned and speechless, his world grinding to a standstill. How could he leave for Holland now, on to-night of all nights? But Catherine would brook no argument:

it was his duty to go. His mind in turmoil, Booth set out for Charing Cross Station, but at Queen Victoria Street he halted the cab to break the news to the shaken Bramwell. He begged him to see the doctors and learn more.

Bramwell moved fast. Before Booth, following two listless meetings in Amsterdam, had even cancelled his tour to return home, he and his mother had sought out other surgeons advised by Sir James. But the second opinions did not vary. One surgeon, Jonathan Hutchison, was uncompromising : he must operate within a fortnight or not at all. Still Catherine hung back.

A woman whose whole life had been the redemption of others, Catherine Booth, typically, thought little of her own pain. About this time a girl eager for Army life called hoping for encouragement. It was an interview the would-be recruit never forgot : Catherine, her face drawn and white, sipping from a tumbler of homœpathic medicine, a shawl draping her shoulders as she slumped exhausted in a velvet-seated wing-chair.

But her words stung like fire. " Have you thought what it means to cast in your lot with us ? " she challenged. " As time goes on you will probably have to see those you love much better than yourself or your own life pushed about or stoned or sent to prison. You will have to see them spoken evil of and written against in the newspapers. You must make up your mind to it all—to it *all* ! "

Though Booth but dimly suspected it, Catherine had dreaded this malign disease ever since it had proved fatal to Sarah Mumford, her mother, in 1869. Yet it was the pain of those who must look on, helpless, that concerned her most. " All my plans are arranged to spare my precious daughters such suffering," she once confided in a friend. " They will not nurse me ; I shall take a little cottage in some lonely place and fight it out without them."

This courageous vow was doomed to failure. At first Catherine pinned her faith in the Mattei globules that went everywhere with her in a little fur bag ; close family connexions like William T. Stead and Frederick Tucker, pioneer of

India, thought the world of them. The invention of Count Mattei, a Bologna nobleman, their liquid electricity was deemed miraculous in cases of cancer. But soon the pain struck across her breast like a scorpion's venom; not even the surgery to which she at last consented could check the cancer now. In the third week of June, 1888, after a stirring speech in London's City Temple, it was one whole hour before they could lift her from the pulpit. Then Catherine Booth resigned herself to die.

To William the irony was almost too bitter. After thirty-three years of perfect marriage he could do nothing to assuage the pain of the woman who had shared his dream. Yet now, because of that chance late night journey over London Bridge, he was on the eve of alleviating the anguish of millions, through a scheme which would deploy social workers not in heathen lands but in Britain's own slums.

Since that historic morning conference with Bramwell, Booth and his officers had not rested—and the reports now piling up at headquarters on his huge leather-covered writing table confirmed that conditions here, in the Empire's capital, were an affront to all mankind. Almost three million people, the " submerged tenth," were dragging out their lives below subsistence level, and for all of them Booth would claim a " cab-horse charter "—the right to food, shelter and work enjoyed by every London cab-horse. As wrathfully as the Lord God of Hosts he would challenge society: " What mean ye that ye beat My people to pieces and grind the faces of the poor ? "

Already, by 1887, many firms, their profit margins pared by an endless cycle of trade depressions, had but one yard-stick: Too Old at Forty. One grey hair in a man's head could spell on-the-spot dismissal. Strikes, unemployment, bloody police clashes were routine—and though unionists drew out-of-work benefits, countless hundred thousand artisans, skilled and unskilled, as yet had no trade union. State medicine, unemployment benefits, old age pensions were unknown. Moved by the plight of 10,000 starving dockers in the great five-week London dock strike of August, 1889, Booth's Army had already stepped in to supply 195,000 cut-price meals.

" In a fortnight we marched farther into the heart of England than in many a twelve-month," was George Railton's shrewd appraisal.

Officers like Elijah Cadman and Frank Smith, former American National Commander, swiftly confirmed Booth's first impressions : London teemed with homeless wanderers, chivvied off the Thames Embankment by the Metropolitan Police, who nightly moved east to trade on the kindness of the City of London Police, sleeping six to a bench on the riverside between the Temple and Blackfriars. Not all were so fortunate : in the small hours of any morning, as Big Ben struck two a.m., the pure white moonlight spotlit scores of men huddled together for warmth in the stone abutments of the bridge at Blackfriars. Some chose the seats in Spitalfields Churchyard or shop doorways in Liverpool Street. One woman slept in a truck in Bedfordbury until the driver, to discourage her, sluiced her from head to foot with icy water. Soon after she died of cold and starvation.

On the nights of 13th and 14th June, 1890, Booth briefed Frank Smith to return again to the Embankment and conduct detailed interviews with a dozen or more dossers. What Smith charted as a result was a truly horrifying map of London's lower depths : redundant men shivering out the long hours of their private hell on hard stone seats while Victorian England slept. There were men workless through cataract or rheumatism, sawyers thrown out of work by machinery, tailors, clerks and builders' labourers. A month later Smith found 368 of them in the mile between Westminster and Blackfriars, stretching out their rootless days with a pennyworth of bread and a pennyworth of soup.

As these pitiable and terrible facts came daily to light it was small wonder that Catherine Booth complained ruefully that she was dying in a house " like a railway station." There was no escaping the problems of a crusading army. Senior officers like Smith and Cadman came and went at all hours on brief imperative errands. Messengers jangled the door bell with urgent telegrams ; meals were served with hash-house ceremony, to be bolted rather than eaten. If William was not departing on a journey, Bramwell was just arriving back.

The furniture grew misty, unpolished, stockings went undarned, and Catherine, who for more than thirty years had taken pride in her meticulous management, grieved over a chaos she now lacked strength to disentangle. Bramwell fretted over finance ; Florence could not sleep for the plight of London's harlots ; Eva, at twenty-three a Commissioner of the London force, had already plumbed the abyss of poverty in a St. Marylebone slum room with two chairs, a rickety bedstead and no running water.

But in sickness as in health Catherine Booth was still " The Army Mother " and her bedroom was the conference room where the finite points of The Army's expanding social policy were now argued and shaped.

To all Booth's officers in these painful months of sifting, pity took on a different guise. For Eva, it was the memory of " Old Bob " that never ceased to haunt her. A chance report had led her to climb a rickety flight of broken stairs to a St. Marylebone garret and behind a warped door that stirred and shivered in the wind she found him—bedridden, pinched with cold, one thin strip of sacking cloaking the iron bedstead. Beside him a cracked cup held his sole sustenance : the dregs of dirty water.

" Thank God ! Thank God ! " the old man muttered, as the tall girl in the blue serge cloak approached him gently. " In the cupboard . . . in the cupboard . . . give it to me quick ! " But when Eva, mystified, probed farther, she found only a days' old crust of bread—so dry and petrified it wouldn't even give beneath her fingers. Reluctantly, as the old man clawed himself upright, she yielded it up. Then she wept uncontrollably for " Old Bob ", before breaking bread, was dutifully mumbling grace : " Oh Lord, for what I am about to receive, make me truly thankful." Then he tore into it like a wolf.

Within minutes, Eve had pelted from the room, fumbling for her purse. She bought kindling, provisions, fresh crusty bread. After she had cooked Bob the first hot meal he had eaten in months, she found an old brush and set to work, clearing the silted ashes from the grate, scrubbing the greasy boards. With true Booth enthusiasm she soon had the floor so awash the tenants below sent up a spirited protest : the " Hallelujah Lassie " was flooding them out.

But the worst of it, Eva knew, was that many fared worse than " Old Bob." Some saw the pavements as their larder, scooping up discarded greengage stones slimed with spittle to crack them between their teeth for the kernels. Most saw casual work in Whitechapel Infirmary Ward as the softest billet, for there they could pick over hospital scraps—fat pork, bones, the burned skin from roasts—which the sick had rejected.

For Bramwell Booth, devoted family man, it was the children who pained him most—children who had known so little affection that " kiss " was a baffling word. The world they knew condemned them to prison for weeks of hard labour for venturing on the grass in the park. For a six-year-old whose sole crime was to be homeless a week's solitary confinement was routine.

It was the plight of the sweated and exploited that most stirred William Booth. Typical was Mrs. Ellen Crowley, a tailoress, who became under-matron at one of Florence's first shelters. At twenty-one she married a mean-minded thug ; only eight weeks in eleven and a half years of marriage passed without a black eye. To keep her husband in drink and her children fed she patched old clothes for a Whitechapel vendor—4d. a coat (four hours' work), 3d. a waistcoat. The sour smell of the garments spread like a gas-attack ; she worked at arm's length, patching them on a table. The Army took her from the brink of suicide ; the landlord who evicted her impounded even the medicine that would have saved her baby's life.

Women like Ellen Crowley took work home every night : shirts, umbrella tassels, waistcoats, artificial flowers. By day, rather than risk the workshop's closure, they endured primeval conditions ; ten red-eyed women hemming and stitching in a room with less than seventy cubic feet apiece. In gaol, even the most degraded convict rated 1,000 cubic feet. And tailoresses, paid 9d. a day against a tailor's 3s. 6d. were rated a better economic proposition than men. In the twenty years before Booth drew up his damning dossier, women employed in the trade increased by thirty-nine per cent.

Others, like Cadman and Frank Smith, found the tenement-dwellers' lot hit them hardest: lodging-houses so cramped that beds were let on the relay system—" Part of a Room to Let " was a common advertisement. If a hotel's night chamber-maid quit her bed at seven p.m. often a bricklayer moved in until dawn. Many of these buildings crawled with vermin from cellar to rafter; at one condemned pile in the Holborn area, even tough demolition-workers struck until the fire brigade arrived with a pump.

Only when a punching white niagara of water had hosed the bugs into eternity would the wreckers resume work.

Other tenements were as terrible. In Southwark, South London, street fish-vendors, lacking warehouse space, lived with unsold boxes of steaming salt haddock stacked in their rooms. Not far away, rabbit-skin pullers battled a different problem; to loosen the fluff during water shortages, they soaked the skins in their own urine, drenching the cracked bare boards on which they lived and slept. For water short-ages were commonplace; many courtyards had standpipes where water was available for only twenty minutes a week. An old woman stood day-long lookout at an upper window, rais-ing a harsh alarm at the first tell-tale trickle.

At sixty, William Booth was still a man profoundly stirred by suffering. Worse, he felt Catherine's day-long agony as keenly as if it had been his own. Often, reeling from her room to begin work anew, he would break down utterly in Bram-well's presence. " I don't understand it! I don't understand it! " he would cry in a paroxysm of grief. But he was no man to be deflected by emotion: at 6 a.m. he rose, for a cold bath and two hours' desk work before breakfast. To the slatternly and shiftless to whom he gave his life he stood in marked contrast. If papers strayed out of place, his secretaries felt the full blast of his wrath. No sentimental do-gooder wringing his hands over the pressures of poverty, his cold card-index brain saw what to do and that he alone could do it.

The sheer statistics bore out his contention. Twenty-five years earlier The Salvation Army had been one man and his wife—without money, with few influential friends, with no more stable place of worship than a tent. Now they were operating from almost 2,900 centres—over £775,000 worth of property, much of it mortgaged. They had raised over £18,750,000 to succour men the world denied a second chance. The " Blood and Fire " banner streamed proudly in thirty-four countries. At International Headquarters, the business of salvation now involved 600 telegrams, 5,400 letters each week.

But Booth had gained more than territory and funds : he had gained the eyes and ears of the world. Each week his 10,000 officers, most of them under twenty-five, punched home the Gospel to the masses at 50,000 meetings. In Britain alone they visited 54,000 homes a week. Their twenty-seven weekly papers reached a thirty-one million readership. As well as an unrivalled publicity medium, Booth commanded a vast intelligence network that could not only assess local needs, but move heaven and earth to fulfil them.

Long before Booth laid his plans before the world, his Army was taking the first steps to prove them practicable. In 1888, four years after Florence's rescue homes and James Barker's Prison Gate Brigades, came the first cheap food depot, set up in West India Dock Road, and two more London depots swiftly followed, in Clerkenwell and Marylebone. This was not the random charity of the soup kitchen, which Booth distrusted, but eating-houses which sold food at rock-bottom prices : meat pudding and potatoes for threepence, baked jam-roll for a halfpenny. Again Booth found old friends were best : the soldier in charge was " Commissary " James Flawn, in whose refreshment rooms he had planned and dreamed twenty-five years back, when the Tent was his sole tabernacle.

But these novel dining-rooms gave shelter too. For fourpence a man had not only washroom facilities—boiling water, soap, towels—but a dormitory warmed to 60 degrees flanked by long lines of mattresses stuffed with seaweed, topped by leather quilts. But not all the guests came with admission tickets; the mattresses were carefully baked each morning.

June, 1890, saw new landmarks in Booth's enterprise. Because workmen and employees lacked all liaison, he forestalled the Government by twenty years, opening Britain's first labour exchange at 36 Upper Thames Street, behind international headquarters. In three months he had placed nearly 200 unemployed; seven years later the total had topped 69,000. Labour yards opened up adjoining each shelter; soon ninety men were working a guaranteed eight-hour day —skilled carpenters making Salvation Army benches, unemployed cobblers patching Army boots.

As Booth saw it, a man's first step towards salvation was to regain his self-respect—so that even men who had touched zero could earn the price of a night's bed and board.

When the poor would not come to Booth, the General had gone to the poor. For six years the lasses of his Cellar, Gutter and Garret Brigade had lived in Whitechapel's filthy tenements, trading in their bonnets and tunics in favour of patched brown dresses and gingham aprons to disarm initial suspicion. Even handkerchiefs, a certain give-away, were forbidden. They cared for old folk and tiny mites in houses where fourteen families shared one water closet; they scrubbed stained kitchen tables littered with bloater heads and onion skins. In summer most, like the tenement dwellers, sat out all night on the doorsteps to avoid the massive stench.

Yet the work, as one lassie recalled proudly, brought results. In London's Drury Lane area, where sixty-nine families at first banded together to pour boiling water on the slum workers, they had won a gradual entrée into thirteen thieves' kitchens.

From the peak of his vision Booth was looking ahead almost sixty years to an age when social security became the watchword—and the words of Christ upon the Mount of Olives embraced his whole credo: " For I was an hungered and ye gave Me meat . . . insomuch as ye have done unto one of the least of these, my brethren, ye have done it unto Me."

Now, with uncanny skill, Booth set out to sell the world his image of to-morrow. A current best-seller set the theme:

months earlier the explorer, Henry Morton Stanley, had rocked the world with *In Darkest Africa*, the story of his abortive 700-strong expedition to rescue Emin Pasha, Governor of Equatoria, cut off by a Moslem uprising. To reach the Pasha at all, Stanley's force had trekked for 160 days and nights on a journey which took toll of 500 lives—dwarfed by dense undergrowth, sweating through the green underwater light of vast forests beyond the Congo.

This primeval backdrop caught Booth's fancy. For mile after mile, trees stretched 180 feet to the sky; no sunlight shafted through to sweeten the decaying air. To the forest's pygmies, there was nothing on earth but this dark world where the rain pattered ceaselessly. A flash of inspiration and the General saw the parallel: weren't there thousands in Britain, too, to whom " the world is all slum " ? His selling-title had come custom-built : *In Darkest England, and the Way Out.*

As ghost-writer, Booth seized on his old ally from the Armstrong case, William T. Stead, who from the General's notes and the officers' dossiers fashioned a trenchant 140,000 word exposé. But Stead, despite his showmanlike traits, was always a man to acknowledge a master's hand. " I did the hack work," was the only credit he would ever take.

Sometimes it seemed that only the will to see Booth's greatest plan launched kept Catherine alive. For a year now they had rented a small villa, Oceanville, at Clacton, on the East Coast, within sight of the sea that she loved. It was here that Booth lived and suffered with her round the clock, working at a rough deal table, scribbling emendations and comments in the great broad-margined manuscript that Stead had prepared for him. But the entries in his diary read as painfully as any Whitechapel dossier :

*My darling had a night of agony. When I went into her room at
2 a.m. she had not closed her eyes. . . . They were endeavouring
to staunch a fresh hæmorrhage. Everything was saturated with
blood. . . .*

Then he had stumbled half-demented into the dark corridor ; he could no longer bear to look.

Day and night, as he scribbled and revised, two nurses were

always in attendance on Catherine, dressing and re-dressing the mutilated flesh in an effort to keep the pain at something near tolerance-level. " Oh God, help just now, help my darling," Booth prayed from the bottom of his heart.

At last on a Sunday morning in September, 1890, a golden day of Indian summer, the epic survey was complete. For a long time the red-bearded Stead sat in Catherine's wing-chair, conning the final pages, before at last breaking silence. " That work," he said, " will echo round the world. I rejoice with an exceeding great joy."

The voice of the sick woman on the bed was barely audible. " And I," Stead heard her whisper at last, " And I most of all. Thank God. Thank God."

Stead's prophecy was true—but Catherine Booth was not destined to see that day. It was a time to say farewells. Twenty senior commanders—among them Elijah Cadman, James Dowdle, the Saved Railway Guard, Commissioner John Carleton of " Self-Denial " fame—took time out of the Salvation war to visit and pray with her. If there had been a Salvation Army in her youth, she whispered, she would have been as good a soldier at ten as she had ever been in later years. Even in those last weeks, Catherine's faith in all God's work remained unshaken. " Don't be concerned about your dying," she wrote to friends, " only go on living well, and the dying will be all right."

Only William Booth, silent in his study, racked by grief, felt the foundations of his faith flawed ; even behind his closed eyelids he saw her brown eyes transfixed with unspeakable agony, the violent unending spasms. " Why does God allow this ? " he tortured himself time and again. " How can it be ? How can it *be* ? " After long agony of spirit, the realisation came to him : difficulties like these recalled God to men and drove men on to God.

On Thursday, 2nd October, 1890, a force 5 gale whipped the North Sea. Icy sleet stung the cheeks and the pure white light of distress rockets spangled the drenching sky as the collier *Larissa* foundered within sight of the windows. Somehow to Booth the sight was symbolic ; on the Wednesday, violent hæmorrhage had set in and Catherine was close to death. Resolved to spend the last moments with her, the General sent everyone, even Staff Captain Hannah Carr, her nurse, from the room.

These were the last hours they would ever pass together on earth ; old triumphs, old disappointments, loomed large in their minds. That first revolutionary walk of William's along Mile End Waste . . . the doubts she had known and stifled as she stared at the glowing coals . . . the wilderness years, both together and apart, when only her twelve-page letters served to bridge the gap . . . anxieties over the children . . . Bramwell's appalling ordeal at school . . . Eva's expected defection to the stage and Kate in prison . . . the brickbat years of Worthing and Sheffield . . . the long parade of the lost and broken who had passed through the shelters and homes they had built between them.

" I have come back to my first love," Catherine whispered, her eyes shining, but Booth, seeing her exhaustion, sought to withdraw his fingers from hers, begging her to rest. But Catherine's hand retained its grasp, as she reproved him gently, " Can you not watch with me one night ? It will soon be over, and what matters a few hours shorter or longer now ? "

And Booth, remembering all the nights that he had not watched with her while the " Darkest England " dossiers piled up and he directed The Army's day-by-day machinery, resisted no further. He sat silent, his hand in hers, sensing that she eased the thin gold band of the wedding ring from her finger to slip it on his own.

" By this token we were united for time," Catherine said, "and by it now we are united for eternity." Humbly Booth acquiesced : he was sixty years old and he would love no other woman this side of Paradise.

By Saturday, the tempest had died. The sea was still and sparkling in the afternoon sun. Along with William at least seven were grouped beside Catherine's bed : Bramwell and Florence, Eva, Marian and Lucy, Staff Captain Hannah Carr, Dutton and Sarah, the servant girls. By now Catherine could no longer speak ; the wasted fingers stabbed at a text that had long hung above her children's photographs massed on the mantelshelf : " My grace is sufficient for thee." Someone took it down and placed it near her, on the bed already draped with The Army flag.

Tenderly, each of her children approached and kissed her. At 3.30 p.m. death came perceptibly closer, as fast-moving as a cloud's shadow across the room, and then Booth was beside her, the grey lion's mane of hair swept back, his lips bending to seek hers. " Pa ! " Catherine said, as William's arms went round her, then died.

Afterwards, enemies were quick to charge Booth with sensationalism. For ten days later, when Catherine's funeral march wound along the foggy Thames Embankment from Queen Victoria Street to Abney Park Cemetery, North London, he did not slump in the passive grief expected of a Victorian mourner. For the entire four-hour journey he stood upright in his carriage, bracing himself against the jolts and jars, conscious that people were craning to greet him, a General acknowledging the salutes of three thousand massed officers.

His soldiers understood, of course, just as they understood the message Booth gave to them beside Catherine's open grave. He had always, he said, on his journeyings or hers, counted the weeks and days until they were together again. What was there left for him, now that she had gone at last ? Morbidly to tally off the years until death reunited them ? No, he was too zealous a Salvationist for that.

" My work plainly," he told them, his voice grave and husky, " is to fill up the weeks, the days and the hours and cheer my poor heart as I go along with the thought that when I have served Christ and my generation according to the will of God . . . then I trust that she will bid me welcome to the skies, as He bade her."

Then Railton, who had opened the burial service with the hymn " Rock of Ages," pronounced the committal sentences as the coffin was lowered, before turning to the vast crowd. " God bless and comfort the bereaved ones ! " he said. " God keep us who are left to be faithful unto death ! God bless The Salvation Army ! " Through the thickening dusk the answer-

ing " Amens " came like a volley ; in the fading light, white
pennants fluttered like moths, white streamers were pendant
from the flagpoles, a white badge gleamed on every soldier's
arm.

This, too, the soldiers understood, because Booth had
taught them: even now Catherine, The Army Mother,
smiled down on them from a heaven where there was no more
pain and the white was a rejoicing, a symbol of her promotion
to glory.

Only once had The Salvation Army ever, in the conventional
sense, worn mourning. This was in the cotton town of
Oldham, Lancashire, seven years earlier, when the stiff-necked
authorities restricted The Army's band to play in their own
barracks. To their fury, the band marched forth unrepentant
but not a drum was heard, not a fanfare of brass split the air.

Instead, in total silence and perfect order, the band paraded
the streets, instruments draped in black, black ribbons adorn-
ing their sleeves—in silent mourning for the stupidity of the
authorities.

William Booth had scarcely anticipated it, but the scathing
criticisms of his deportment at Catherine's funeral were as
nothing compared with the storm that soon raged about him.

Overnight *In Darkest England* became a runaway best-
seller and for the first time the public saw Booth's plan for
what it was ; a literal attempt to apply the Christian ethic to
industrial civilisation. If the State neglected the poor, Booth
claimed, the public's Christian duty was to step in where the
State had failed. The people of " Darkest England " deserved
no less than this : a £100,000 fighting fund subscribed by the
public, with a steady £30,000 a year to maintain the work of
re-shaping men in the image that God had created them.

Soon Booth's daring blueprint had made him the most
talked-about man in Britain. Within a month, 90,000 copies
were in print ; a year later, 200,000. For the first time, scores
who had viewed the General as one more eccentric evangelist
learned of his new labour exchange, his slum brigades—and
that these were just the first planks in his platform. He dreamed

of a farm colony where men from his labour yards could take another giant stride towards redemption, a planned emigration scheme, an overseas colony peopled by families with new reasons for living.

And Booth had other projects. Because over 9,000 people dropped from sight in London each year, he had opened a missing persons bureau—with his 10,000 officers as potential sleuths. Next on his agenda came Poor Man's Metropoles—high-grade lodging-houses where men finding their feet could have private cubicles, sitting-rooms, even kitchenettes. He planned a Poor Man's Bank, modelled on France's Mont de Pieté, with credit facilities for artisans. Supposing a carpenter for whom The Army found work had his tools in pawn, Booth submitted. This bank could advance the money to redeem them—once a man signed over part of his weekly wage as repayment.

An eternal visionary, Booth pioneered another benefit : a legal aid scheme for the poor, embracing every issue from breach of promise to probate. The destitute widows of East London knew no more dogged champion than the General. In one typical case The Army had tracked down a young governess's wealthy seducer, threatened him with public exposure and prised a £60 down payment from him, an allowance of £1 a week—and a £450 life-insurance policy in the girl's favour.

But some of Booth's denunciations fell harshly on ears attuned to imperial fanfare. If his whole scheme needed £1 million to put it in full working-order he asked, what then ? The misguided jingoism of the Afghan War had cost £21 million. Then, too, his radical criticism of laissez-faire cut to the Victorian quick. "It is religious cant," he charged, "which rids itself of the importunity of suffering humanity by drawing unnegotiable bills payable on the other side of the grave."

Within days, Booth's fighting words set the pot of controversy seething. Critics scoffed that his scheme was "a childish impracticable Utopia," that no one ever yet changed a loafer into a useful member of society. Booth was ignoring the fluctuations of business prosperity. He would hamper the flow of free labour, whittle trade union membership, cripple existing religious societies. The Army would end the family's dominion, invade personal rights, usher in an era of despotic socialism.

Spearhead of the opposing force was Professor Thomas Henry Huxley, biologist and agnostic, who more than any man had won public acceptance for Charles Darwin's theories. A tall aloof man of sixty-five, Huxley chose the letter columns of the London *Times* to launch an all-out attack on Booth and his beliefs. Someone, he claimed, had given him £1,000 to donate to the " Darkest England " fund—if he thought fit. In twelve hard-hitting letters—14,500 words in all—Huxley outlined his objections. He saw Booth's sway over his soldiers, involving " the prostitution of the mind," as a worse evil than harlotry or intemperance. His campaign to make men sober and hard-working was a ruse to drive " washed, shorn and docked sheep " into his " narrow theological fold."

It wasn't that Huxley, a brilliant academic, was opposed to the betterment of the poor ; as an East End medical officer he had opined that New Guinea savages had greater scope for happiness than any slum-dweller. It was merely that he saw social welfare tied in with political and secular theories : God had no part in it.

Huxley's hostility, Bramwell thought, all stemmed from the gentle fun Booth once poked at the evolutionists in a public address. It all began, the General explained, poker-faced, in a patch of mud. After a long time—" ages and ages and *ages* " —out of the mud came a fishy creature something akin to a shrimp. Time yawned—" ages and ages and *ages* "—before the shrimp turned into a monkey.

And then ? " Ages and ages and *ages* passed," Booth would drawl, his eyes now twinkling, " before the monkey turned into—*an infidel* ! "

Relayed back to Huxley, legend claimed, this story so piqued him that he thereafter saw Booth as his implacable enemy. But other opponents of " Darkest England," nettled by the General's home-truths, were quick to follow Huxley's lead. *Punch*'s nickname, "Field-Marshal von Booth" was a damp squib alongside one paper's depth-charge : Booth was "a sensual, dishonest, sanctimonious and hypocritical scoundrel." "Brazen-faced charlatan," "pious rogue," "tub-thumper," "masquerading hypocrite"—if Booth's enemies were sparing with alms, they were generous with invective.

When Bramwell grew angry over such abuse, his father, shrugging, always delineated his first-things-first policy : "Bramwell, fifty years hence it will matter very little indeed how these people treated us. It will matter a great deal how we dealt with the work of God."

How Booth dealt with God's work was dramatically demonstrated within months of his book leaving the press. Research had brought home to him that some of Britain's most important match-manufacturers treated their 4,000 employees worse than Siberian salt-miners and the General set out to stir the nation's conscience.

His chief investigator, Colonel James Barker, "Prison Gate" pioneer, soon came up with a burden of appalling proof. One case spoke for all : a mother and two children aged under nine were slaving a sixteen-hour factory day to make 1,000 plus match-boxes for take-home pay of 1s. 3¾d. Unable to pause even for meals, they gobbled dry bread as they pasted and cut. But there were direr evils than sweating. Though many countries compelled their match factories to paste harmless red phosphorus on the side of the match-box, Britain lagged behind. To flood the market with vast quantities of cut-price wax-vestas, manufacturers dipped their match-heads in deadly yellow phosphorus—of which three grains could prove lethal.

At the rock bottom price of a penny per dozen boxes, these "strike-anywhere" matches were a tempting bargain for the tight-pursed.

For these fat profits others paid with their lives. So toxic were the fumes of yellow phosphorus that Barker found scores of women workers plagued by severe toothache : unknown to them the phosphorus was attacking the jaw. Soon the whole side of the face turned green, then black, dis-

charging foul-smelling pus. This was "Phossy Jaw"—
necrosis of the bone—whose one outcome was death.

The Army was swift to act. As early as May, 1891, Booth's
airy well-lit model match-factory for 120 workers opened at
Lamprell Street, Old Ford, East London. From the first his
"Lights in Darkest England" match-boxes held only safety
matches tipped with harmless red phosphorus, then only made
in the proportion of one to a thousand. At peak this factory
was turning out six million boxes a year.

But Booth was not in business for its own sake : he was out
to reform the industry from top to bottom. Soon James
Barker was piloting conducted tours of newsmen and M.P.s
round the factory-workers' homes to demonstrate the grim
price of matches at twopence farthing a gross—as against The
Army's regulation fourpence. At the climax of each visit,
Barker would lean forward to snuff out the gaslight and a low
gasp of horror stirred in the room.

In the eerie darkness, the victim's jaw, even her hands and
blouse, glowed greenish-white like a spectre's, as the phosphorus rotted her while she lived.

The campaign was no overnight success : conservative
Britons still prized "strike-anywhere" matches above the
new-type Swedish safety-matches but, not for the first time,
Booth had pointed the Victorians towards recognition of the
need for modified State intervention. By 1901, managing
director Gilbert Bartholomew of the Bryant and May match
factory, gave promising evidence to the Home Office Lucifer
Match Committee : his firm had not used one ounce of yellow
phosphorus in ten months.

But Booth, a year earlier, had closed down his own factory,
aware that "Darkest England" had scored its first victory.

Although the initial £100,000 Booth sought was subscribed
within months, the scheme was still sore-pressed for money.
The annual £30,000 never was forthcoming ; at most the
public contributed £4,000. Worse, the scheme's detractors had
broadcast a hurtful rumour : after salting away £2 million of
other people's money, Booth would abscond like any nimble-
fingered financier. To allay public fears, Booth assented to the

London *Times*'s suggestion that a five-man committee under the Earl of Onslow, former Governor of New Zealand, should check on the fund's legal and financial aspects. Eighteen sessions later, the committee summed up : Booth had drawn no income from mission or Army funds in twenty-seven years as an evangelist. Almost his sole support was the £5,000 trust-fund set up for him by the Tasmanian Henry Reed ; even his book's phenomenal £7,383 profit had been ploughed back into the fighting-fund. Twenty-two years later saw Booth's final vindication—when his will revealed assets of a scant £487 19s.

But ceaseless trial and error saw his venture taking shape. In London, all City and Metropolitan police stations had finite instructions : men found wandering abroad should be sent to Salvation Army Shelters. Soon so many were flocking to The Army that Booth found an overcrowding problem ; fully 1,200 men could not be housed. They complied with the letter of the law by evolving double-decker bunks in which one man slept above another.

All through the 'nineties there was the ever-present need to find work for the workless. Indefatigable, Booth explored avenue after avenue : brick-making, paper-sorting, a cabinet factory. By September, 1891, an officer was *en route* to Sweden to purchase timber first-hand and rule out middle-men ; the Hanbury Street labour yard alone was turning out 150,000 bundles of firewood a week. Sample matchboxes from Old Ford reached Booth on tour in Africa ; in Canada, a sample brick. Coffee made from grain was sold at 6d. a tin. Down-and-outs found new purpose making shaving-mugs and tea-caddies bearing Booth's image, cutlery with blood-and-fire crests, musical clocks that jingled popular Army songs. *The War Cry* advertisements offered dress lengths, skirts and Norfolk jackets " all made by pure and holy hands."

At Hadleigh, Essex, on the Thames estuary, Booth's farm colony was the next step up the ladder : a small township of 260 men, farming 3,000 acres of pasture and market-garden, tending kilns that baked two million bricks a year. In spring the massed pink-and-white blossom of 15,000 fruit trees glowed beyond the mud-flats ; rabbits cropped the grass over ten closely-wired acres. The white Wyandottes from the poultry runs were chosen to improve Queen Victoria's own stock. Among 250,000 emigrants aided by Army loans, thousands were men who had learned their pioneer skills at Hadleigh.

Despite an initial £4,000 a year deficit, Booth saw this as a drop in the bucket compared with society's saving in gaol upkeep and pauper hand-outs. Drafted to Hadleigh from the London labour-yards—elevators, Booth liked to call them— some men at first had strength only to sort and bale waste-paper ; weeks passed before they found stamina to wield a spade. Typical was the degraded sneak-thief who had tattooed the Devil over his heart ; after a harrowing session at the Penitent-form, a skilled tattooist was brought in to transform it into an angel.

Booth never once claimed that his reclamation programme was the sole answer—but somewhere a start must be made. " When the sky falls," he answered his critics, " we shall catch larks, no doubt. But in the meantime ? "

One aspect of the scheme had unviable teething troubles. Despite Bramwell's marathon study of soils, climates and economic conditions, The Army's own overseas colony, de-signed to re-people the dominions with redeemed city dwellers, never became a reality. A promised 20,000 acres dwindled to 2,000. No worthwhile crops could be raised in Canada be-cause of early frosts. As late as 1907, Bramwell was closeted with Winston Churchill, then Under-Secretary of State for the Colonies in the Campbell-Bannerman Administration, urging that the Government should underwrite The Army's venture. Churchill, though warmly in favour, knew the final decision lay with Prime Minister Sir Henry Campbell-Banner-man—who might have reservations. Did The Army propose to send only bad men ?

Bramwell denied it. They wanted to send people who would be bad if The Army didn't take them in hand ; people did not become bad all at once. To his puzzlement, Churchill, in a confidential aside, confessed : " No—*I* did not."

Despite the goodwill of men like Churchill, Booth and his social works were long suspect. All through The Army's July, 1890, jubilee, held in the grounds of London's Crystal Palace, a British Secret Service agent prowled amid 60,000 red-jerseyed Salvationists, ears cocked for seditious propaganda. The Charity Organisation Society were unblinkingly hostile : " The hunger of the mass of the people can only be met by their own exertions." Another implacable foe was the great reformer Lord Shaftesbury, to whom The Army's titles and tambourines were anathema. Urged that Booth and his soldiers were in deadly earnest, he blazed : " Was not the Devil himself in earnest ? There is no need of gymnastics to enforce Christianity."

But slowly the value of Booth's great concept won him notable supporters. The head of the Roman Catholic Church in Britain, Cardinal Manning, a warm admirer since the Eliza Armstrong case, went on record : " I am very sure what Our Lord and His Apostles would do if they were in London." As the Cardinal saw it, " the spiritual desolation of London alone would make The Salvation Army possible." To Charles Haddon Spurgeon, famed Baptist preacher who drew crowds of 20,000 at a time, The Army was irreplaceable—" five thousand extra policemen could not fill its place in the repression of crime and disorder."

And more and more countries, it seemed, in the months that followed, were prepared to give Booth's idea a sporting chance. Already the Government of Victoria, Australia's, co-operation had shown what could be done : within the space of years the main tenets of the " Darkest England " scheme had been accepted on the Continent. The bitter winter of 1890, when The Army opened its halls to frost-pinched down-and-outs turned the tide in Holland and France : from now on the city fathers were stirred to make buildings over to The Army at peppercorn rentals. Germany, too, saw The Army's value when Cologne's pioneer " Drunkards' Brigade " went into action ; armed with stretchers and lanterns, a captain and four soldiers nightly toured the streets, carrying fuddled men back to their quarters and sobering them with strong coffee. Soon the men they had redeemed were staffing a small workshop. Shelters were opening in Brussels and Copenhagen; soon The Army's work would be recognised and financially assisted by twenty-four governments.

Inevitably, public fancy endowed The Army with a slogan which has stuck ever since : " Soup, Soap and Salvation ! "

And The Army's selfless devotion won American co-operation too. Though they took no stand in the great strife between capital and labour that marred the 'nineties, their work for strikers' families stirred many hearts. At Fall River, Massachusetts, in the winter of 1894, Captain Alexander Lamb found a situation past enduring : three months' strike action against a local textile mill had brought many families to starvation point. Small near-naked children roamed the streets, crying bitterly for food.

Then a local merchant came up with an offer : if someone would prepare and serve up dinners, he would donate $25 worth of meat and vegetables every day for the duration. Lamb acted fast. He offered The Army's barracks as a dining-room, then secured a kitchen. Since his corps officers were out of work he had a full contingent of cooks, dishwashers and waiters ready to hand. On the first day, over 500 famished youngsters had gorged themselves on meat and vegetable soup, with bread and jam to follow. By week's end, 1,050 were showing up for the meal. " Jimmy," Lamb was touched to hear one five-year-old tell his friend, this is more than good."

In Chicago, in this same year, Captain Wallace Winchell, a sturdy bespectacled man called " The Bishop of the Bowery " was shocked by Governor Peter Altgeld's exposé of the misery following the two-month strike in George M. Pullman's Model Town—a veritable feudal manor where the sleeping-car king, who outlawed unions, owned every foot of ground, every worker's house, every church. Though 100,000 railroad workers voluntarily quit work in the biggest strike America had then known, the true scapegoats were Pullman's 3,000 wage-slaves who had revolted against slashed wages and soaring rentals. As the strike petered out, Pullman called for

new employees willing to sign " yellow dog " contracts—
total disavowal of a union. In cold and fireless houses, men
saw their wives and children grow haggard with starvation.

At once Winchell hastened to the Governor with a plan to
aid them. A blizzard of Salvation Army handbills descended
on Chicago, entreating food, even clothing to help Pullman's
hapless citizens. The Princess Skating Rink was opened as a
collection point for cash donations. Soon horses and trucks
choked Haymarket Square as Winchell's wagon-train of
supplies set out to Pullman's relief.

Chance begot the idea which has become almost The Army
image in America. Depression gripped the west coast and
Captain Joseph McFee, one-time sea-captain, operating a San
Francisco soup-kitchen for unemployed longshoremen, was
at his wit's end : how to find funds to keep feeding them ?
Pacing the waterfront one winter's day in 1894, he spied a
huge soup kettle suspended from a crane outside a ship's
chandler's shop. On an inspiration, McFee hired both crane
and kettle, transferring them to the foot of Market Street.
Passers-by paused, intrigued by his lusty cry : " Keep The
Kettle Boiling ! "

By the winter of 1895, thirty Army Corps along the west
coast had seized on the kettle as a fund-raiser. Then McFee's
idea spread east : in Boston, Army kettles provided Christmas
dinners for 150,000 needy men, women and children. The day
was in sight when 5,000 bright-red Army kettles, some
mounted on tripods twenty feet high, would not only symbolise Christmas to millions of Americans but at times enrich
the fighting funds by $20,000 a district.

That winter, William Booth returned to New York to a
hero's ovation ; through its slum work, The Army was fast
assuming its unique position in present-day America. Car-
negie Hall was packed to hear the man many regarded as an
American tell of his " Darkest England " scheme in a voice
that at times rose clear and strong, with a timbre that sent
shivers down their spines.

" It isn't wicked to be reduced to rags," Booth told them.
" It is not a sin to starve, to pawn the few sticks of furniture

to buy fuel and pay the rent. It is a misfortune that comes to people, honest and good people, in hard times, or when work is hard to get. It is such people that the social scheme means to help."

This time America saw more of William Booth—and what they saw they approved. At the close of his tour, for those who liked them, he reeled off the statistics : he had travelled 18,453 miles to hold 340 meetings in 86 cities. He had spoken to 437,000 people and 2,200 had flocked to the Penitent-form. In twenty-four weeks he had spent 847 hours in a train.

Not to be outdone, his soldiers chalked up some statistics of their own. By March, 1891, the six lasses of the Garret, Dive and Tenement Brigade, operating from one tenement-room in Manhattan's vicious Cherry Hill district, had visited 5,500 families, fed over 600 of them, clothed almost 1,000 more.

What Ballington Booth and his wife began, his successor, Commissioner Frederick Tucker, enlarged. Known after his marriage to Emma Booth as " Booth-Tucker "—each of the General's sons-in-law added Booth to his own surname to enable the wife to use it—his clarion-call was " Work for the Workless." He sent down-and-outs with push-carts all over New York City foraging for salvageable junk. He contracted with some of Chicago's city wards to keep them garbage-free. At Boston and Houston he set up woodyards where unemployed men collected, sawed and delivered wood. By 1898 he had eight Salvation junk-shops selling secondhand clothes at knock-down prices, and five flourishing woodyards.

As ready as in India to explore native customs, Booth-Tucker, in ragged jumper and broken boots, his face blotched with engine-grease, spent a restless night in a New York flophouse before pioneering the first of 125 American hostels for men—with dormitory beds at 10 cents, private cubicles for 15 cents.

By June, 1895, when the present national headquarters building, dedicated as a memorial to Catherine Booth, towered eight stories high at 120-124 West 14th Street, the *New York Tribune*'s laudation spoke for all America : " Nearly all the people in and out of the Churches whose opinion is worth anything frankly acknowledge the good it has done and is doing."

What Booth-Tucker and his officers achieved in the United States was as nothing to the transformation they wrought in the criminal tribes of India—a story as strange as any in Salvation Army annals. For centuries these scattered nomadic tribes, almost three million strong, had lived in villages or wandered like gipsies, but all had one thing in common : an aversion to work. Thieving was so inbred in them that at birth babies born of criminal parents went down on the police register. When " Crims," as they were known, deigned to work, it was always as pedlars—a sure way to prospect for pickings.

As far back as 1871, the Government of India had laboured to regenerate them through reformatory settlements—without avail. One " Crim " grievance was their lack of land—but given land they rented it to local farmers, went on stealing. Reproved, they were guileless : what use was land without bullocks to plough it ? Given bullocks, they sold them ; bullocks were a costly luxury without seedcorn. The seedcorn they ground into flour for bread—and went on stealing.

The tall soldierly Lieutenant-Governor of the United Provinces, Sir John Hewett, was at his wit's end. Finally, like many a man before him, he laid his problem before William Booth : from 1895, following relief-work in famine-ridden Western India, The Army's status had been paramount. Hewett could promise no easy task : to date, the Crims' cut-and-run guerrilla tactics had outwitted 150,000 policemen, 700,000 village watchmen.

Booth, unable to resist such a challenge, readily accepted. The Army would make a start at Gorakhpur, United Provinces, where 300 members of the Dom (pronounced "dome") tribe were penned under police supervision in barrack-like compounds.

At first sight of these tall muscular men, with their dark-grey hairy coats and round greasy caps, Booth-Tucker's heart sank. Rowdy and evil-smelling, they swarmed from the gaol's rose-pink walls in an all-out effort to terrify him, screaming, stamping and shaking their fists. Though his quiet patience at length won him a hearing, the screaming redoubled at the news that work was involved—and at coolie rates of four annas (fourpence) a day.

" Four *annas* ? " screeched a spokesman, " when we can go out any night and get a thousand rupees (£66) *without* working ? What do you take us for ? "

And in the faces of the red-turbanned Indian police, Booth-Tucker read only outright scepticism. How could amateurs check these wild-willed charges—when even the police couldn't stop them slipping over the fence after roll-call for a profitable night's pillage ?

Only monumental patience won the day. No Dom believed in washing ; when their clothes shredded into rags, they stole fresh cloth. Family life was irregular ; when a man went to gaol, his wife took a second husband, " to protect her virtue." If the successor contested the first husband's return a battle to the death ensued. Parental confusions multiplied. In The Army's Gorakhpur boarding-school for Dom children, one small girl, Mahadaya, was claimed by two fathers *and* two mothers. The child suffered no personality-disorder, Booth-Tucker acknowledged reluctantly : on visiting day, Sunday afternoon, all four brought her sweetmeats.

Worse, the Dom's clear pre-notion of Heaven scarcely accorded with William Booth's : Heaven was any place without police stations, where a translated Dom could gamble all day with tiny shells called cowries. At a Dom's funeral the vital ceremony was wedging a tiny piece of gold in the dead man's mouth—his first stake for the other side of the river.

From the outset Brigadier John Hunter and his wife Jessie, overseers of the first Dom settlement, faced a crucial problem : how to find the Doms suitable work ? At Gorakhpur they won the municipal contract for garbage-disposal and many Doms became scavengers ; others, with grim irony, were employed making hessian bags for the local Treasury.

It was a mighty work of faith, destined to encompass a full quarter-century. In time, Hunter's success with the Doms spawned other settlements—in Madras, the Punjab, Bihar, Orissa, Bengal—but each tribe had its own villainous skills to rise above. Some were expert horse-thieves, who fitted pads to obliterate hoof-marks from the sand ; others coined fake ingots, planted them on the highway, then chanced along to claim a share of the finder's reward. A few presented knottier problems. At Moradabad, the Haburah tribe cost one officer and his wife countless hours of sleep ; each night, from two a.m. to three a.m. they squatted on their haunches, howling like banshees, to propitiate evil spirits. Local big-wigs viewed their presence sourly ; to scavenge the street-refuse they relied on jackals, but the Haburahs saw a jackal as gourmet's fare, heaven-sent for the cookpot. Undaunted, The Army set the tribe to work and gradually, as their earnings soared, their diet grew more conformist. Finally the police commissioner paid his supreme tribute :   " You've done wonders with the Haburahs ! The jackals are back."

Afterwards, Booth-Tucker reflected wryly that this was perhaps the one time the success or failure of an Army mission was judged by a prevalence of jackals.

How did The Army work its wonders with such improbable material ? Mainly because the key-note of each settlement was that laid down by John Hunter at Gorakhpur : trust. Once a " Crim " knew The Army believed in him and hoped for him, he often took the first giant step towards self-reliant manhood. " I don't know how you can bear to live among these people," one Indian official confessed. " To us, they're cattle, just cattle." Replied Hunter simply : " To us they're immortal souls."

And they were souls The Army soon knew with unrivalled intimacy. Accepting charge of a batch of " Crims " involved complete re-registration : family details, finger-prints, wounds or birthmarks, occupation—always listed as " beggar." But presently tribes began seeking The Army of their own free-will, some glad to find a settled place of shelter, others because they felt secure obeying orders. One gang sent word that they were turning themselves in to seek refuge from the police, hiding in the jungles by day, travelling by night.

Few tribes stopped short at murder—but Booth-Tucker's officers, lacking weapons, found the armour of God their safety. One squad of fifty Doms was brought to Gorakhpur from a colony forty miles away; they arrived roped together in ranks, guarded by close on 140 heavily armed police. The potential killers were then signed over to John Hunter and four of his officers, who already had charge of 250 other incorrigibles.

As Booth-Tucker saw it, Bible classes and prayer meetings were a vital redemptive factor. Often groups of " Crims " sat together over a Bible, reading verse by verse in turn. At one settlement, a scavenger even pressed for a Bible in lieu of wages. Another Dom, Roshan, progressed so well he was among the first to merit the privilege of unescorted travel, with a Salvation Army pass; until then, no Dom in police custody could travel without an armed escort. Returning after a week's visit to friends he explained how he had duplicated The Army's nightly meeting in his host's home, recounting such stories as the Prodigal Son.

Hunter was gratified. " So you took your Bible with you ? "

" Oh, no," said Roshan airily. " I knew all the stories by heart."

As one old Dom woman summed up with touching dignity : " To think of God as One instead of millions of gods and spirits is in itself restful."

By 1904, following his return from America, Booth-Tucker was trying to aid India's impoverished villages by setting up home industries. Now, bent on finding his "Crims" worthwhile employment, he redoubled his efforts—a harbinger of the mid nineteen-thirties when 10,000 " Crims," converted into skilled artisans, were peopling thirty-five Army settlements.

Always the terrain was the guiding factor. In Bezwada, Madras Presidency, stone quarries were there for the working ; elsewhere 1,500 acres of swampy ground were turned over to millet and rice under Adjutant Robilliard, one-time Malayan planter. One tribe converted land given by Sir Harold Stuart, Government Secretary at Ootacamund, into fifty fertile acres of tomatoes and cocoa-palms; christened Stuartpuram in honour of its donor, it became a settlement so large it now has its own railways and schools, a judicial council made up of settlers. Most are now free from the Criminal Tribes Act's provisions and can live where they please; as in five other still-existing settlements they opt to stay with The Army.

At Changa Manga, in the arid Punjab, Booth-Tucker's boldest experiment was to take over a dense mulberry forest ten miles square, setting " Crims " to fell and cord the trees for sale as firewood. But Booth-Tucker's sights were set higher. From France he imported three million silkworm eggs; from Kashmir, famed for its glowing shawls, he summoned skilled experts. Reared on their habitual diet of mulberry leaves, the silkworms ate seventy hundredweight a day, transforming them into countless yards of silk that were woven each year in The Army's settlements.

The man above all others who worked to make this possible, Major Frank Maxwell, a 38-year-old ex-engineer, had once proved one of William Booth's biggest headaches. As a teenager, pneumonia had left his voice so weak and piping he was inaudible ten feet away. Finally commissioned at thirty-six—far older than most robust young cadets—his open-air meetings were an ignominious failure.

But Maxwell, whose gentle steel was typical of many Army officers, saw a way out. Fired by Booth-Tucker's zeal to improve the villagers' lot, he attended twice-weekly weaving classes for a month. Learning, he pondered. The hand-action by which the weaver threw the shuttle often damaged the warp —the threads stretched lengthwise in the loom. Already the ex-engineer was seeing room for improvement.

As a staff officer at The Army's boarding-school for boys at Ahmedabad, Gujarat State, 280 miles north of Bombay, Maxwell took time out to study Indian weaving methods. His verdict: primitive and time-wasting. In direct competition with factories, village weavers earned a pittance;

few could even reach a speed of 60 picks—as weavers call the casts of a shuttle—a minute.

Out of Maxwell's brooding and book-work came an invention which in its final shape was destined to become one of the few radical innovations in the history of textile machinery : a simple automatic two-pedal handloom, thirty inches wide, built from rough packing-case wood.

When this won first prize in a local industrial exhibition, Maxwell, encouraged, went on to construct the cam-action autoloom which made him famous. Cheap yet easy to manipulate, light yet strong, it scored over Western hand-looms ; most were too heavy for their frail-boned Indian operators. Beyond a width of sixty inches, English handlooms needed two men to work them ; Maxwell's was operable up to 100 inches by one man. In Calcutta's 1907 Exhibition it won first prize over sixty other looms.

Soon, with the loom adopted by The Army's settlements, 10,000 " Crims " were busy weaving millions of yards of cloth and silk ; in later years even the Duke of Windsor (when Prince of Wales) was ordering silk for his personal shirting. And soon the loom's benefits extended beyond The Army. To Maxwell, in 1911 came an urgent summons from Mahatma Gandhi in his *ashram* (half farm, half monastery) outside Ahmedabad. This new patent loom seemed the very thing for his Swadeshi (Home-industry movement); thousands might be needed.

Small, bald, spectacles perched on his pointed nose, the Mahatma, reclining on a string bed, at first rhapsodised over Maxwell's invention. And all seemed set fair in The Army's favour ; as a privileged prisoner, Gandhi had been a regular attendant at Salvationist Bible classes while incarcerated in Bombay gaol.

But suddenly Maxwell's heart sank, for the Mahatma, uncoiling from his bedstead had exclaimed decisively : " No, I can't do it after all, Maxwell. Ours is an all-Indian movement. I couldn't use a loom invented by a white man."

With the stubborn persistence of the meek, Maxwell drove his arguments home. The looms were made entirely by Indian craftsmen from best Burma teak-wood. He himself had only oversight of the manufacture.

It wasn't that Maxwell stood to gain as much as one rupee from the Mahatma's contract ; as a true disciple of Booth, he had voluntarily made over his patent's soaring turnover to The Salvation Army. But his pride as an inventor as well as a Salvationist was in question.

Still the Mahatma was inflexible. " My movement could *not* adopt your loom. You see, the cotton is grown by us, and spun by us and woven by us—all by Indians."

A man whose disability rendered him grudging with words, Maxwell was yet lynx-eyed and his probing glance had taken in every corner of Ghandi's stone-walled room.

" Grown, woven and spun by Indians," he whispered painfully, " and then sewn—on a Singer sewing machine."

The Mahatma's hands, already raised in rebuttal, dropped slowly. After one long moment, he submitted with good grace. " I'd never thought of that."

Thirty years after that momentous interview, Ghandi's followers were still using Maxwell's simple looms : in time, weaving schools led to co-operative societies, enabling villagers to buy them to use in their own homes. Through their shuttles flew not only gauze for The Army's hospitals but countless yards of shirting for their leper colonies.

This was the spirit of the 10,000 strong Army through whom Booth sent the precepts of " Darkest England " around the world : anticipate, improvise—and always have the last word.

"Go for Souls, and Go for the Worst"

1891-1910

After Catherine's death William Booth felt freer to travel abroad. The man whose parish had once been the rookeries of Nottingham was seen across the world, following the trails his soldiers had blazed for him. No country was too remote, no people too barbarous, for the General and his shock troops. " Go for souls," he told them as succinctly as always, " and go for the worst."

At seventy, William Booth was a lonely man, estranged from almost all his children. January, 1896, saw the secession of Ballington and his wife, Maud, to found a rival organisation, the Volunteers of America, denouncing their General's " despotism " ; five years later, Kate, who had married her Chief of Staff, Arthur Clibborn, complained bitterly that Orders and Regulations strangled a Territorial Commander's initiative and followed suit. " I am your General first and your father afterwards," was the rugged old man's farewell to his daughter. A year later, Herbert, voicing the same griev-ance, took the same step.

But Booth was adamant. " The Salvation Army does not belong to the Booth family," he told his soldiers plainly. " It belongs to The Salvation Army. So long as the Booth family are good Salvationists, and worthy of commands, they shall have them, but only if they are. I am not the ' General ' of the family, I am the General of The Salvation Army."

Only Eva, who became National Commander of the United States in 1904 and Bramwell, his devoted Chief of Staff, remained close to their father. Vehement, impulsive, moody, Booth still found the perfect complement in his calm, cautious, steadfast son. Often he would cut short a discussion, " You are like her, Bramwell—your mother," and Bramwell's eyes would hold his father's while a silence fell between them. " Well, Bramwell," was the old man's frequent greeting, " Have you brought along anything to cheer me ? "

Yet to some, Booth's estrangement from his own kin seemed inevitable. Once, when Bramwell asked his father the secret of his strength, Booth revealed how, as a boy, he had knelt at a bare table in the schoolroom of Nottingham's Broad Street Chapel and vowed " that God should have all that there was of William Booth." And Eva, in after years, would add the rider : " That wasn't really his secret—his secret was that he never took it back."

By 1891, fully 10,000 of Booth's officers had made this same decision. Now established in twenty-six countries, they time and again, with sacred principles at stake, courted head-on clashes with the forces of evil.

Three years after Catherine's death, a young Japanese travelled half across the world to press his country's needs on Booth ; two years later The Salvation Army " opened fire " in Tokyo. Opposition, at first, was slight ; to the people of Japan, Booth's was true Bushido religion—worship of God and service of the people. Two of The Army's leading officers won high esteem—Colonel Henry Bullard, who took command in 1900, and his assistant, Captain Gunpei Yamamuro. Bullard, who pioneered India with Booth-Tucker, was a man so ingenious he once escaped from an ugly mob disguised as a saloon-keeper's girl-friend, in a fashionable ulster with ostrich-plumed Duchess of Devonshire hat. Yamamuro, a 23-year-old farmer's son, had resigned his duties as an assistant-pastor to work as barber, farmer and architect's assistant. That way he could reach coolies, bricklayers—people who never came to the little mission church.

Go for Souls, and Go for the Worst

Early in July, 1900, Bullard and Yamamuro watched in silence as a weird procession wound through Tokyo's streets; carriages piled with flowers that flamed and shone in a hundred different hues—blood-red peonies, camellias, tiger-lilies, chrysanthemums, frail pink cherry-blossom. Behind, tripping delicately on high lacquered sandals came scores of lovely olive-skinned Japanese girls, their hair adorned with enormous tortoise-shell hairpins, clad in kimonos of rich silk brocade. Their faces, powdered and painted, were as haunting as death-masks.

Bullard was puzzled. Ordinary women wore only three hairpins—these girls sported fully a dozen. And while the average housewife who shopped on Tokyo's fashionable Ginza wore the customary obi (a big sash) behind her, these girls wore them in front.

Yamamuro didn't mince words. These were the mandatory badges of prostitution. This annual procession, The Feast of the Lanterns, held in honour of a famous harlot, was a token that Japan accepted the degraded profession as the natural order of things.

Main stronghold of these unhappy girls was the Yoshiwara, or " Meadow of Happiness," a mile from the city's centre. Built almost three centuries earlier, this great walled city, a mile square, housed almost 5,000 girls. And though the selling and buying of girls had been declared illegal in 1872, little had been done to enforce the law.

Most girls became prostitutes with their parents' full knowledge; her body was the price of the loan they accepted in time of famine. But with interest that doubled yearly, this loan was never written off; most of the girl's earnings went towards her board or to buy her expensive clothes. Only the Lock Hospital or death by hara-kiri could release her from the horrors of this infamous stockade, guarded by gloved and sworded police, whose blazing lights drew over 100,000 customers a week.

Bullard spent precious hours mulling over Japanese law. He, too, would go for souls and for the worst. As he saw it, the operative clause of the 1872 edict was this: no one's

person must be held for debt. But no man had thought to pu
this into colloquial Japanese that the girls could understand—
a world away from the classical language used in official
documents. When Yamamuro had completed a translation,
Bullard splashed it across the front page of a special edition of
Toki-no-Koe, Japan's *War Cry*:

AN OPEN LETTER TO THE WOMEN IN
LICENSED QUARTERS

As I think of your misfortune, I cannot keep silent. . . .
Even if you work in a rice-field, you have nothing to be
ashamed of in your poverty . . . but *you* are like birds in a
cage .   your bodies seduced by drunkards, liars, thieves.
. . . You *must* resolve to give up this way of life. . . . No
living person, no matter how heavy his debt, can be
forced to do painful service against his will. . . . Contact
us, we are prepared to take care of you. . . .

Then, summoning his fifty officers to The Army's hall in
Kanda, a Tokyo suburb, Bullard knelt with them in a long
night of prayer amid piled copies of *The War Cry*. They knew
that within hours they would gamble all their lives in a savage
war with the brothel-keepers and their satellites.

Next morning, 1st August, 1900, " Blood and Fire " banner
flying, drum pulsing steadily, The Army set out to storm the
Yoshiwara—Bullard and Yamamuro accompanied by Major
Charles Duce, their Chief Secretary, New Zealander Annie
Smyth and several score officers and soldiers. Past the fleet of
waiting jinrikshas, through the high gateway, flanked by a
feathery weeping willow-tree and giant scarlet lanterns, they
wound past the high four-story houses, deploying on street-
corners. To the steady tocsin of the drum, Yamamuro and his
Japanese-speaking officers broadcast their proclamation like
town-criers. Soon sleek black heads peeped from the paper-
panelled shutters of the upper storys. A sea of kimonos—
some scarlet, or mauve starred with white flowers—surged
about them. Then, doling out their copies of *The War Cry*,
Yamamuro let fall the gage. Any girl renouncing her life of
sin would be welcome at The Army Rescue Home, that he and

his wife had opened. Why not come now—this very day?

Pandemonium followed. Up the sandy street a task force of close on 300 bullies came doubling. Screaming, the girls bolted for cover to watch the battle with bated breath from the great picture windows where each night they knelt to display their charms. Staves and batons flailed; stones and white porcelain saké bottles came hurtling to find their mark. Crows rose raucously from the giant lacquer trees; The Army banner hung in limp blue shreds. Hastily, a posse of police broke through and manhandled Bullard's bloody panting warriors to safety from a side gateway.

Briefed to expect a badly-bruised husband, Kiye Yamamuro, already caring for seventy girls, showed the right spirit: " It is an honour that my husband has been wounded for the cause of Jesus Christ."

But Bullard sought not only honour but results. Next day, as he had anticipated, the Press arrived in force at Bullard's headquarters—among them the vernacular *Mai Nicki*, the British-owned *Japan Daily Herald*. To a man, the editors shared The Army's view and gave it front-page treatment: any girl seeking to regain her liberty should be free to do so. On the scene to report a new kind of battle was the famous war correspondent, Richard Harding Davis, who wrote: " There is no place where The Army's women fear to enter, nor are the men less courageous."

And The Army needed courage. For one whole year, the houses of Bullard and his staff officers were guarded by special police. Plain-clothes bodyguards shadowed them from street to street. Once Charles Duce was dragged by strong-arm men before a committee of thirty brothel proprietors who menaced him for hours on end. Duce was unmoved. " I am ready to die," he said calmly, " and fear not your sword and stones." He escaped with a cruel beating.

As word of The Army's campaign spread, results were heartening. Time and again visitors whom the Yoshiwara's bullies mistook for pressmen took savage hazings; trade slumped sharply. Enraged, gangs of thugs invaded two leading newspaper offices and wrecked their plant. By now all

Tokyo was at fever-pitch. Those papers still in business issued two, even three editions daily. " March on, Salvation Army," applauded one, "and bring liberty to the captives."

By October the Japanese with typical thoroughness followed the course reserved for supreme national emergencies when Parliament was not in session. An Imperial Ordinance drawn up by Ministers of State and signed by the Mikado, Mutsuhito, became irrevocable : any girl desiring her liberty could state her wish at the nearest police station and her name would be removed from the register. With no financial liability to her employers she would then be free. Any keeper hindering a girl who wished to leave was guilty of criminal action.

Even now, Yamamuro and Bullard didn't cease fire. They ran off 10,000 leaflets urging the girls of the Yoshiwara to give up their abject lives—leaflets which disgruntled brothel keepers tried to buy up at 10 sen each. It was a futile gesture ; one year alone saw 12,000 girls place themselves in Army hands. By 1902, revulsion had swept the country : 14,000 prostitutes had renounced their calling and brothel visitors, over a million in 1900, had dropped to less than half.

Years later, in 1920, when a roll of honour listing " the benefactors of Japan " was prepared for national records only five Europeans were numbered—but among them, to mark a nation's gratitude, were Henry Bullard and Charles Duce.

The tribute was in keeping. Thirty-five years of persecution had passed like an evil dream and now statesmen and crowned heads vied with one another to do Booth and his Army honour. 1898 saw him open the U.S. Senate with prayer ; 24th June, 1904, saw him at Buckingham Palace, with King Edward VII, shaking him cheerily by the hand, avowing " You are doing a good work—a great work, General Booth." And how the King wanted to know, did the Churches now view his work ? " Sir," replied Booth, with the humour that never failed him, " they imitate me." When the King, chuckling, begged Booth to write in his autograph album, the old man bent forward to sum up his life's work :

Go for Souls, and Go for the Worst

Your Majesty,
Some men's ambition is art,
Some men's ambition is fame,
Some men's ambition is gold,
My ambition is the souls of men.

From that day on many British papers quietly dropped the quotation marks which until now had always bracketed Booth's title.

But if Booth walked with kings he kept his bearing : he never lost the common touch. A brisk laving of his hands in a workman's pail was his sole preparation for that first meeting with King Edward. Newspapers might urge that " this Caesar of evangelism, this Napoleon of the Penitent-form " rated a peerage—but in October, 1905, when the City of London conferred their freedom on him, his journey to Mansion House showed the measure of the man. He could not ride in triumph through streets where he and his officers had succoured the poor ; instead he must walk. Beside him trudged a task force of officers until Bramwell, struck by the symbolism, urged " Fall back—fall back and let him walk alone ! " Suddenly, with deep humility, Booth swept off his top-hat and the watching crowds saw the autumn breeze ruffle his fine white hair. At that moment one aide, Lieut.-Colonel George Jolliffe, was riveted to see a hansom-cabby perched on his box—weeping openly, like scores of others, without shame.

But even the splendour of Mansion House couldn't deflect Booth's sense of The Army's purpose : soon the City fathers were listening raptly to his telling apologue of The Army's Boer War work. One besieged town had food in plenty but to simplify distribution the community was hived off according to religions. The Anglican clergyman told off his flock, the Baptist assembled his—but at the end a large crowd still stood dumbly, with the mute appeal of stray dogs.

" Then," Booth wound up, " the next man to step forward was The Salvation Army captain—' All you chaps who don't belong to anybody, follow me '."

Despite his humble origins, Booth mixed readily with men in high places ; only a lavish torrent of donations could keep his mighty ship of faith afloat. Men like Viscount Northcliffe, the "Napoleon of the Press" and founder of the London *Daily Mail* proved powerful allies from the first; as a boy, legend claimed, Northcliffe had knelt at the Penitent-form, and once confessed as much to Booth. Though Booth chaffed him "There wouldn't have been room for both of us in the same Army!" in truth he knew Northcliffe as The Army's staunch supporter. Often Northcliffe's Rolls-Royce carried Army officers on honeymoon. Once, at a dinner party aboard an ocean liner, when someone spoke scathingly of Booth, Northcliffe went white with anger.

"Gentlemen," he said rapping his glass with his knife, "all the religion I have I owe to General Booth, and I will not permit anything derogatory, either to him or to his Army, to be said in my presence."

And Booth numbered many such friends. George "Bloater" Herring, a wealthy retired bookie, gave thousands of pounds to the social work for men; though no Salvationist, he proudly preserved an Army cap in a glass case at his hunting-lodge. Sir Abe Bailey, the South African magnate, gave as generously to Army funds as Britain's great Empire-builder, Cecil Rhodes—who, as Premier of Cape Colony, presented The Army with a 3,000-acre farm north of Fort Salisbury. A keen student of Booth's Hadleigh Land Colony, Rhodes still found his absorption in degraded men a puzzle. Booth had to confess it: "To me men, especially the worst, possess the attraction of gold mines."

But what touched Rhodes most deeply was that Booth, on their return journey to London, knelt in the railway carriage to pray for the great pioneer. When Rhodes died in 1902, William Booth to him was still "the only one who believes I have a soul."

No sycophant, Booth was more than a match for any tycoon. "I'm going to give you a thousand pounds, General," Lord Rothschild told him once. "When will you have it?" "Now!" rapped out Booth with such authority that Rothschild lost no time fumbling for his cheque book. To Booth, ends justified means. When a high-minded Christian scolded him for accepting a donation from the Marquis of Queens-berry, a professed agnostic, the General was unrepentant. " We will wash it in the tears of the widows and orphans and lay it on the altar of humanity."

No man who met Booth in these globe-girdling years ever quite got over his frugal fare. Once in Germany, Booth found himself at a millionaire's table winking with crystal and gold plate. The bishops and burgomeisters flanking the board, licked their lips in anticipation ; in Booth's honour, the host had imported a chef all the way from Paris. Then, politely, Booth apologised. He was a tiresome eater and moreover, on a bland diet. The rich man thought he understood. Spit-roasted quails *could* be rich—but how about some consommé, poached salmon with Hollandaise sauce and a glass of white wine ?

" Thank you, sir," replied Booth courteously, " just a little bread and milk."

After that a printed menu went ahead to warn every host : what nourished the General was one meal each day at 4.30 p.m. —a pot of strong " Triumph " tea, The Salvation Army's own blend, with boiling milk, thin crisp toast and a few fried mush-rooms. Once, seeing Booth about to tackle this formidable concoction of fungi and tannin at his office desk, author Rider Haggard was awed : " Never before had I understood the height, depth and breadth of your faith in the Heavenly protection." One host, hearing that Booth was a vegetarian who neither smoked nor drank, asked an aide : " Good heavens ! Has the General *no* vices ? "

What hit them even harder was the way Booth drove him-self : the clammy heat of the Red Sea or the glacial silence of the Arctic were the same to him. Secretaries like 35-year-old Major Fred Cox could barely keep pace with a dynamo of 70 who habitually felt his best after 7 p.m. ; for a man who wrote thirty-five articles on one outward voyage to Australia, no day was ever long enough. An unwavering perfectionist, Booth would preach only in wide well-ventilated halls with a stout, tintack-free platform-rail to support his weight—and it was Cox's job to check up on them. When Booth rose to speak,

Cox, far to the rear of the hall, clutched a white handkerchief: a gentle flutter, and the General knew that every word was carrying.

If Booth began the day with 6 a.m. paperwork, midnight had chimed before Cox read him to sleep—but often he woke to three nocturnal calls: to turn Booth's pillow, to darken his room, or to take 4 a.m. dictation.

No secretary ever slept on unawares—for sixty feet of wire linked the electric bell beneath his pillow with William Booth's bell-push.

An insomniac, his stomach always in pain, Booth was no easy taskmaster. By 1902, Cox had 200 daily duties—from testing Booth's bath-water with a thermometer through keeping sodium bicarbonate at the ready to peeling and coring his apples. When The Army's tailoring department, bewildered, asked why Cox's uniform needed forty-three pockets, Cox could list a need for every one—from travel tickets to cough lozenges and spare dentures.

Even railway carriages became offices as Booth, his back to the engine, seated farthest from the wheels, donned carpet-slippers and travelling cap and opened up his portable wooden desk for three hours' non-stop dictation. If the train rolled, Cox knelt on the floor with the typewriter on the seat—and Booth, strapped to the hat racks by holdall-straps, wrote grimly, pad on arm. It was now, Eva always believed, that his eyesight began rapidly to wane.

But all over the world Booth found Salvationists driving themselves the same way—accepting primitive life as they found it, living as God had called them. In New Zealand he saw officers seeking souls by canoe, carrying Maori shields and spears. On the tiny island of St. Helena, Captain George Harris and his wife jog-trotted along dirt roads on donkeys, *War Crys* strapped to the cruppers. Salvation outriders ranged the pampas of the Argentine, steering through the low blue islands of eucalyptus trees, the horse's tethering thongs bound tight round their wrists lest they toppled senseless from sunstroke. By night they crouched at the gauchos' camp-fires, hacking sizzling chunks of mutton with a clasp knife from a

whole roasted sheep, a guitar's plangent cry accompanying
Army songs. Far away in Hawaii, Major John Milsaps learnt
to summon converts in the age-old tradition of the islands—
a long blast on a conch-shell.

Where pioneers went, The Army was never slow to follow.
The seven Salvationists mustered by Eva Booth who in
April, 1898, set out from Skagway, Alaska, over the Chilkoot
Pass to Bennett, British Columbia, journeyed not for gain but
for God. Five hundred miles away, beyond the dangerous
Five Finger and White Horse Rapids, lay Dawson City,
Yukon territory, bursting its seams with 20,000 men, lured by
the gold-rush of Bonanza Creek on the Klondike River.
Under the dazzle of the Northern Lights, where the thermo-
meter plunged to seventy below, lassies and men paddled
their canoes for thirty-five interminable days, resolved to bring
God to the gold rush.

With fingers so blistered and bleeding each paddle-stroke
seared like fire, they reached Dawson City somehow on 22nd
June, 1898. Almost $50 of their first collection was in pure
gold-dust.

" It's the chance of a lifetime," Eva wrote excitedly to Kate.
" We are straining every nerve to seize it to the full. . . ." The
true perils she kept to herself : at Skagway, Alaska, five armed
killers led by " Soapy " Smith, a local saloon-keeper, had
invaded her camp among the pines. Only the chance discovery that the tall dour killer had attended Army meetings
as a boy averted an ugly situation. Gently, Eva spoke of a
salvation that meant victory even over death, while the out-
laws sat, incongruously, sipping steaming cocoa. Five days
after " Soapy " Smith and Eva had knelt in prayer, a rival
killer gunned him down on the wharfside.

A town ablaze with gold-fever, the largest most lawless
city west of Winnipeg, had work for The Army to do. On
one evening alone, 2,000 prospectors stampeded to nearby
Dominion Creek to stake their claims, then queued all night
outside the Recorder's Office. And eighteen thousand more
were spending to the hilt : because he liked milk, a Front
Street saloon-keeper calmly paid $1,000 in gold-dust for a

Holstein cow. Typically, The Army's first convert had gambled and boozed his way through $7,000.

Though Dawson's churches used planks for pews and whisky bottles as candelabra, primitive conditions didn't deter The Army. Ever resourceful, they held their first service in a marquee 2,800 feet square, loaned by two eccentric American ladies who had come as tourists—along with two great Danes, a zither, a portable bowling-alley and an ice-cream freezer. But soon their meetings had transferred to a rough pine-wood barracks seating 150, which the miners had built with their own hands.

Only The Army, the miners came to see, would have served up piping hot Christmas dinners to 300 shivering men who had staked and lost their all. Only The Army would have persevered to rehabilitate and find work for men on the brink of delirium tremens, who had drawn no sober breath in Dawson.

Sometimes The Army's intentions were misconstrued. Colonel Robert Hoggard and his troops, pioneering Korea, saw recruiting reach an all-time peak—then realised that their peasant converts, clamouring for promotion and arms, were signing on for a war against Russia. Months later, Hoggard still heard baleful mumbles : " That man promised me a gun and a captain's pay. . . ." In South Africa, the five young stalwarts Booth hand-picked to wage Salvation war in Zulu-land found all the odds against them. Rumbling by ox-cart from Pietermaritzburg, Natal, over 100 miles of red, rutted roads they were set down on a snake-infested ten-acre site by the Amatikulu River amongst the proudest warrior tribe in all South Africa—who hotly resented their coming.

To The Army's leader, Captain Allister Smith, a mop-headed young Scot, one thing was plain : a handful of men held the Zulus in thrall as their British conquerors of twelve years back never could. Witch doctors, in theory outlawed by the British, were still dreaded and revered for their occult power to divine ill-wishers. Only many gifts would induce a greedy witch-doctor to work his " ten-goat magic," raving and beating his body with a whisk of animal tails. But the hapless man he " smelt out " was roasted to cinders over a slow fire.

Though a tiny trickle of converts came to the primitive brick-built hut which The Army themselves erected, Smith knew that progress would be minimal while the witch doctors reigned. The huge 40-stone Chief Tshingwayo, who ruled Amatikulu district, had abiding faith in them. Covertly he instructed his head men to keep their people from Army meetings.

Not until August, 1892, did Smith's chance come. Then drought ravaged Amatikulu country. The crops wilted in the fields ; the lush grass of the river valley shrivelled like fine brown hair. The dairy cattle were like stumbling skeletons and their milk yield dwindled. Soon children began to die.

Though no friend to The Army, Chief Tshingwayo was still the father of his people. According to his lights, he now did the best he could for them. He summoned the finest rain doctor and paid him handsome fees.

On the appointed day, Zulus from all over the district tramped to the Great Kraal to see the rain doctor subdue the skies. They watched in silence as he threw the bones of divination. They saw him dance before the ancestral spirits and saw foam well from his lips. They heard his command, high, nervous and staccato, as he shook his fist at the sky : " Rain ! I, the Great One, command you to come from the Heavens ! "

But from the " Great-Great," as the Zulus called Smith's God, there came no answer. In despair and anguish the people saw the discomfited rain-doctor driven from the kraal.

Tshingwayo was in a quandary. He saw The Salvation Army as a threat to his powers, their teachings as subversive. Their strange notions of the sanctity of womanhood fell harshly on his ears ; women's place was in the fields while men waged war. At best The Army were unwelcome guests of the British Government. Yet could *their* God bring rain to his drought-stricken land when the witch doctors were impotent ?

Early one morning two Zulus in grey cast-off military greatcoats reported to Smith's quarters. These were Chief Tshingwayo's envoys. " Our hearts are dried up within us."

one confessed, " our courage is finished. The Great One has called the rain-doctor, but he has failed to overcome the dry devil who beats us with his rod of hot air."

Humbly they voiced their request : if The Army would hold a Sunday prayer meeting to the White Man's God, all the Chief's people would be ordered to join them. What word should they carry back to Chief Tshingwayo ?

It was a daunting challenge, but one that Smith must meet. For the first time a new force had claimed these people's attention—prayer. Of course, answered prayer would turn the tide—but what if The Army's prayers went unanswered ? This risk he must accept.

" We shall do our part," Smith told them. " We have spoken. Go in peace."

No officer of Booth's Army ever prayed harder than Smith did now. Sunday saw hundreds of Zulus trudging across the parched valleys and plains, squatting on the forlorn brown grass outside the Catherine Booth settlement. To his secret joy, Smith saw that at least one Zulu, despite the crowd's scoffing, had brought a vast umbrella.

" You could shelter your family under that tent, Jojo ! Do you think it *will* rain ? "

As the banter died, the upright old man replied demurely : " Well, we are here to-day to pray for rain, *and it might rain* ! " It was an answer, Smith thought, to shame many a Christian.

Then, rising before his vast audience, he taught them a short simple prayer in the Zulu tongue : " Our Lord, send upon us the rain in Thy mercy. Help us with rain. Shower it upon us, O Great-Great."

At once Smith's handful of converts began fervently to pray. Uncertainly at first, the Zulus followed. Voices rose and fell in exhortation, dying sometimes to a mumble as one man prayed alone, rising again in massed volume to seek God's intervention. Three hours passed. The sun was white and pitiless in a blue, brassy sky and Smith prayed on. Suddenly, from far to the east, towards the Indian Ocean, came a heavy rumbling. Rapt with awe the congregation saw, piling inland from the sea, massed thunderheads moving inexorably towards Amatikulu. The sun from the west blazed upon them and they shone like high and snow-capped ridges.

As the thunder rolled louder, louder rose the prayers. Feet away from Smith, a searing flash of forked lightning ripped the ground. Again thunder crashed, unbearably loud, drowning out all human sound. In solemn silence the congregation crouched. *Nkulu-nkulu*, the Great-Great, was speaking with a warrior's majesty.

Warm, wet drops of rain, as large as pennies, spattered on the Zulus' upturned faces. Hastily, with a last devout prayer, Smith brought the meeting to a close : soon the rivers and streams on the homeward journey would be raging white torrents. He dared not of course, look ahead to a moment, not far distant, when Chief Tshingwayo and all his kraal, even the witch doctors, would themselves profess salvation. Nor could he envisage the first Army-sponsored Zulu school, where pupils from six to sixty came to learn not only to read and write but brick-making and husbandry. Fat oxen, broken into the yoke, drew ploughs which The Army helped the Zulus to purchase. The unfair burdens thrust on the women became properly those of men. Sewing-machines hummed busily, with the neat calico garments of practising Christians replacing the filthy skin kilts of savage life.

All this lay in the future. On this August Sunday, Smith saw only the people rise and run in all directions, laughing and singing as the rain their prayers had brought beat on their naked bodies. Louder than any sang old Jojo, trudging homeward beneath the vast canopy of an umbrella justified by faith.

Once, groping to express the larger concept that his father's social work had given to The Army, Bramwell Booth dubbed his soldiers " the servants of all "—men and women so transfigured by glory they cheerfully shared the direst hazards of the peoples they lived among.

In all the world, no better example existed than Captain Emil Ovesen of Harstad, Norway.

Along the north Norwegian coast for 150 miles, stretch the

five islands of Lofoten, storm-lashed granite mountains rising 4,000 sheer feet, ending where the Narvik Fjord winds inland. From mid-February to April's end, comes the cod-fishing season which spells survival to the Lofoten folk, when shoals of fish 150 feet thick teem coastwards from the Atlantic, and even youngsters in their teens set out with the fishing smacks to help in the hard work of drying and salting. Emil Ovesen, a solemn, brown-eyed youngster, was fourteen when he made his first trip. At fifteen, already a convinced Salvationist after attending seamen's meetings, he found himself sole support of his mother and eight young brothers and sisters. A force 8 gale, slamming with hurricane force along the knife-sharp reefs, had swept his father overboard and engulfed him.

Emil studied navigation and gained his pilot's certificate. He made a down payment on a boat and for seven years, as its skipper, fought the black teeming water off 1,100 miles of coast from Kirkenes, near the Finnish frontier, as far south as the famous fishing port of Bergen. Though Ovesen did not know it, he was mastering invaluable skills for the work to which God would soon call him.

As far back as 1888, George Railton and Commissioner Hanna Ouchterlony, the handsome blonde Territorial Commander for Sweden and Norway, had cherished a dream : a Salvation Army lifeboat. But this would be a craft with a difference, for to launch a lifeboat from the coast against a six-knot tide was to court disaster. This boat would dog the wake of the fishing fleet, riding out storms for days, even weeks on end ; a boat manned, above all, by blood and fire Salvationists. No insurance company would underwrite the job ; few other contenders seemed likely.

Memos and messages passed from Hanna Ouchterlony in Oslo to her old friend Bramwell in London. Suggestions, modifications, winged from Booth in Melbourne, Jerusalem, Bombay, back to Bramwell, on again to Hanna. Meanwhile, one of Hanna's officers, touring the fishing ports, had hit upon Emil Ovesen, fishing-smack skipper and Corporal in the *Frelsesarmeen*, as a likely man for the job.

Then disaster struck. On the night of 13th October, 1899,

force 10 gales turned the North Sea into icy towering mountains of water. Two days later, when the gales died, the choppy blue-grey waters were littered with the bobbing driftwood of over twenty-nine vessels. Fully 140 lives were lost. From Bergen to Lofoten Islands the bells tolled and the glassy mirrors of the fjords trapped the slow black defiles of mourning women.

But now the Salvation Army had the answer. On 19th February, 1900, after eight weeks at a training-home qualifying for officership, Captain Emil Ovesen and his three-man crew strode up the gangplank of the *Catherine Booth* in Laurvig harbour.

She was a craft worthy of her namesake. By agreement with Bramwell, Hanna Ouchterlony had hired Colin Archer, builder of Fridtjof Nansen's famous *Fram*, to pit his wits against the weather. Now Ovesen took over a 50-ft. yawl built of solid oak, lined with air-tight compartments, so scientifically built that even if her decks smashed in and her hold filled with water she would neither capsize nor sink.

Every inch of her interior was padded with reindeer hair, which has a special supporting power in water. Her cork cushions, even the mattresses in her berths, were dual-purpose life-buoys, each supporting two men. Other noteworthy equipment included a cannon to fire life-saving rockets and drums of oil to calm the sea when inching nearer a wreck.

All her nails were copper or brass, all her iron galvanised. While other ships heeled under closely-reefed canvas, the *Catherine Booth* crested the waves with her sails outspread. Pitching north from Laurvig to the Lofotens, she arrived already towing a damaged fishing-vessel.

Over the months and years, Ovesen pioneered other techniques. Lofoten fishermen used the old Viking build of boat—open, shallow, peaked fore-and-aft. Rigged with a square, single sail, they ran easily before the wind; if they capsized readily they didn't sink. Soon Ovesen had shown them how, if a boat turned turtle, to clamber astride the upturned keel, then plunge their long-bladed knives into the timbers and hang on for dear life. Trial and error proved that this way a man could survive for twenty-four hours—long enough for the *Catherine Booth* to reach him.

Sometimes she limped back to Harstad with four boats in tow at a time—after riding seas so turbulent the deck officers had only hung on by lashing themselves to the mast. In time of calm, by tranquil contrast, she drifted gently up the fjords carrying the Gospel story to 7,000 fisherfolk a year. Thirteen years after her launching, when Ovesen handed over command, the statistics showed the measure of her value; by 1913, 1,772 boats had been brought safely to land, the sea cheated of 5,000 lives. Ninety times Ovesen himself, half-blinded by salt water, collapsed after dragging men to safety from the heaving keels of capsized boats.

The Army's first full-scale baptism of disaster work came on the early morning of 18th April, 1906. For one awful moment —a third of the time it takes to boil an egg—the four square miles of San Francisco city shook and trembled. The skyline danced and billowed as people crawled like bugs on all fours, caught up in America's greatest disaster since the Chicago fire. On Market Street, epicentre of the greatest earthquake then recorded, 30-inch water mains snapped like dry sticks: street car tracks hung suspended ten feet in the air. Soon a leaping wall of orange fire moved inexorably across a city of 450,000 souls—whose entire water supply was now cut off.

The Army's Colonel George French, onetime Bristol cobbler, was swift to act. Though The Army's provincial headquarters and twelve other buildings— $150,000 worth of property—were wiped out, his first thought was for others. While desperate Italians flung wine into the holocaust and other men stood vainly urinating, Salvationists under Staff Captain " Happy Bill " Day were setting up a refugee relief camp across the bay in Beulah Park, three miles from Oakland. They stood by as ambulance workers, searchers for the dead, inquiry agents.

From a city where more than 28,000 houses— $400,000 worth of property—had been gutted or wrecked, 16,000 shocked and fearful refugees, diverted to Beulah Park, found The Army's ordered sanity the tonic they needed. In San Francisco, the Mayor, announcing the death penalty for looters, had called in 1,500 U.S. soldiers—but in Oakland The Army's blue serge tunics maintained all the law and order that was needed. " Our uniforms count for more than a millionaire's millions," Colonel French summed up.

It was small wonder. For five days of fear and apprehension, no officer even removed that uniform to sleep. In one day, Captain Elsie Alleman of San Francisco's Chinese Corps, doled out 1,500 gallons of milk in 24,000 cupfuls. Her Chinatown Salvationists worked as valiantly, serving up beef stews and chicken dinners by the barrel to people who hadn't eaten for four days. They begged soap, towels and chloride of lime from Oakland's Chamber of Commerce. They clothed almost 6,000 near-naked people.

And others played their part. Eight Salvationists, briefed by the Los Angeles city authorities, racketed through the night to 'Frisco on a priority relief train ; until they had reached their destination all other trains were sidetracked. On the Sunday following, Eva Booth's mass meeting at Union Square, in the heart of New York, raised over $12,000 for an Army relief fund ; a month later, the fund topped $15,000 including $1,000 from William Booth in London. " The prayers and sympathy of our people the world over are with you," he cabled President Roosevelt.

From high-ranking Commissioners to unknown Salvation soldiers, this was an Army imbued with the spirit of William Booth—a man who now walked with kings yet who, on his visit to Palestine, could humbly kneel outside the Garden of Gethsemane to kiss a leper's hand.

Though William Booth's impulsive gesture was inspired by pity, it was in many ways symbolic. Whether for lepers or social pariahs, his Army's first care was for people the world passed by.

The man who initiated The Army's work for lepers, General Johannes Van Hutsz, Dutch Governor-General of Java, was

himself a Roman Catholic—but one furlough in the Nether-
lands inspired the solution to a problem that had beset his
government for years. On a visit to friends, he noted their
main topic of conversation was the virtues of their Salvationist
housemaid. Shrewdly the General pondered : why shouldn't
The Salvation Army put Java's house in order ?

Sounded out, Booth seized the chance with both hands, and
in 1909, The Army, wholly financed by the Government, took
over their first colony at Pelantoengan, Central Java.

Almost 100,000 Javanese had known this blinding moment
of trauma—the first tell-tale white spot that spelt leprosy, a
dreaded ailment marked by ugly evil-smelling wounds which
could rob a sufferer of his limbs or rot away his face. Soon,
thousands came to know the next stage of the disease ; the
moment when the train, rolling up the long mountain grade
from the port of Semarang, chuffed into Weleu terminus. As
the leper stepped from his solitary wagon, coolies with sedan
chairs made tracks towards him. Soon the sedan was winding
through pale-green rice fields, past the darker green of coffee
estates and tea-plantations. At length the perpetual green was
broken by the white-walled bungalows and grey-shingled roofs
of Pelantoengan Colony.

As the traveller stepped out, the coolies, hastening the
sedan to the river's edge, burned it to feathery grey ashes.
Not from Pelantoengan—or from any of The Army's three
other colonies—did any traveller return.

Though The Army could find no cure for leprosy, their
officers—Dutch, German, British, Hungarian—could still, as
they phrased it, " lighten the lepers' load." When medical
research showed that children born of leper parents are rarely,
if ever, infected, at birth, their Poeloe, East Sumatra, Colony,
pioneered a bold experiment : patients could intermarry if
they would yield up all new-born children. Beyond the
boundary of infection, the babies grew up in an Army home
—where officers took home movies to keep parents briefed on
progress. Parental presents, bought by proxy, were taken
direct to the home.

Cut off from their fellow officers in primeval wilderness,

Booth's fighting priesthood battled round the clock.   At
Semaroeng, East Java, Lieut.-Colonel Thomas Bridson and
his wife Marjorie had no helpers save the patients themselves ;
each day they bandaged the sick and twice each week gave
injections—quinine for malaria, morphine to deaden pain.
Most lepers died slowly—one reached 80 after 40 years in an
Army colony—and others, hopelessly deformed though no
longer infectious, the famous " burnt-out cases," needed equal
care.

Dramatic incidents proving the risk they ran occurred with
alarming frequency.   Often the disease struck through to
patients' brains and they grew violent.   In East Sumatra, fifty
lepers armed with sickles on long poles gravely wounded a
party of Government soldiers.   One Salvationist was wounded
in the back by a hatchet ;   another was almost strangled by a
patient.

But Bridson and his fellow-volunteers never lost heart.
They organised cinema shows, sports days, feasts of sweet-
and-sour fish bought from native restaurants, even produced a
Malay version of *Hamlet*.   And they strove for their spiritual
welfare too.   Many patients were as young as Soetomo, son
of a government inspector of schools, yet when doctors
ordered him to Pelantoengan colony, The Army were as
reluctant as his father, a strict Moslem—for no Salvationist
ever tries to wean a man from his religion.   But soon the father
was so inspired by Soetomo's joyful letters he gave them
rights over the boy.

A youngster who had set his heart on becoming an architect,
Soetomo pleaded to learn more of the Gospel—and what he
learned he took literally.   "In my father's house are many
mansions," he read, and at once took fresh heart.   In that case
they would need architects in Heaven to build those mansions ;
he must go right on studying.

When Soetomo died, Sister Christine Stewart, who had
helped all along to maintain this illusion, was moved almost to
tears to open a long stoutly-wrapped parcel from the boy's
father.   Inside, the proud Moslem had packed the last requisite
for his son's grave :   the cross of Christ.

Best known of all Java's pioneers was Dr. Vilhem Andreas Wille, the young Danish eye-specialist who landed at Semarang as early as 1907. Already his native town of Køge had been startled by the spectacle of a doctor who went his rounds in full Salvation Army uniform; one reading of Catherine Booth's biography had decided Wille on his life's work. Within twelve months he had presented his fine town house to The Army and left for London to train as a full-time officer.

A dark thatched barrack, split into five compartments little more than twelve feet square, seemed an unlikely surgery in which to make medical history—but in time Wille achieved that distinction. As resident medico to a Salvation Army colony for destitutes outside Semarang his consultations, in 1908, topped 7,000—and five years later had risen to 41,000. More than 5,000 of these were eye patients; almost half the 2,700 operations he performed each year were serious.

What earned the surgeon his niche in medical annals was his diagnosis of an eye disease which had cost thousands their sight, many of them ailing four-year-olds. Known as xerophthalmia, many doctors mistook it for a simple eye-infection, evidenced by night-blindness and a dulling of the cornea. Then, within days, they were appalled to see the whole cornea melt away like wax. Wille, delving into close on 300 cases, confirmed a theory first postulated by other Danes: this was no infection, but a wasting disease caused by avitaminosis—deficient diet. A steady intake of full cream milk, butter, eggs, ox-liver, cod-liver oil—all rich in A and B vitamins—produced miraculous three-week cures.

Few surgeons ever assembled a more colourful waiting-room of patients. One blind boy was so delighted when sight returned to his right eye he dashed from hospital before they could fix the other. He was followed to the operating table by a Sultan's son with flowing robes and a diamond-studded crown. A Dutch admiral's daughter, Wille's first patient one morning, was replaced by a Javanese convict, his iron ring and chain still round his neck. As his fame spread, patients flooded in from India, China, even Australia. From one

Manila hospital came a ten-month old baby whose eyelid had been eaten away, imperilling her sight. With three nurses, Wille saved it and through plastic surgery gave her a new eyelid, minus only the lash. A deformed and syphilitic beggar got the same treatment.

If rich men who could pay their fees in full complained that Wille gave preference to the poor, the bearded doctor replied patiently : " Sir, you are able to pay any medical man practising on the island—these have no one else to whom they can go. I shall be happy to do my best for you—if you will be good enough to wait your turn."

For despite his gleaming up-to-the-minute operating theatre where he could sit while working and allow his hands freedom, Wille was Salvationist as much as surgeon. Before each operation he knelt on the tiled floor, beseeching God's help. The surgery accomplished, a prayer of thanksgiving followed, with an interpreter on hand to explain the gist if Wille didn't know the patient's language.

Trail-blazing medical work of this calibre in time led to the growth of over 150 Salvation Army hospitals and medical units, but The Army never lost sight of their first goal : above all they were surgeons of souls. One of the most adept was Colonel William McIntyre, a modest bespectacled Canadian Scot who, in the years that Wille worked the jungles of Java, worked the asphalt jungle of New York's East Side. For fourteen years before prohibition, McIntyre, under Eva Booth's direction, waged a bitter battle against alcoholism— the first step towards twenty-one Harbour Light centres The Army operate to-day.

New York's first intimation of what was afoot was dramatic. Through the dreary streets of " Hell's Kitchen " roared a procession of green double-decker Fifth Avenue buses. Outside saloon after saloon, they ground to a halt, discharging a task force of swift-moving Salvation Army officers. Within seconds they were back, piloting a few more stumbling red-eyed bums expertly aboard. One hour later bystanders packing the city's sidewalks gaped at an eye-popping spectacle : a monster three-quarter mile long procession of mounted officers and five brass bands, led by a walking papier mâché whisky bottle ten feet high, to which a ragged reeling man was held fast by chains. Behind came a city water-wagon, packed with bleary befuddled bums, uniformed Salvationists marching alongside to keep them " on the wagon." Borne by the bus-load to The Army's Memorial Hall on Thanksgiving Day, 1909, and sobered with strong black coffee, 1,200 hopeless homeless Bowery bums were inaugurating New York's first-ever " Boozer's Day."

Until the Eighteenth Amendment no campaign spotlit so mercilessly the alcoholic's true plight. From the gallery, watching newsmen and magistrates at first blenched at the putrid odour that hung above the audience like a fog—then stayed to marvel at a meeting which saw more than 200 men seek out the Penitent-form. Many of these, cut to the heart by old hymns like " Nearer My God To Thee," unheard since childhood, broke down in paroxysms of weeping. Others gave proof that God, through The Army, was working His pur-pose out, testifying to their impassioned change of heart : " If the whole Atlantic were whisky and I had to spend my life swimming around it, I wouldn't open my gills for a drop."

Aside from *Darkest England*, no one Army reform re-ceived such world-wide publicity. One clipping-service estimated that New York papers alone devoted thirty-six yards of single column space to one convention. At Inter-national Headquarters, the furore was so great William Booth anxiously cabled Eva for details—then cabled back " Fully approve."

McIntyre's most notable convert, who more than any man publicised the work, wasn't won over until " Boozer's Day " 1910. At forty-nine, Henry Milans had spent two-and-a-half years tasting degradation to the depths. A flabby mountain of a man, whose collar size was twenty, turning the scales at 250 pounds, alcoholic addiction had cost him everything—his marriage, his hard-won job as managing editor of the *New York Daily Mercury*.

In 1908, blacklisted from the newspaper world, he sank to

the Bowery. He joined the " skins," the " no-gooders " in a street once known as " the livest square mile on the face of the earth "—more truly called " the bottom of the bottom." Each yard of its grimy sidewalks, lit by flickering gaslight in red and blue globes, became his world, and the stench that was the Bowery's own—garlic, pretzels, Bologna sausage, limburger and stale beer. He foraged its gutters for discarded pigs' knuckles ; he bummed drinks in cheap saloons, where better-heeled citizens choked down four dozen oysters, soused in pepper sauce, at a sitting.

Degradation taught new values : a dollar was no longer four 25-cent pieces but twenty drinks. Anywhere from Cooper Square to Chatham Square, six blocks by seven blocks wide, where 200 saloons served 50,000 citizens, the same standards held good : a slug of " third rail " whisky or a 5-cent schooner of beer entitled you to a bed for the night—on the floor of the back room, where men and women lay criss-crossed like the dead on a battlefield. On this street every saloon offered a bargain : for a nickel Milans got not only beer but free food—pickled fish, sauerkraut, rye bread—wiping his mouth on the big communal towel, steel-clamped to the rail of the bar.

This was the street Salvationists knew well, housing more than half New York's cheap lodging-houses ; in most they burned a pound of sulphur a day to destroy the bugs. It was a street of contrasts, where prostitutes wore virginal white and carried revolvers, where " millinery store " was the polite euphemism for a brothel. Above all, it was the street of bums, who came in many grades, but the lowest of all was Milans, who at night slept out on a loading platform near Brooklyn Bridge, wrapped only in a Tucson blanket (newspaper). Often enough it was his own *Mercury*.

Milans had reason to despair. Taken unconscious to the alcoholic ward at Bellevue Hospital, where 200 fresh cases daily tortured the air with their screams, he had wakened to hear a professor from Cornell University Medical School lecturing clinically on an alcoholic's predicament : " You are looking, gentlemen, at a hopeless incurable. . . . The only

peace he will ever find will be a drunkard's grave." When
Milans opened his eyes he saw professor and students grouped
at the foot of his own bed.

Months later, at dawn on Thanksgiving Day, 1910, Milans
again opened his eyes, chilled to the bone by the raking wind
that blew from the East River. Now he was amazed to find an
Army lassie beside his loading platform, her face tender with
compassion. "Aren't you tired," she asked gently, "of your
life of degradation ? " Milans stared at her without interest,
without hope. "The doctors and specialists have declared I
am incurable," he said bleakly.

But the lassie, impatient, brushed this aside. "Of course,
they can't cure you there ! " she retorted. "Yours is more than
a physical disease ; it is a sort of heart disease that they can't
touch. But listen, Jesus can cure you and make you a good man
if you will let him."

Milans was fearful and he knew why. "Boozer's Day"
meant free coffee and doughnuts and the pre-dawn chill was
like a block of ice inside him. Always before he had held out
against The Salvation Army, some hard brave corner of his
mind too proud to become a " mission stiff "—a tramp who
sang fake Hosannahs in return for beef stew. That day, as
soon as the Memorial Hall service was over, he slunk away,
afraid he would be called on to " get religion."

Yet night after night, despite himself, he drifted back to the
Memorial Hall. Through the private hell of the years he knew
he had lost hold on God, but The Army's unquenchable love
of souls struck a response in his fogged brain. He felt suddenly
less despairing, less alone. When he shrank from Envoy Kate
Roberts, afraid lest she become infested, she assured him :
" Never mind moving—I'm not afraid of your condition. But
I want you to come with me to the Penitent-form and let
Jesus cure you of those terrible habits that have spoiled your
life." But somehow Milans could not go just then.

Next night he was back once more, though wary in case he
was moved to surrender ; again, as soon as the meeting ended,
he hastened for the door. This time it was Captain Lena
Jackson who caught his arm : " Please come back to-morrow

night—will you ? . . . Last night at the quarters we couldn't sleep, so we got out of bed and prayed for you."

Within a week of " Boozer's Day," Milans knew that God *could* help him. What no psychiatrist or specialist could achieve, three young envoys of the Lord, who cared for a dirty depraved bum, had done between them. He went meekly to the Penitent-form and with a new serenity felt the lost years slip away.

Within weeks he had found work with a Jewish printer, earning enough to re-outfit himself. He became Penitent-form sergeant at The Army's Memorial Hall. Later, as prosperous manager of a larger printing press, he was reconciled with his wife. But Milans now knew the Salvationists' secret : his life would have real meaning only if he helped other sufferers. He began work with William McIntyre on his week-end campaigns. With the rank of Envoy—though nicknamed " The Colonel " —this mammoth man opened a veritable correspondence school of Salvation, mending the troubled and broken lives of people all over America.

On his eightieth birthday, in 1941, The Army baked him a special cake, the massed candle-power almost melting the frosting—but Milans, despite his years, was a warring Salvationist still. Even three years later he was achieving record results on Detroit's Skid Row, mingling with the outcasts whose lot he had shared thirty years back, eating where they ate, pleading with and winning over audiences of 300 a night —a living example of what Salvation surgery could achieve.

"For all Lands are my Father's"

1907-28

The year of " Boozer's Day " was 1909 and William Booth was eighty years old. While his aides worried over the merciless way he drove himself, the General grieved for the world. As early as August, 1904, inspired by the advent of the motor-car, he sought to reach more people still, launching out on a twenty-nine day car tour of Britain, covering 1,224 miles, addressing 164 meetings. His passion to reclaim the lost was boundless : " To reach and gather these, I must make a big sound and paint with a big brush—big as the stars."

And his impact was electric. Soon, the old General in his dark-green, ankle-length motoring coat, a peaked motoring cap replacing his favourite silk topper, was a national institution ; all over Britain crowds packed the highways fifteen deep as the white open Napier tourer with red wheels wheezed triumphantly past. By July, 1907, after three such tours, Booth had clocked up over 5,600 miles, addressing close on 400 meetings, speaking for anything from twenty to seventy minutes.

For an old frail man, well into his seventies, it was a gruelling endurance test. As the cavalcade, six cars strong, bounced and balked across Britain's rutted roads, blinding clouds of white dust rose from the wheels, coating passengers and hedges alike. Often, as he rose to address a wayside

meeting, Booth's lips were thick with dust, his clothes like a
miller's smock. Going uphill was even worse ; because the
reverse gear was the lowest, the procession usually wound up
backwards.

The faithful aides who travelled with him—among them,
George Railton, Elijah Cadman, John Lawley—never forgot
those journeys. It was as if Booth, brought closer to an
audience than at any time since Christian Mission days, burned
with the flame of God. Once, journeying northwards, his car
was halted by factory workers who had playfully blocked the
street with a rope. Yet as he rose from his seat, Booth's voice
seemed to hold them mesmerised : " Some of you men never
pray—you gave up praying long ago. But I'm going to say
to you, *won't you pray for your children*, that they may be different ? "

Within minutes, the General's grandson, Wycliffe recalls,
the street was an unending vista of bared heads as fully 700
men knelt in silent worship.

Often, as if sensing the end was close, Booth seemed increasingly obsessed with the work still left undone. " My life
has been an uninterrupted trial," he told the inmates of a
Sussex workhouse. " Often I cou'd weep myself to sleep."
When one aide, Lieut.-Col. William Haines, exulted at a
meeting's close : " Wonderful, General—did you see them ?
A hundred to the Penitent-form in ten minutes ! " Booth was
sombre, " I saw the hundreds going out, having rejected
Christ." More than ever the agony of dyspepsia made eating
an unlooked-for penance. " They bring me eggs for breakfast
and right now children are starving," he burst out once.

From 1907, with Adjutant Helen Treen as his housekeeper,
he lived on alone at his modest six-room Hadley Wood villa,
which The Army had built for him and on which Booth paid
them a scrupulous 4 per cent. Bramwell, quartered with his
family at The Homestead nearby, never failed to pay a
faithful good night call on his father if he saw a light still
burning. Once, making his way to Booth's ground-floor study,
Bramwell and Captain Evan Smith, the old man's secretary,
found the General, in a long fawn Jaeger dressing-gown,

girdled with red, pacing distractedly with folded arms, a wet towel coiled round his forehead to alleviate a headache.

" Ought you not to be asleep ? " asked Bramwell concerned, but Booth shook his head. " No, I am thinking." At first Bramwell was puzzled : was he thinking of anything in particular ? Sadly Booth placed his hands on his son's shoulders. " Bramwell, I am thinking about the people's sins. What will they do with their sins ? "

But it wasn't only Britain's sins that worried Booth now ; his parish was the world. Stockholm, Melbourne, Johannesburg, Jerusalem, Tokyo—half a century before the jet-age, Booth was spanning the world as doggedly as any globe-trotter. At Boston, in September, 1907, on his last tour of the United States, some felt his time was almost done. Several times at one Press conference he bowed his head on the table, fighting for strength. At meetings he seemed testy and on edge, checking all hand-clapping abruptly. Once, stopping in mid-sentence, he stabbed an imperious finger at a woman in the front row : " You will kindly refrain from fanning if I am to keep on talking."

At his official farewell, on 8th November, 1907, he seemed in worse shape still ; escorted by a police inspector and fifty patrolmen, he stood on the steps of New York City Hall, where twenty-seven years back Railton had been refused the right to preach in the streets, to address a crowd 2,500 strong. But now the old General's voice was too weak to carry beyond the steps ; three officers with megaphones boomed his message to the wintry air : " Maybe I will see you again—who can tell ? I won't say good-bye for good then, but only for a little while. I will see you again if I live, and if I am dead I will try to see you anyhow, if they will let me."

Softly massed Army bands played " God be with You Till We Meet Again," as New York said good-bye to William Booth.

But Booth's hold on life was tenacious—as none knew better than secretary Evan Smith. If he was sometimes woken by the General six times in one night, the old man kept going somehow through day-time cat-naps at the billet of his current host. Huge notices : " Hush ! the General sleeps," loomed like off-limits signs on his door. Now the light pained Booth's eyes so acutely that his bed was turned away from the window —with its glass, even the mirror, plastered with huge sheets of black paper. To make Booth's notes for corps councils as legible as possible, Smith took infinite pains—using an old four-bank Remington typewriter with extra-large type, allowing a double margin, double-spacing every line, under-lining main paragraphs in black, subordinate paragraphs in red. Often this grotesquely-spaced agenda covered 300 pages.

Deeply compassionate, even if exacting, Booth let slip no opportunity to do a kindness. When, in October, 1910, the trial of wife-murderer Hawley Harvey Crippen monopolised the world's headlines, Booth took thought of Crippen's dupe and mistress, Ethel Le Neve, whom the jury acquitted. At once he contacted Alfred Tobin, K.C., Crippen's counsel; could The Salvation Army help the girl ? As a result, Ethel Le Neve began a new life in one of Florence's homes. And he was solicitous in small things, too. Once, dining alone with a wealthy hostess to discuss Army finance he was disturbed to find the housekeeper economising on Captain Smith. Four hours later, at midnight, Smith struggled from sleep to answer the General's bell. To his bewilderment Booth, un-wrapping a silk handkerchief, solemnly pressed on him two smuggled slices of fried bread.

Christmas was Booth's most cherished season, when Smith or Major Fred Cox, given a £5 note, set to work devising treats for Bramwell's seven children—perhaps a giant cracker, looped with coloured streamers, which burst apart in a shower of miniature crackers. Inside was a present for every child. No one tugged at his allotted streamer more heartily than William Booth—or joined with more gusto in the Blind Man's Buff and Musical Chairs that followed. On Christmas morning the garden of The Homestead came alive with scurrying warmly-wrapped children, bound for a carol recital at Grandpa's house nearby. But no matter how many new carols they had learned, no recital was ever complete without Colonel John Lawley's " When Jesus was born in the

Manger." Then Booth's deep voice joined in most loudly, rising above the children's piping trebles.

But one Christmas morning, the General's grandson Wycliffe still recalls, plans went awry : the children, after a small-hours' forage into their stockings, overslept. The first thing they heard was Booth's stentorian voice hallooing from the hallway : " *Christians awake !* " The first thing they felt was the ferrule of their grandfather's walking stick, playfully seeking out their ribs as they squirmed and squealed beneath the bedclothes.

Christmas 1908, saw a break in the tradition. At last Booth had learned the truth about his failing sight ; both eyes were affected by cataracts and already his right eye was ripe for operation. The General did not hesitate ; there was still God's business to be done, more travels lay ahead. Following a successful operation at Guy's Hospital, London, Booth was soon in Norway to meet King Haakon. A fortnight later, in mid-March, he was received by King Gustav of Sweden.

A warrior to the last, Booth was not giving up his travels—though the schedule he set himself would have finished a lesser man. At times, alarmingly, he lapsed into something akin to coma. " Where are we, Smith ? " he would murmur, as his " motorcade " wound through sooty streets, lined with wildly-waving crowds, and Smith, perturbed, would answer : " Newcastle, General."

" What are we doing here ? "

" You are going to preach to-night."

" What on ? "

" Judas, General."

" Judas ! Ah, yes, Judas ! "

Then the sight of the theatre, its portals lined with his soldiers bearing smoky flaring torches of rosin, seemed to galvanise him with new power. If his sight was so weak that broad bands of white ribbon, lashed to each end of a railing, prevented him stumbling from the platform's edge, he could hold a vast theatre—Berlin's Circus Busch or Toronto's Massey Hall—spellbound. Across the packed silent house his voice crackled, as if charged with electricity.

" Ah ! Who is this ? " he asked, almost whispering, conjuring up a vision of a man come suddenly into view. " What is this man doing ? He is—*counting*. Coming up close to us, a hellish gleam in his eyes, he whispers, ' See, see, one, two, three, four, five, six, seven, eight, nine, ten, twenty, thirty ! ' "

Then, like a lost soul, his cry rang out, " Ah ! THAT WAS WHAT I SOLD HEAVEN FOR—THAT WAS WHAT I SOLD MY SOUL FOR. See those lights gleaming up yonder. There is the gate of Heaven, there is the throne of God, shining in the faraway distance. Ah, for this I sold it all, I sold it all ! That is Judas, the prince of backsliders. And if ever you go to Hell, he will come to you, and count his silver over in your ears—AND YOU WILL SHOW HIM THE PRICE YOU PAID FOR YOUR SOUL TOO ! "

In the long sick silence that followed, the audience, coming slowly back to earth, heard Booth's whiplash finale : " What shall a man give in exchange for his soul ? What are you giving ? You, *you*, YOU ? "

For all his vehemence, the old man's sense of fun was unflagging. Once, following a lively discussion on prison reform with his old friend Winston Churchill, then Home Secretary, Churchill joked : " Well, General, am I converted now ? " At once Booth flashed back : " Oh no, I wouldn't say you're converted but I think you're *convicted*." Shafts of earthy humour lit every speech—like his favourite story of the man confessing between sobs : " I'm a convert, all right, General, but when I came into this place I'm damned if I had any idea of getting saved." And at Liverpool, when a traffic jam held up his carriage on the way to a meeting, Booth soothed his distressed hostess, " Remember what the prisoner said to the warder on the way to the scaffold—' They can't start this performance without me '."

His magnetism never failed. If a signal stalled his express train, plate-layers or porters would crowd the carriage window for a word with the ever-accessible General. On one tour, Booth waved and smiled briefly to a woman at her garden gate. Hastening indoors she promptly arranged a codicil to her will bequeathing The Army £1,000. One man, surprised in his bath, was still determined to see Booth : dashing naked to the door, he waved wetly as the car drove by. At a wayside meeting for children, a small girl gazing at Booth, her eyes shining, whispered finally : " Isn't he like Father Christmas?"

But all Booth's meetings, in a sense, were children's meetings ; he knew that people like to learn by picture, not by precept. Seldom did he use a word a child of primary school age couldn't have understood and because of this the flying shuttle of the years wove his message in the hearts and minds of millions across the world. " Use words that Mary Ann will understand," he counselled his officers, " And you will be sure to make yourself plain to her mistress. If you speak only to her mistress you will very likely miss her and Mary Ann as well."

An essential showman, whose filing cabinet held 300 classified sermons, Booth time and again hit the target with deadly aim. After one stirring Saturday night address in Rotterdam, a man bent on shooting his rival in love repented and brought his revolver to the Penitent-form. On the Sunday afternoon, his girl friend joined him. Sunday night saw them again at the Penitent-form—with the rival lover in tow. Smiling through tears, the would-be killer turned to the girl : " Now you can have whichever of us you like ! "

Thereafter the revolver became one of Booth's most treasured souvenirs.

More dramatic still was the reaction of a guilty citizen at Birmingham's Town Hall. With mounting intensity Booth was portraying the dilemma of a seducer on Judgment Day : " Here she comes—the woman he seduced ! Her golden hair is falling over her shoulders—she is screaming ' That is the man ! That is the man ! ' " Suddenly, to the horror of all, a voice from the gallery cried in torment " My God—he means *me* ! " Then, with an appalling crash, he leaped clean over the balcony to the floor of the hall, stumbling miraculously unhurt up the aisle to collapse at the Penitent-form.

Game to the last, Booth fought stubbornly the notion that his race was run. At 81, visiting Germany, he scornfully rejected the comfortable armchair offered him : " That is

meant for an old man ! " The closest he would come to
admission was a wry jest shared with George Railton : " I
sometimes fancy, you know, that I may be getting to a halt and
then "—a broad grin—" we shall have a chance to see what
some of *you* can do." But the chance was closer than he knew.
At Newport, Monmouthshire, in July, 1909, Booth's sixth
motor tour, planned to cover 1,460 miles in five weeks, came
to a disastrous close. His right eye in anguish from the ever-
present grit, Booth sought medical aid in his billet but the
doctor was final. Booth must abandon the tour.

But suddenly Booth's voice cut across the diagnosis :
" Doctor, I can't see you," and his aide, Colonel Hugh
Whatmore, thought he knew why : just prior to the doctor's
entry he had turned the old man's chair from the window,
dimming the gas to relax his eyes. " Turn and look at the light,
General," he advised. There was a pause while Booth turned.
Then, with no emotion, no fear, the old man said : " I see no
light. I am blind."

" Yes, General," the doctor admitted, " I am afraid you
are."

To Whatmore it seemed the silence would stretch for ever,
until Booth, still calm, replied, " Doctor, God has helped me
through many a storm and He will help me through this."

In fact, Booth was not yet totally blind ; his left eye, though
dimmed by cataract, was unaffected. On 21st August, a
surgeon at Guy's Hospital removed his right eye, but
typically, Booth's first call on returning home was for his
fountain pen. What he wrote he could still decipher and that
was good enough : a half-blind General could still toil for God.
By 6th May, 1910—the night Edward VII died—he was
preaching in Zurich. Vertigo made him sick and dizzy ; it did
not cut short his travels—to Holland, Denmark, Germany,
Switzerland, Italy. Back in England he flung himself into his
seventh and last motor-tour.

On the face of it, his will to wage war was undauntable.
On 26th January, 1912, Bramwell and Smith were horrified
to see him stumble over the cord of his dressing-gown and
tumble headlong downstairs, striking his head as he fell. " I

always told you my head was the hardest part of me," was all he said as Bramwell picked him up unhurt. But three months later on 9th May, 1912, 7,000 Salvationists, crowding London's Albert Hall, saw the old white-maned warrior admit temporary defeat; he was, he told them, " going into dry dock for repairs."

Incredibly, even now, no amplifiers were needed as he made his last, perhaps his greatest speech, a war-cry to kindle the heart : " While women weep as they do now, I'll fight ; while little children go hungry as they do now, I'll fight ; while men go to prison, in and out, in and out, I'll fight ; while there yet remains one dark soul without the light of God, I'll fight—I'll fight to the very end ! "

Brave words bravely spoken—but two weeks later, prior to an operation on his left eye, carried out at Hadley Wood, a premonition haunted Booth. " Chief," he blurted suddenly to Bramwell, " I shall not get through this." " If you feel like this, don't let us have it," Bramwell advised, distressed. " No," Booth decided finally. " I shall go through with it now."

To his soldiers' relief, first bulletins were optimistic, but three days later, complications set in ; the eye was irrigated under anæsthetic. Soon surgeon Charles Higgens, who had performed both operations, had called in another consultant, Edward Treacher Collins. While they conferred downstairs, Booth lay quietly in his huge double bed, nervously locking and unlocking his fingers. " Well, General," said Higgens quietly as they returned, " what do you want us to say to you?"

" You must know what I want you to say to me," the old man said pitifully. " I want you to say that I shall have my sight again."

Now Higgens couldn't answer and it was Collins, as gently as might be, who broke the news : " Well, General, that is what we all hoped for but I fear there is not much chance of your seeing objects any more."

Sensing that it was Bramwell who knelt at his bedside, Booth took his son's hand. " I shall never see your face again?"

were his first words. Then, after a moment, resolutely, " God must know best. Bramwell, I have done what I could for God and the people with my eyes. Now I shall see what I can do for God and the people without my eyes."

But Booth was very close to death. Perhaps he knew it. Once, when Eva, on a flying visit from America, described the glory of that evening's sunset, the General said thoughtfully : " I cannot see it, but I shall see the dawn." Even sightless, his eyes were fixed on the white fields of harvest which were derelict humanity ; the problem of the homeless obsessed him. " I want you to do more for the homeless of the world, the homeless men," he urged Bramwell repeatedly. " Mind, I'm not thinking of this country only, but of *all* lands."

" Yes, General," Bramwell promised patiently. " I understand."

" The homeless women—ah, my boy, we don't know what it means to be without a home."

" Yes, General, I follow."

" And the homeless children, Bramwell, look after the homeless. Promise me."

And Bramwell promised, but Booth, even in sickness, must have the last word : " Mind—if you don't I shall come back and haunt you."

On Sunday, 18th August, he lost consciousness. Next day, he grew worse ; a slight paralysis of the throat set in and he could take no solids. Tuesday he was weaker and a cough racked his old frame. Among the faces that came and went stealthily to the sick bed was Colonel Theodore Kitching, who for a moment stood transfixed : the August sunlight spilled from the window on the white patriarch's head like an aureole of silver fire. Booth was still ; not moving, not speaking. Death was roosting in the room.

By 9 p.m. on Tuesday, 20th August, his heart and pulse skittered, seeming to stop. The breath came sharp and rasping, stirring the " Blood and Fire " banner that lay atop the coverlet. Only the white tapering fingers remained restless, counting, always counting, as they had done when he was still conscious. Fifty-two, fifty-three, fifty-four—he was somewhere far away from Hadley Wood, perhaps at Mile End, and souls were moving up to the Penitent-form. He did not see the white faces massing the silent, dimly-lit room : Bramwell and his children, Florence, Lucy, Kitching, Major Fred Cox, Dr. Wardlaw Milne, his physician.

Fifty-five, fifty-six, fifty-seven . . . the fingers lay still upon the counterpane.

Bramwell's whisper, tight with grief, broke the silence : " This is death, Doctor ? "

" This is death," Dr. Milne agreed.

" Now he is with our mother," Bramwell said, and he bent, kissing the white brow, placing Eva's cablegram " Kiss him for me " between the limp fingers. Then he bent again, kissing his father's forehead for the last time.

At 9 a.m. on 21st August, staff officers arriving at International Headquarters, were stunned to read this simple message in the window : " The General Has Laid Down His Sword."

He had lived eighty-three years, four months and ten days.

At midnight on 21st August, 1912, Cadet-Sergeant Bernard Booth had the strangest sense of living through history. Already he had seen several officers, including Bramwell, his father, and Commissioner Randolph Sturgess, who headed the social work for men, bearing the weight of his grandfather's casket towards the motor hearse drawn up on Rookstone's gravelled drive. After that Bramwell had turned to Colonel Theodore Kitching, ordering, " Well, you know what to say—you can release it now " and Kitching had hastened to the old-fashioned wall telephone. Now the twenty-three-year-old Bernard, riding in the front of the hearse alongside the driver, guessed that in Fleet Street and Downing Street and all over Britain, telephones were ringing, and soon the bells would toll.

But what struck him most forcibly on this never-to-be-forgotten night was that as the cortège, followed up by rattling car-loads of pressmen, wound through ten miles of midnight streets towards Clapton's Congress Hall, brilliant oases of light glowed suddenly from the darkness. Outside police station after police station, the lights were ablaze—and inspectors and constables, heads bared, stood ranked in silent spontaneous tribute to William Booth's memory.

And the homage was nation-wide. At the three-day lying-in-state at Clapton's Congress Hall, fully 150,000 people filed past the old warrior's casket—many of them officers who approached Major Fred Cox with a folded handkerchief and a last poignant request. Would Cox take it and wipe the casket's glass lid, to afford them a last personal souvenir?

On Tuesday, 27th August, when Booth was borne to Olympia, a vast exhibition hall on Hammersmith Road, West London, 40,000 people flocked to his funeral service—and to many it seemed the General's spirit filled the hall with peace and purpose. Officers on furlough from all over the world—among them Eva, arrived post-haste from New York—knelt beside the casket to re-dedicate themselves to God and The Army. Along with them, knelt thieves, tramps, harlots, the lost and outcast to whom Booth had given his heart.

Unknown to most, royalty was there too. Far to the rear of the hall, almost unrecognised, sat Britain's Queen Mary, a staunch admirer of Booth's, along with her Lord Chamberlain, Lord Shaftesbury. At the last moment, as Lord Shaftesbury later told The Army's Colonel Isaac Unsworth, of Headquarters Staff, the Queen had elected to come without warning and there was no other seat to be had. Beside her on the aisle seat was a shabby but neatly-dressed woman. Shyly she confided her secret to the Queen: once she had been a prostitute and only the Salvationists had saved her from death. Years later, at a meeting, General Booth had heard her story and told her gently: "My girl, when you get to Heaven, you'll have a place of honour, because Mary Magdalene will give you one of the best places."

The Queen was curious: was it this that had brought the woman here? That, the woman confessed, and the flowers—the three faded red carnations that all through the service were the only flowers that lay on Booth's casket. She had come early to claim an aisle seat, guessing that the casket would pass within feet of her—and as it did she unobtrusively placed the flowers on the glass lid.

Deeply moved, a Queen heard a prostitute pronounce William Booth's epitaph : " He cared for the likes of us."

Next day, Wednesday, there followed a scene that none present would ever forget. Through the doorway of International Headquarters, where it had rested all night, the casket was borne to a bier drawn by two chestnuts : above it in triumph fluttered the white palms of victory. As it moved off, 10,000 uniformed Salvationists fell into step behind ; the massed might of forty Army bands crashed into the " Dead March " from Handel's *Saul*.

Back through the crowded city streets where he had succoured the friendless, past the Mansion House, where the acting Lord Mayor of London stood in silent salute, William Booth passed on his last journey to Abney Park Cemetery. As the August heat struck heavily on the marching throng, pot-boys in green baize aprons ran from the same pubs where his soldiers had been reviled with water to cheer and refresh them.

City offices were dark and shuttered ; the flags of all nations had slipped gently down to salute him. On this day of tributes, when the London *Daily Mirror* produced its own memorial number, the *Daily Telegraph* avowed : " He belonged to the company of saints." " No man of his time did more for the benefit of his people," claimed the *New York Times*. Around his grave like a vast carpet of flowers lay wreaths from the King and Queen, from Queen Alexandra, Kaiser Wilhelm of Germany and American Ambassador Whitelaw Reid, and high on the hill above Abney Park Cemetery were the thousands whose presence bespoke their grief, packing the streets in a dark unending mass.

As the procession neared journey's end, the international staff band struck up a new song, and a gasp ran through the crowd. The tune, though not its Army lyric, was known to all :

> *Home, home, sweet, sweet, home,*
> *There's no friend like Jesus,*
> *There's no place like home.*

Tears filled the eyes of many. The significance of that well-loved melody drove deep into their hearts.

At the graveside stood Bramwell Booth to point the course The Army would take : " I loved him, and you loved him, and he was our leader. He led us and we are going to follow him."

For without the ranks breaking step for an instant The Army had lost and found a General. As early as 4 p.m. on 21st August, less than twenty-four hours after his father died, Bramwell, along with senior lieutenants like Cadman, Railton and Sturgess, had attended a meeting at International Headquarters. There The Army's solicitors, Dr. Alfred Ranger and William Frost, had opened an envelope sealed by William Booth twenty-two years earlier. Within, in accordance with the right he had claimed under the Deed Poll of 1878, Booth had nominated Bramwell as The Army's second General.

The last words of William Booth to his son had been a grimly accurate prophecy : " I'm leaving you a bonny handful —but Railton will be with you."

It was a " bonny handful " indeed. In sixty years as an evangelist Booth had travelled five million miles, preaching almost 60,000 sermons—and his hypnotic spirit had drawn 16,000 officers to follow the flag in fifty-eight countries, to preach the Gospel in thirty-four languages. In 1881, when Booth first moved to Queen Victoria Street, headquarters staff thought themselves hard-pressed with a thousand letters a week. Now they were engulfed by a floodtide of a thousand letters a day.

But just how much of a handful he had inherited Bramwell couldn't know. Within a year, worn out by strain, George Railton had died of a heart-attack at Cologne Railway Station ; two years, and World War One had swept across Europe. A fever of hatred for all things German gripped Britain. The Duke of Edinburgh's great-uncle, Prince Louis of Battenberg, was driven from his post as First Lord of the Admiralty. Only the personal intervention of King George V scotched the barely credible suggestion of Lord Fisher : for every air raid on Britain, batches of German prisoners should be systematically shot. Dachshunds were stoned through the streets. Demagogue Horatio Bottomley went further: why not raid the St. George's Chapel at Windsor and forcibly impound the Garter banners of all Royal houses at war with Britain?

Thus to Bramwell the war was a challenge The Army could not shirk; its whole concept of international unity lay at stake. There were Salvationists in Germany, too—but could The Army march on its way unhating without the risk of being hated for its stand? Did they face their greatest crisis since Bramwell and William Stead had risked ostracism in the Eliza Armstrong case?

Then, in a flash, it came to him: William Booth had faced this problem too. Fifteen years back, at the outset of the Boer War, the distracted old man had cried: "I am like a father with a divided household. My children are on both sides. Whoever wins I lose." And his solution was characteristic: a party of four led by Mary Murray, an Indian Army general's daughter, had gone to minister to both Britons and Boers.

Though the party pared their personal expenses to five shillings each per week, they gave yeoman's help to both armies—acting as stretcher bearers, conducting burial services, preaching from pulpits of piled biscuit-tins. Within sound of the guns of Ladysmith, Mary and her team did night cocoa-picket for sentries—then went on to dig graves.

"You have given us an example of how to live as good soldiers and how to die as heroes," Lord Kitchener told William Booth.

Within days Bramwell had taken his unflinching stand. An army which recognised no barriers of colour or sex must rise above racial hatred. As in World War Two, sub-editors slashed the word "enemy" from every page-proof of Army copy. "Keep it in mind that you are international," Bramwell briefed one editor, "as Jesus Christ was. . . ." His Press conference made The Army's position crystal-clear: "Nothing can save any nation but a return to God." At the close of 1915 he rallied his troops with the reminder: "Every land is my Fatherland, for all lands are my Father's."

For all Lands are my Father's

Eleven days after war broke out, he sent Colonel Mary Murray to reconnoitre the Flanders front. By September, Swiss-born Commissioner Ulysse Cosandey took charge of all relief operations for Belgium. Nor were the Germans forgotten. One bilingual twenty-five-year-old, Captain Sidney Carvosso Gauntlett, travelled 17,000 miles a year visiting P.O.W.s, addressing over 50,000 men.

In truth Bramwell's most stubborn opponents were not the British public but the British War Office. When, early on, the plight of Tommies stranded at railway terminals was brought to his attention, he sent off staff and bedding post-haste to a hired apartment by Liverpool Street Station; within weeks, thousands of men were supping and sleeping in Army hostels. But despite The Army's front-line work with ambulances and canteens, not until 1918 would the War Office allow four Salvation Army officers to do duty as regimental chaplains.

" You see," the Secretary of the War Office, Sir Reginald Braid, explained distastefully to Theodore Kitching, " you're so religious."

Bramwell could only reflect wryly that the United States was approximately twenty years ahead of them in time. Armed only with a blanket and an umbrella, the first Salvationist U.S. Army chaplain, Major John Milsaps, had braved the dangers of the Spanish-American war as far back as 1898, helping wounded and needy Filipinos as readily as U.S. troops, suffering months of griping indigestion, living mostly on high-priced (75 cents a pound) horseflesh.

But despite War Office hostility, The Army were still William Booth's soldierly Samaritans—" the servants of all." Invited by the Red Cross they bought and staffed a fleet of thirty Buick ambulances, costing £400 apiece : one vehicle alone carried over 1,800 wounded men. " These drivers can be trusted better than any others to carry out their duties conscientiously," was Sir Robert (later Lord) Baden-Powell's verdict as a frequent visitor to the front. But the British Expeditionary Force took longer to convince. At Harfleur, near Le Havre, Adjutant Thomas Wells and his wife who took over The Army's first 50 ft. by 20 ft. hut found senior officers less than cordial : to make their feelings plainer, they sited The Army hut facing the latrines. Denied transport, Wells, a small sparrow-active man, had to trudge from town to camp weighed down by bulky cases of condensed milk. But Wells clung doggedly on ; by war's end he not only had transport but a hut housing 1,000 men at a time.

All over Flanders fields, the shock troops of God showed the same tenacity—often under more rugged conditions than any Salvationists had faced since the brickbat era of the 'eighties. Wet feet, sunless cellars and biting winds were routine, and greatcoats so caked with thick grey mud they turned the scales at 100 pounds. But Salvationists like Adjutant Mary Booth, Bramwell's eldest daughter, felt even the labour of cooking 1,000 kippers a day was worth it to hold the last service before a great battle : the dim light of an old oil lamp shining on the faces of men at peace with God, though death was shouting their names. Often they stumbled from the hut at Étaples *en route* to the firing line wearing Army ribbons and badges, and the last song that drifted back through darkness was an old Army favourite, " When the roll is called up yonder I'll be there."

Then, to the day-long rumble of guns, Mary's helpers from Dunkirk to Le Havre went on with the job of tracing missing relatives, working with the firing parties, taking photographs of the graves they tended. The sad shrill notes of The Last Post would be part of their lives for ever.

Some Governments, more progressive, had fully twenty Salvationist Chaplains attached to their forces from the first— men who remained an inspiration long after Armistice Day. Outstanding among them was Lieut.-Colonel William McKenzie, the 17-stone beetle-browed Chaplain whom the 1st Brigade of the Australian Expeditionary Force knew as " Fighting Mac."

Armed against bullets and sunstroke with no more than a swagger stick and a bandanna handkerchief, the 6 ft. 2 in. McKenzie was fighting on his troops' behalf long before the bloody shambles of Gallipoli in April, 1915. Posted to Cairo he grew fearful that rot-gut liquor and tawdry brothels would sap their morale before they ever reached the battle line. Soon one sight became familiar in Cairo's back-alleys : McKenzie's great frame storming into clip-joint after clip-joint, appealing to the better natures of fuddled men, forcibly dragging many from the premises. Soon " Fighting Mac " became the fulcrum of a long rumbunctious chain of drunks who almost tore his arms from their sockets as he steered them towards a tram.

But McKenzie pulled more weight than he knew. When he swore wrathfully that the whole red-light district of Wassa deserved burning to the ground, his lusty " Diggers " took him at his word and left nothing to chance. Firemen arriving to battle the blaze found only slashed hoses with which to do it.

If any man had doubts of McKenzie's fibre, Gallipoli swept them aside. From the rocky headland that masked the Turkish trenches, less than sixty yards away, a torrent of fire swept the Australian positions—and McKenzie, as he read the burial service, often had to crouch on all fours, bullets whipping wildly through his hair, once piercing his cap-shade in three places. Strain—and the sheer physical effort of burying 170 men in ten days—stripped five stone from his hulking frame.

Eight weeks of this cruel campaign cost the Brigade's 4th Battalion alone 600 casualties—but all who lived to see it through came to worship " Fighting Mac." On Sunday at 4 p.m. the Turkish artillery habitually grumbled into silence ; at this hour men grew used to seeing McKenzie striding down " Shrapnel Valley," lustily carolling a hymn. On all sides, heads popped like jack rabbits from crumbling dug-outs— following trustingly after Mac until he had picked a sheltered spot for his service.

No wish a man cherished was too much trouble for McKenzie to fulfil. Once stretcher-bearers complained that a slippery zig-zag path over the hills added needless peril to ferrying the wounded. Within days, McKenzie had hewn clear-cut steps every inch of the way—a route that was soon

symbolic when a burial party went by. " Another Digger,"
men would say, " gone up old Mac's steps."

August saw the desperate daylight feint against Lone Pine
to mask the British onslaught at Suvla Bay, when the Aus-
tralians won seven Victoria Crosses for the cost of 4,000 lives.
Among the first over the top in this vicious no-holds-barred
slaughter amid the Turkish trenches was William McKenzie.
When men marvelled at the Brigade's bravery, McKenzie
quipped : " The boys came running after me because I was
carrying their money in my belt."

But McKenzie was hiding grief so deep he secretly yearned
for death : the silent dead and the screaming half-dead, piled
tiers deep, had cut him to the heart. Over three days and nights,
his sole sustenance three biscuits and six billycans of tea, he
buried 647 men. When his men begged him not to run
needless risks " Fighting Mac " had one answer : " Boys,
I've preached to you and I've prayed with you—do you think
I'm afraid to die with you ? "

These horrors were not fleeting ; for years McKenzie fought
their memory. But when the 1st Brigade went to France,
" Fighting Mac " went with them—to endure Passchendaele
and the whole terrible winter of 1917 on the Somme. He lived
in a sea of mud so thick that men and horses died from sheer
exhaustion fighting its suction—" willing " as he joked, " to
peel potatoes or pray with penitents, save a soul or sell a
saveloy ! " Often his lusty Salvation services could be heard
half a mile away. But other work called for grim stealth :
snaking on his belly by night, McKenzie penetrated into no-
man's-land, far beyond the reach of the burial parties, sifting
valuable personal details. Always he returned to camp with a
thick cluster of identity discs hanging from his belt—each one
representing a man buried with his own hands.

Few of the 3,000 " Diggers " who were converted by
McKenzie's examples realised the pitiful toll that the work
took of him : until his death in 1947 few hours of sleep were
free from nightmares. Afraid to trust himself in bed he slept
on the floor, prayers, cries and sobs tumbling from his lips for
three hours at a time : " Yes, Jim, I'll tell them . . . yes, I'll

kiss them for you . . . here, lad, drink this . . . God be with you . . . God be with you."

" Simple thorough-going seven-days-a-week Christianity " was the sole explanation of 250 officers and Salvationists, posted to France from New York, for their impact on the U.S. Army—but this was only part of the story. The first group to leave New York on the *Espagne* on 12th August, 1917, marked the climax of a clash of wills between Eva Booth as National Commander, and General John Pershing, commander of the American Expeditionary Force. Pershing, who had vetoed a visit to the front by evangelist Billy Sunday, at first saw no reason to make an exception for The Salvation Army. Like millions of other Americans—save for city slum-dwellers and wealthy patrons—the General rated The Army as street-corner hot-gospellers, more adept with a tambourine than a tampon.

But though Pershing had relented, his soldiers had other ideas. The sight of the first officers in their regulation khaki, trench hats bearing the red Salvation Army shield, aroused only suspicion : given one inch of encouragement, they'd be peddling religion. At Demange, Lorraine, in the American 1st Division sector, Salvationists fresh from office chairs toiled manfully in pouring rain to build a hut twenty-five feet wide by a hundred long for the troops' benefit. No man gave them the time of day, far less lent a hand.

Even the Salvationists' commander, Lieut.-Col. William Barker, had all his work cut out : his one limousine served as office, bedroom and to shuttle workers to their stations. Often when Barker bedded down for the night, the car drove on until dawn, purring at a considerate 40 m.p.h. its roof piled high with canteen supplies, passengers clinging precariously to the fenders. No one offered The Army more transport.

What swung the troops to The Army's side was sheer practical example. Neither lasses nor men went near an officers' mess, for Eva Booth had forbidden it : they were in France to serve soldiers. They squelched to the " chow-line " to queue with the " dog-faces " through thick grey mud like

Portland cement; at Gondrecourt, where the troops lacked even a dining-room, they ate in the rain as well. At Ansauville, in the Toul sector, the lasses endured cold so bitter that shoes were thawed out over a candle each dawn; milk for the breakfast coffee froze two yards from the stove. The long-suffering lasses of the Baccarat sector fared as badly; water was so scarce they cleansed their faces with cold cream. For three long months baths were an unknown luxury.

Sector after sector came to acknowledge the lasses' worth. At Demange their first meeting was held in an open-air boxing-ring at the height of an air-raid: no man present ever forgot the strange muted throb of the planes, the winking flash of signal lights, the girl whose clear sweet voice sang "Nearer, my God, to Thee." Others were won by their trust system; as new huts sprang up, the lasses willingly gave "jawbone"—credit—for goods purchased and kept no accounts. A man was trusted to say what he owed. Often a hut had thousands of francs outstanding, but never after pay-day.

When it came to improvising they showed rare ingenuity. At Montiers, though not a stove or a field-range could be found, the lasses wheedled some Mexican border veterans into making an adobe fireplace and roofing it with sheet-iron. Three lengths of old sewer-pipe linked together, and they had a stove. Except when the wind was in the west it smoked woefully but the lasses could still make fudge enough to feed the entire personnel of an ammunition train.

But what won The Army pride of place in American hearts was the brain-wave born of dire necessity at Montiers after thirty-six days of rain. Supplies were at lowest ebb; only flour, lard and sugar remained. Ensign Margaret Sheldon, a capable officer-nurse from Chicago's slums, voiced the suggestion that went down to history: "Why don't we make them doughnuts?"

They had no rolling-pins or cake-cutters and gales had blown down their tent, but Salvationists thrive on challenges. Along with Ensign Helen Purviance, a dark forceful New Yorker, Margaret Sheldon crouched in the rain to prepare her dough; an empty grape-juice bottle did duty as a rolling-pin. In lieu of a cutter they used a knife, to twist the cakes into cruller shapes.

Those first doughnuts, cooked over a wood fire, were a triumph of improvisation. To keep the deep fat hot enough for frying was always a frantic race to pile the fireplace with kindling. But on the first day, with a pan too small to cook more than seven at a time, they still served up 150 fat, sugary doughnuts.

Next day's batch topped 300, with the time-honoured hole punched out by the inside tube of a coffee percolator, and soon the idea spread like a prairie fire; at Sanzay, in the Toul sector, homesick "dog-faces" with time on their hands, sometimes queued five hours to tuck in to one free doughnut. "If this is war, let it continue!" one man whooped. But soon the troops realised that even in the firing line the Salvationists wouldn't neglect them. When lassies like Ensign Florence Turkington crawled under shellfire through muddy trenches to dole out doughnuts and coffee, letters lauding The Salvation Army began flooding home to the States. *Stars and Stripes* broke into lively verse:

> *Tin hat for a halo!*
> *Ah! She wears it well!*
> *Making pies for homesick lads*
> *Sure is " beating hell"!*
> *In a region blasted*
> *By fire and flame and sword,*
> *This Salvation Army lass,*
> *Battles for the Lord!*

Overnight, the bewildered lasses found themselves national heroines. Soon their output was 5,000 a day—so many that some went down with "doughnut wrist"—and the *New York Times* special correspondent filed the dispatch that prophesied The Army's enormous latter-day grass-roots support: "When the memoirs of this war come to be written the doughnuts and apple pies of The Salvation Army are going to take their place in history."

But the "doughboys'" deep regard for the "doughnut

girls " stemmed from more than hunger. Their cool courage was legendary ; at L'Hermitage, near Nancy, an ammunition dump went sky-high as officers and lasses worked calmly to unload a hundred dozen eggs from a truck. Though mammoth detonations from the dump a hundred yards away rocked the earth they worked carefully on : eggs were five francs a dozen. Another officer, Major John Atkins, " The Little Major," was 53 when he opted to live in the front-line trenches with Major Theodore Roosevelt's 26th Infantry Battalion, carrying a 70-lb. pack like any soldier, bedding down on a chicken wire bed. To search out writing-pads, soap and candy for his men, he would trudge twenty kilometres at a time ; often, when he removed his socks, lumps of flesh peeled from his puffed blistered feet.

Protestants, Catholics, Jews—" The Little Major " would pray with them all, but what won the Battalion's undying respect was his spiritual impact on a man who had cursed life itself. A private soldier so violent he was kept in chains, pending execution for a horrifying murder, the killer had refused all religious aid until execution day. Inexplicably, he now asked for Atkins. " The Little Major " entered the cell to confront a man like a wild animal—unshaven, degraded, with the crazed eyes of a fanatic.

" You must be in great trouble, brother. Can I help you ? " said Atkins in his steady gentle voice.

The man rounded on him viciously : " You call me brother! You know what I'm here for, and you call me brother ! Why ? "

Patiently, Atkins explained : Christ had endured his agony on the Cross to save all mankind. Atkins, the killer, and every mortal man were " brothers for whom Christ died." Tears streaming down his face, the soldier cried in torment, " Could I be made a better man ? " Soon, kneeling at Atkins's side, he searched painstakingly through the shabby catalogue of his sins before he said : " It's true what you said. Christ *has* pardoned me. Now I can die like a man ! " He walked smiling to the gallows.

All through the Fall of 1918, as a million and a quarter

Americans strove to drive the Germans from the Argonne
Forest along a ninety-mile front, the Salvationists' legend
grew. Thousands of proud-pursed doughboys lived to bless
Eva Booth's money-order blanks, issued in France, and cash-
able at any one of 1,000 Salvation Army posts in America.
Tens of thousands of dollars in pay that would have gone in
hard liquor went to support wives and young children. Men
who fought in the Mondidier sector at Gisons and Froissy,
spoke of the cool courage of " Smiling Billy " Hale and his
lasses who, unable to secure front-line permits, jammed into a
covered 3-ton truck and followed the troops into battle any-
way.

Whatever the dangers, Salvationists proved eager to share
them. At Neuilly, in the Argonne, a lassie lamed by a shell-
splinter felt that a visit to hospital might result in all front-line
work being vetoed. She limped bravely on, complaining of
corns. At Baccarat, lasses worked so close to the German lines
they couldn't even whisper for fear of listening-posts ; the
" sermon " that came up with coffee and doughnuts was a
friendly squeeze on the shoulder. They took infinite pains :
trucks jolted all through a pitch-dark night along 200 miles of
front to meet one battalion's fancy for oranges. Ingenuity was
endless ; when a plague of flies threatened gangrene at Mont
Fontaine hospital, in the Joan of Arc country, Lieut.-Col.
William Barker vainly combed all Paris for mosquito netting.
Unperturbed he bought up $10,000 of white veiling from
swanky fashion-houses like Schiaparelli and Molyneux.

" The Salvation Army has had no new success," Eva Booth
protested, as the tributes redoubled, " We have only done an
old thing in an old way." But most Americans were seeing
The Army for the first time : by August, 1917, they knew, the
Salvationists had spent $900,000 on rest-rooms, hutments and
hostels—some of them with monster doughnuts eighteen
inches in diameter slung above the porch. At one post-war
Washington parade, 200 wounded men from a base hospital—
some limbless, others blind—groped to their feet and cheered
like furies as the Salvation contingent marched past. From
coast to coast the nation endorsed that tribute—subscribing an

unprecedented $13,000,000 to wipe The Army's slate clear of debt.

In London, Bramwell Booth knew no such good fortune. The Army's Central Fund—devoted to new development and properties—alone needed £200,000 ; hostels for troops and the work in Flanders was costing fully £50,000 a year. Above all, filial instinct urged him to follow William Booth's last injunction ; to spread The Army's work still farther afield, to Russia and even China. By strange irony, though *The War Cry* subscribers numbered such eminent Russians as Count Leo Tolstoy, already world-famous for *War and Peace*, Czar Nicholas II, right up to his abdication in 1917, had resisted The Army for fear of offending the Church. The Church, the Dowager Empress (formerly Princess Dagmar of Denmark) explained to William Booth over tea at Buckingham Palace, was the last bulwark against Bolshevik revolution.

But China was virgin land. " Promise me that you will begin the work in China," William had begged, and reluctantly Bramwell had promised ; though The Army was now reputedly a £30 million concern, money was chronically lacking. Constantly Bramwell warned the head of his subscribers' department, Colonel George Jolliffe : " I shall need another £10,000 next year, Jolliffe."

Jolliffe groaned : the strain of Generalship, he knew, had visited Bramwell with his father's insomnia but often, it seemed, he spent those sleepless nights thinking up ways to unbalance Jolliffe's budget.

Thus in Tsinan in 1917, alarmed rumours swept the British Club : a uniformed German officer was standing on a soapbox in the native quarter haranguing the coolies in fluent Chinese. It was British Consul John Pratt who set them to rights : the officer wasn't a German but an emissary of the " Save-the-World Army," whose 40-strong force had aptly arrived at Peking's Ch'ien Men Railway Station on the eve of Good Friday.

It was a task which might have daunted William Booth himself. By Bramwell's reckoning, the first three years' work would swallow up £60,000, but money was the least of his officers' problems. Before they could claim any true success, pioneers like Captain Hal Beckett, a tall auburn-haired Canadian and Colonel Charles Rothwell, a clever voluble Lancastrian, went through the wringer of every problem from linguistics to famine—in a country racked by the bitter chaos following the fall of the Manchu dynasty. From 1911 on, 400 million near-illiterate Chinese suffered twenty years of government by war-lord—and in the midst of it all toiled The Salvation Army.

At Cheng Ting Fu, remotest of all The Army's out-posts, 200 miles south-west of Peking, Hal Beckett learned what it meant to be sole pastor to 800 square miles of China. The nearest European—a doctor—was 100 miles away; in no time at all Beckett and his wife Violet were talking, even thinking, in Chinese. But mastering twenty-five verses of the Gospel of John didn't allow for the nuances of idiom. At one meeting, held by North China's Territorial Commander, Charles Jeffries, blank bewilderment greeted the news that The Salvation Army rescued people from the gutter. To his dismay Beckett found the interpreter's translation was quite literal: "In the great Commissioner's country, people are so degraded they lie about in water-gullies until The Salvation Army lifts them out."

Even the concept of Christ Himself proved a puzzle. "Have you prayed to the Lord Jesus?" one Chinese kneeling at the Penitent-form was asked. With the air of a man fast losing patience he replied: "Just which of the white men on the platform *is* Lord Jesus?"

But in the soldiers' souls was exultation: if William Booth had cried for China, they would spare no effort to alleviate its distress. Within a year of their arrival, The Army in Tientsin faced just such a task: floods had swept away the homes of 7,000 people. Promptly they assumed responsibility for a hundred huts and 400 refugees. "These are the people who have love in their hearts for their fellow-men," said one old woman approvingly.

Typical of the harsh conditions prevailing was one news item featured by the *Far Eastern Times*: in the first twenty days of February, 1918, Peking's police had given pauper burials to 479 unidentified folk frozen to death in the streets. At once The Army went into action: renting vacant ground in the heart of the city, they set up a makeshift lean-to of plaited straw matting, installing a battery of boilers to cook millet porridge, the staple food of the poor. Here hundreds of lame, blind, smallpox-ridden men were daily nursed back to life.

But Peking's needy numbered thousands, not hundreds. The Army opened a second kitchen, then a third. Then Beckett, prospecting for land to house a fourth, ran into trouble. The only site available was the yard of a Buddhist temple—and the priest was blatantly hostile.

But God was just then working for The Army in the heart of General Chao Er Hsun, one-time Governor of both Manchuria and Mongolia, a fine old Chinese aristocrat, who grieved bitterly for the poor. His servants were at their wits' end: though the frail old man was past eighty, he refused to eat or be covered with warm quilts at night until someone had first fed and warmed the poor. One day, in a state of high excitement, a servant rushed in: someone *did* care for the poor. He had chanced on a Salvation Army porridge kitchen.

"Tell the coolies to harness the horses to the chariots," the General commanded, "let four servants in livery accompany me, and take me to this place of refuge for the poor."

Within the hour the General stood in silent wonder at the sight of a white woman, a 24-year-old Salvation Army Captain, doling out porridge to a long shuffling line of derelicts. Regretfully the Captain explained she had no time to show the distinguished visitor round: she was giving a dinner party for 600 guests.

At the sight of her thin cotton Chinese coat, General Chao spontaneously slipped off his blue flowered *ma-kua*, lined with snow-white lambswool, draping it gently round her shoulders. Then he ordered his servants: "Take me to the headquarters of the Save-the-World Army."

When the General heard of the coveted temple yard he ordered Beckett to take him directly to the spot—then ignoring the priest, asked Beckett to outline his plans. Beckett complied. Here would be kitchens; the courtyard, matted and heated, would be the assembly point for guests. In a third sector they would file past for food.

The old diplomat nodded. Then, turning to the priest, he crisply ordered: "Sir priest, from the first day of the next moon this section of your temple yard will be a Save-the-World Army porridge kitchen."

The priest knew when he was beaten. Bowing to the dust he whined: "This unworthy courtyard will become virtuous because of the great General's benevolent acts!"

From that time on, General Chao was one of The Army's most powerful friends, raising as much as £1,500 annually to aid their work.

Smallpox, cholera, typhus—The Army wrestled with them all. Often the calm of Cheng Ting Fu's narrow streets was broken by the old medieval plague cry: "Bring out your dead." The Salvation Army's first hospital, 700 miles away at Tingchow, was always rushed off its feet. Next floods engulfed Chihli Province, cruelly outpacing women with bound feet, swallowing up men who stayed on to save their cattle. Famine followed: women made loaves, eking out their last handfuls of meal with leaves, chopped tree-bark, even soil.

Along the Yellow River, in the 'twenties, conditions were worse: a famine so terrible that human flesh was sold openly in the markets. Parents, burdened by young mouths they could not feed, cast their children adrift in the forests to starve to death. At peak period, The Army was serving up 50,000 pots of millet porridge a day.

In theory, Beckett's living quarters housed sixty Chinese children. In practice, he often outstripped his own cablegrams home; once, after a twenty-four-hour journey by train, ox-cart and junk, he arrived home for breakfast along with thirty-seven destitute Chinese girls. The wire he had sent to break the news to Violet gently never was delivered.

Amid such harassments The Army had to contend with the advance of warring armies, bent on loot; peaceful services broke up in panic as officers and converts scattered to hide up in outhouse bales of hay, scarcely daring to breathe while bandits searched the building. But there were compensations. Village meetings had a colourful charm of their own, held in a circle of mud-brick houses while black hairy pigs rooted in the soil. The annual Thanksgiving Feast for beggars was a poignant season, when blind boys led blind grandfathers by the hand and lepers advanced their rice-cans on the end of long bamboo poles, that none need touch them.

Another such moment was Hal Beckett's first Christmas in Cheng Ting Fu—an event which meant less to China's children than the birthday of Confucius would to Canadian eight-year-olds. Christmas Eve saw no excited speculations about Santa Claus ; the children went tranquilly to bed. Then Hal and Violet got busy. They promised themselves that if they worked all night, this would be a Christmas for Cheng Ting Fu to remember. It was 1 a.m. before they filled their own children's stockings and crawled to bed.

At 6 a.m. on Christmas Day, the rising bell jangled ; all unawares, the children clustered in the courtyard for prayers before scattering to routine house chores. Splitting up, some raced to the dining-hall, some to the school-room. And they paused transfixed.

A forest of paper festoons, scarlet and gold, wreathed and twined from wall to wall. A monster Christmas tree, laden with coloured parcels, bulked in the dining-hall. Tiny Japanese celluloid dolls, with gay silk skirts that Violet had run up, dangled saucily from the branches. At every table the rice-bowls were piled with nuts, crystallised sweets, lychees, dried melon seeds.

" Oh ! *Ai-ya* ! Who has been here ? " was the chorus on all sides until one of the brighter spirits remarked, " *This* is the Christian Festival they have told us about." At this moment Hal and Violet Beckett looked at one another afraid to speak. They had known many good Christmases but the faces of boys and girls alive for the first time with the meaning of Christmas would warm their hearts for ever.

Too soon the rustle of parcels and the joyous melody of carols gave place to bedtime—and it was at evening prayers in the little girls' dormitory that Violet Beckett saw the most moving sight of all : a row of children robed in white, black shining pigtails beautifully braided, hands clasped in prayer. "Dear Jesus, we do thank You for this *lovely* day," was their united chorus, "the first day we knew You *had* a birthday."

Months later, when Self-Denial Week approached, the children learned for the first time of how William Booth had needed funds and of John Carleton's determination to go without pudding. That night in the dormitories there was much excited whispering. Could white men have given up food for a whole week just to keep the children of Cheng Ting Fu alive ? For sheer wonder it ranked with the stories of the Bible.

Next morning, to Beckett's dismay, a deputation of youngsters was early at his door. "We have decided," said a spokesman carefully, "to deny ourselves dinner every day next week to help other children in need."

Both Becketts protested vigorously. All the children need do was pray for the fund's success. They would imperil their health if they gave up food. And everything else they owned—clothes, books—The Army had given them.

"We have *decided*," the spokesman said firmly, "If you supply dinners, we shall not eat them."

The Becketts agreed to temporise. The children could give up dinner for just one day. To be on the safe side they would provide extra food at tea-time.

At noon on the first day of Self-Denial Week, sixty uproarious children, ignoring the open doors of the dining-hall, raced shouting into the playground and romped and played as they had never done in their lives. One day, Beckett thought, would see a change of heart, but as the week passed there were no dinners and no requests for dinners. At the week's end, the deputation returned.

"When we lived in our village and food was scarce," the spokesman announced, "we ached inside, but we have had such a happy week and never felt hungry at all. It must be because we did it for Jesus. We have come to say we want a second Self-Denial Week."

Beckett was horrified. "Certainly not," he said firmly.

"You have done marvellously—but one week is quite sufficient."

But there was no outdoing China's children. Thirty minutes later a deputation of small determined girls again crowded into Beckett's office. Holding her hands like a cup, the eldest firmly addressed Hal and Violet: "Father and Mother, all we have you have given us: all we know you have taught us ; all we are you have made us. The only things that are ours by right are the worthless trinkets we brought with us. Will you sell them to your foreign friends as souvenirs and add the money to what we saved not having dinner—and give it all to Jesus as a present ? " There on Beckett's desk she showered from her cupped hands a shining flood of brass rings, enamel ear-rings, pins and brooches.

A few days later, when the international Self-Denial Fund was swelled for the first time in Army history by forty Chinese dollars, Beckett's eyes were wet. There was nothing he could say, nothing at all.

By 1928, The Salvation Army in North China had 212 trained officers, women as well as men. Slowly their work was taking root in eighty-four centres ; no one could envisage the bitter set-backs it would undergo in the Sino-Japanese war or The Army's heart-breaking 1951 expulsion from Red China. They saw themselves as trail-blazers along the path that William Booth had pointed.

But meanwhile, in London, The Army and its General were facing a crisis William Booth had never believed could come to pass.

"Now the Door is Opening"

1928-

On 6th March, 1928, two days before his seventy-second birthday, General Bramwell Booth entered his wife's office at Queen Victoria Street, pale and shaken, a letter clutched in his hand. " My darling," Florence always recalled his first words, " Here is trouble."

As Bramwell saw it, the letter, signed by nine of his top lieutenants, struck a blow at the whole concept of The Army laid down by William Booth. A firm but courteous round-robin, it urged the General to take serious thought on a current proposal of Eva Booth : that Bramwell should announce himself the last Salvation Army General to nominate his successor. Though many were among Booth's earliest pioneers—John Carleton, innovator of Self-Denial Week, Frederick Booth-Tucker, David Lamb, an early Hadleigh Farm Colony governor—all were of one mind : The Army stood in need of a life-saving transfusion of democracy.

In a sense, despite Bramwell's perturbation, the issue was not entirely new. As far back as 1920, Bramwell and Eva, as U.S. National Commander, had disagreed fundamentally ; after sixteen years in America, Bramwell warned his sister, she must shortly expect a transfer. Eva's bitter protests won her a two-year respite but in 1922, when a recall was again mooted, Eva's was not the only voice raised in protest. Top U.S. businessmen like John Wanamaker, department store chief and Republican Leader, threatened covertly to withdraw financial support, in a cable of protest signed by twenty men of the calibre of Herbert Hoover, Henry W. Taft and Rabbi

Joseph Silverman. Three thousand miles away in London, it was hard for Bramwell to realise that for millions of Americans his dramatic red-haired sister, whose vibrant voice had been coached by Nazimova, personified The Salvation Army.

And Eva's pressure for long-due reforms found favour in American hearts. When she pleaded the right to appoint her own Divisional Officers—which William Booth's rules had forbidden—most Americans agreed. Within The Army ranks, an unidentified pamphleteer urged that if The Army's General was British, his Chief of Staff should be American. Wasn't almost half The Army's world property holding sited in the United States?

Anxious to avoid the situation which had saddled William Booth with three Salvation Armies Bramwell gave in. Eva could stay on in New York.

But Eva was too much of a Booth to yield a principle. In October 1927, as spokesman for the reformers, she arrived in London with a fifteen-point memorandum—the bulk of them variations on the cardinal Point Four: " It is almost universally hoped that the present General will be the last one to be appointed by his predecessor."

And Eva pressed her point home: if other religious bodies could change their constitution, why not The Salvation Army? The post-Christian Mission frame-work, whereby every officer was content to entrust William Booth with sole authority, couldn't go on for ever. Future generals should be chosen by a closed conclave of top lieutenants called the High Council.

Strangely, two world-famous men—a Victorian statesman and an American tycoon—had played unwitting roles in the drama that followed. The High Council was the virtual brainchild of Britain's Prime Minister William Ewart Gladstone who, as far back as 21st December, 1896, had chatted with William Booth in the vast library called " The Temple of Peace " in his home at Hawarden, Denbighshire. In passing Booth had mentioned that the Deed Poll of 1878, which wrought The Christian Mission into The Salvation Army, gave each General sole right to appoint his successor.

Gladstone, heaping fresh logs on the fire, paused aghast. "Now excuse my asking," he said, "but suppose some General becomes unworthy ? Suppose he becomes a heretic or loses faith ? " Even the Pope, he pointed out, enjoyed no such authority ; his successor was the elected choice of the Sacred College of Cardinals. What provision was there in Booth's constitution to remove such a General ?

William Booth had to admit it : there was none. But, he defended his system, the General was in law a trustee of Army property. If he failed in his trust, an appeal to the law could remove him.

Gladstone shook an impatient head. Any such appeal would be cumbersome and costly—and in the meantime an unfit General would be sole overlord of the £1 million concern The Army had by then become. Why not a system whereby a General, if proven unfit, could be deposed by a majority consensus ?

At the time Bramwell himself cordially approved this proposal. At Booth's bidding he went into a huddle with Britain's three most brilliant lawyers : Lord Haldane, Herbert Asquith (later Lord Oxford and Asquith) and Charles (later Lord Justice) Sergant. Seven years' high-level negotiations resulted in the concept of a High Council, made up of active Commissioners and all territorial commanders, whatever their rank—a conclave which if convened by the Chief of Staff and four Commissioners, or by any seven Commissioners, could adjudicate on a General's fitness for office.

This Salvation Army Magna Charta had laid down that any General mentally or physically infirm, adjudged bankrupt or guilty of misconduct could be deposed by a two-thirds majority.

Hence Eva's resolute stand—for her contact with leading American luminaries revealed nothing but amazement that an autocracy, however benevolent, had survived well into the twentieth century. President Calvin Coolidge, on hearing that American Salvationists lacked even an ambassador in London, could, typically, find no words. On another occasion, conferring with John D. Rockefeller, Eva explained how The Army's Generals were chosen.

Rockefeller stopped short in blank amazement. " Then your coming General is produced for you out of a bag ? " he asked incredulously. " He can put his hand on you all and you don't even know the colour of his hair ? "

But Bramwell was unyielding. A loyal son—to him, William Booth, even after death, was always " the General "—he could not find it in himself to tamper with his beloved father's creation. Firmly he had told Eva as much—but now on 6th March, 1928, the Commissioners' joint letter made it plain that others shared Eva's views.

On 12th April, 1928, Bramwell closed his official diary : " Left for Hadley Wood." Though he could not then know it, he had crossed the threshold of 101 Queen Victoria Street for the last time. Within days, blood pressure and nervous strain had forced him to seek treatment. The doctors advised him to take a break from the office, coping with essential work only at his Southwold cottage, on the Suffolk coast.

The crack-up wasn't surprising. At 72, Bramwell still drove himself as hard in The Army's service as ever William Booth had done. In a typical year he granted 1,000 interviews, attended eighty council meetings, spoke at about 150 others. If he reached his desk at 7 a.m. he thought nothing of settling to decode and answer twenty-one telegrams at 11 p.m. His idea of holiday relaxation was typical : correspondence dwindled down to thirty essential letters a day.

The Army, his family noted, had become his life ; even a game of chess tapered by degrees into a discussion on Army affairs. His officers' welfare was always paramount ; once, lynx-eyed as always, he noted that several taking tea with him bit on only one side of their jaws. Promptly, at his own expense, he sent them to his dentist. He introduced the payment of minimum salaries for field officers, half-salary pension scales for the retired, allowances for children under sixteen.

By autumn, 1928, neuritis was almost crippling his right arm. A martyr to insomnia, his weight dropped alarmingly. Soon a specialist forbade even walks ; only complete rest in bed could avail. By mid-November Bramwell was sleeping only under narcosis. The fear that his illness might precipitate a High Council Convention obsessed him.

Once, at dead of night, he stole downstairs to lock himself in his study and consult his dictionary. What did "unfit" *really* mean? These words leapt from the printed page: ". . . loss of the strength, skill or qualities required for any task or purpose; to be disabled or disqualified, as, for instance, sickness unfitting a man for labour." From that night on, those close to him thought, the fear of ill-health served to magnify his pain.

Bramwell was then too ill to know it, but The Army was fast hardening in favour of reforms. From Australia, forty-three leading officers had urged him to fall in with Eva's proposal. Thirty-one New Zealanders wrote in identical terms. On Wednesday, 14th November, faced with the demand of seven commissioners to summon the first High Council, Commissioner Edward Higgins, Bramwell's tall, handsome Chief of Staff, saw no other choice.

As The Army's leaders saw it, succession was not the only issue at stake. Racked by neuritis, hardly able to move and speaking only with difficulty, Bramwell was now so unfit as to leave The Army without a head. The house that William Booth built was now a complex of vast trusts—which, under the existing system, only one man could legally administer. Bramwell could sign his name only to the most important of the scores of documents awaiting him, yet The Army's work must go on.

On 8th January, 1929, the sixty-three men and women who made up the first Salvation Army High Council met at Sunbury Court, a fine Georgian mansion on the Thames, to draw up a memorandum regarding the General's deposition. Many of them, weeping, could barely sign their names to it; nothing but pity was in their hearts but the work that William Booth had pointed them to do was something, they knew, bigger than them all.

It was characteristic of The Salvation Army that as they set their house in order a mighty crusade impelled by Bramwell was approaching zero hour.

Eight months had now passed since Ensign Charles Péan, a lively dark-bearded 27-year-old, received an urgent summons to the Paris office of Commissioner Albin Peyron. Facing France's ascetic, silver-haired Territorial Commander, Péan squirmed uneasily. Notorious for his high spirits—once he'd snipped off half a fellow cadet's moustache while he slept and returned it to him by post—Péan wondered just which of his pranks had reached his chief's ears.

"How much do you know," Peyron asked suddenly, "about Devil's Island?"

Péan thought fast. As much, he supposed, as any Frenchman knew—that the infamous settlement of French Guinea, the *Terre de Bagne*, was a living grave for 10,000 men. If many were condemned to the horrors of "The Dry Guillotine," few returned to talk about them.

Peyron was explicit: for eighteen years the crying wrong of Devil's Island had never ceased to haunt him. But appeals to successive Ministers of Justice to allow Salvationists to work in the colony had fallen flat; his letters had even gone unacknowledged. Then a chance contact with the Minister of Colonies had tipped the scales and Bramwell Booth, fully in sympathy, had urged the instant dispatch of a young English-speaking officer, a bachelor with all his wits about him.

"Now the door is opening," the Commissioner told the astonished Péan, "and *you* are to go."

But as Péan embarked on the *Puerto Rico* at St. Nazaire on 5th July, 1928, he had little concept of what lay ahead. Three weeks later, as he passed through the curved stone gateway of St. Laurent-du-Maroni, capital of the settlement, his heart sank. Not even in nightmares had he pictured such misery as this—the worm-eaten hutments, the wolfish half-naked men, clad only in sun-bleached sacking, the stinking mosquito-haunted swamps.

Péan's first meeting was with the Deputy Governor of Guiana, Jean Galmot. "It seems impossible in the twentieth century," he burst out, "that France has over 400 employees working in a penal service whose only result is the physical and moral degradation of 10,000 men."

The Governor shrugged. " I agree with you, Ensign. But it's no use. This is a little hell no man can conquer." He smiled wearily. " Perhaps it's even too big a job for God."

" That, your Excellency," said Péan grimly, " remains to be seen ! "

For all his youthful high spirits, Péan was as practical as a knife and fork. He knew the most telling weapons in his armoury would be facts. If the French public cared so little about conditions in the *Bagne*, it was because they knew less. He must visit every camp, every settlement, and see things for himself.

For three long months he lived up to his resolve—travelling by pirogue, a narrow tree-trunk canoe, gliding through a damp malarial maze of mangrove swamps, where tiny luminous yellow butterflies flitted from leaf to leaf. Often for miles only the plash of paddles, the harsh cries of green and red parrots broke total silence. Filling a small bookshelf of school exercise books with his notes, he sought out every settlement— even Devil's Island itself, a seventeen-acre site fortified thirty-four years before to imprison Captain Alfred Dreyfus.

In fact, every island was the Devil's province. The convicts who died on them were buried in their chains, but there were greater torments than death. A man attempting escape could still be sentenced to a torrent of two hundred lashes on his naked buttocks. Until recently the overseers in their blue, silver-braided uniforms had a punishment all their own to spur on refractory workers : stripped naked they were coated with molasses and staked all day to an anthill.

On all sides Péan saw sights to rend the heart. At St. Joseph's Camp, men sentenced to solitary confinement rotted in their cells for three months at a stretch ; the thin partitions that screened them from the insane could not blot out the nightlong screams and howls. Self-respect was so low that one hundred men would apply for the executioner's privileged post. Hospital contact-men did a lively undercover trade in the leprosy virus and tubercular bacilli, for the chance of lying up in a hospital bed outstripped all risk of infection. At sick parades patients' hands were often strapped behind them ; a detected malingerer wouldn't stop short of murder.

What he endured has marked Péan all his life—physically as well as mentally. Often after gulping down the same foul-smelling messes as the convicts, he hastened away to vomit painfully. Once sunstroke toppled him senseless in the street. Each time he tried to speak of hope, the sight of the waxen-faced consumptives, the syphilitics, the men with running cancerous sores, stopped the words in his throat. As his pile of jam-packed notebooks grew thicker his spotless white uniform was blotched with blood, as the mosquitoes tormented him. A sharp attack of malaria almost cost him his life ; the convict-nurse had sold the quinine prescribed and substituted unsterilised water. The outcome was recurring internal abscesses for which Péan three times underwent major surgery.

Now Péan made an appalling discovery : close on 3,000 men faced a blacker future than the convicts. Under the infamous system of *doublage*, or double time, the pathetic *libérés* (free men) were forced to live on in Guiana for a time equivalent to their original sentence. A law of 1852, passed by the Emperor Napoleon, had a two-pronged purpose : the provision of white slave labour once the French Empire had abolished slavery, the segregation of habitual criminals into life-long quarantine.

" When freedom is gained," ran a *libérés'* saying, " then your sentence begins."

The free man's plight was brought home to Péan by Albert Vignon, a dapper man in a white suit carrying a leather brief-case, who introduced himself as President of the Liberated Men's Club. Guiding the Ensign to the club-room on the first floor of an empty house in Cayenne, he introduced him to its fifteen members—neat self-possessed men, all of them skilled tradesmen who had found employment. " But we are ostracised by the civil population," Vignon explained. " We are not allowed to sit down in a café. There are special places for us in the cinema."

Now the Door is Opening

Outside in the street, where the thermometer stood close to ninety, Péan saw a harsher reality: scores of homeless, workless, free men sitting on the kerb in the shadow of the market "lined up like swallows on a telegraph wire." Fearing they would resent his youth and vigour he tried vainly to avert his glance. "You'd do better to give us a crust than stare at us as we rot," one derelict snarled.

But to Péan these men needed more than bread; they needed hope. Nine-tenths of them were workless, unskilled, on the brink of starvation. Serving convicts at least received board and lodging; free men had to find their own. Their status was so degraded that even the Church was forbidden them; a free man who died was brought perfunctorily to the church porch for the priest to sprinkle holy water on him.

What clinched Péan's resolve that the free men rated priority was the moving farewell which climaxed his visit. On the day he left Guiana, a small deputation waited on him— to solicit the honour of carrying his trunk as far as the pilot boat. "You see," one explained simply, "It is as if God had come amongst us." To his amazement, lined up on the shore, Péan saw more than 300 free men assembled to say good-bye. Some pressed letters to their wives and children on him, another a bouquet of tropical flowers. Then, as the whistle shrilled for the pilot boat to pull out to the steamer anchored beyond the shallow harbour, 300 men cried out as one: "Come back, come back! Please come back!"

All through the long voyage home those cries rang in Péan's ears. "Those forgotten men," he recalled later, "were crying not only with their voices but with their eyes and their hearts." Frantically his pen raced over the paper, detailing in his official report the horrors he had seen. He yearned to go back before the year's end—little knowing that his unlucky injection would render him a semi-invalid for almost two years. But Commissioner Peyron now had ammunition enough to launch his split-level campaign—to establish reasonable living conditions in Guiana; to bring French public opinion to the boiling-point that would demand the total abolition of the *Bagne*.

Meanwhile, in Britain, The Salvation Army's High Council

had with sorrow and reluctance deposed General Bramwell Booth by 55 votes to 8. Though Bramwell was convinced that his health, given time, would recover, Commissioner Gunpei Yamamuro, of Japan, summed up prevailing feeling: " It would be cruel, cruel, to impose the burden of office on him again." Seven Commissioners made the long cold journey to Southwold through snow-carpeted countryside to gently break the news. The sight of the shrunken, ageing man, tortured by neuritis, only confirmed them in their decision. But it was typical that at this last meeting Bramwell should have prayed to God to guide them. " Lord, this is a special occasion. Help them to help me now. Help them to do the right thing and to do it in the right way. . . . Bless the Council —Give them a special blessing. . . ."

By forty-two votes to seventeen, the Council elected Commissioner Edward Higgins, Bramwell's Chief of Staff, General of The Salvation Army—since confirmed by Act of Parliament as the standard mode of selection—but three more Generals, including Eva Booth herself, were to be elected before the work Bramwell had begun had been accomplished. Not until 1933 had public opinion in France advanced far enough for Minister of Colonies, Albert Sarraut, to sanction The Salvation Army beginning work in French Guiana. On 5th July, Péan and six other officers set out on a mission which was to endure for twenty long years.

At first the venture promised well. The first hostel Péan opened on Cayenne's Rue Malouet was renovated by the free men themselves—while Péan hired others as cooks and helpers for the dining-room and dormitories. One, a Left Bank artist who had killed his mistress, painted a sign for the portal: " L'Armée du Salut : Le Foyer." Soon, though, crises were sprouting like weeds. Péan's plan to mark the shelter's in- augural with a free meal for all-comers went wildly awry ; by 10 a.m. on opening day his cooks and waiters were already dead-drunk on tafia, a neat rum made by distilling crushed sugar-cane. Faces crimson, Péan and his officers stripped off their tunics and themselves served up the meal to 2,000 famished guests. That night the guests returned to steal most of the provisions, the cutlery and china, the cords for the flag-staff and the chef's cap.

And at first, few free men were disposed to work at all. Many had sunk so low their sole ambition was to loaf through their *doublage* in a waking coma of alcohol. Unhelpful, too, was the Government's strange policy of reserving plots of land for serving convicts; often men who sought to strike out as cultivators couldn't even get a land grant. Others were too weak or sick to perform more than the lightest chores.

But Péan would not relinquish what he now saw as his life's work. At Montjoly, eight miles from Cayenne, he leased an abandoned overgrown farm, setting a lieutenant and twenty free men to hack through the sprawling undergrowth. Each yard of ground was a battle in itself; soil, when cleared, was next burned to neutralise acidity, then ringed with ditches to ward off armies of ants. Nor was this all—often the wind carried powder from butterflies' wings, causing an eruption of red itching pimples on the sweating flesh. Vampires sucked the blood of the colony's pigs; a stout wire-netting stockade was run up round each sty.

Painfully, yard by yard, Montjoly's acres yielded. The free men built a hen-house and created a fishery by netting off a creek and collecting the fish at low tide. Meanwhile, in a clearing at the top of the hill, bungalows, huts and sheds the free men built, were mushrooming.

Within months, the staff had doubled, and Péan had land under cultivation: a pineapple plantation, citrus and banana groves, with a fruit-packing station to market the produce in Cayenne. Each year the banana trees alone yielded six tons of creamy fruit. As the colony grew, others worked to make benches, chairs, folding beds. By October, 1933, Péan had extended the work, opening a carpentry shop at St. Laurent-du-Maroni, 150 miles away.

Ill-wishers to the scheme were never lacking. The receivers of stolen goods, tafia peddlers, prostitutes, corrupt prison guards—all saw Péan's crusade to win the minds of men as a potent threat to their graft. Often he opened his morning mail to find one more anonymous threat: Get out of Guiana

—or else.   Salvationists were waylaid at night by tough-muscled assailants.   One lieutenant's jaw was broken in three places.

But slowly converts were won—many because of the unswerving trust Péan placed in them.   An embezzler was set to balance The Army's books ; a man who had poisoned his wife became Montjoly's first cook.   One officer, when absent on business, set a rapist-killer to guard his wife.   Other sceptics came round when they realised the officers drew no higher salary than the free men they employed.

For his weaker charges, Péan evolved a scheme in a thousand : Salvation-lepidopterists.   Encamped in deep jungle, with iron rations, free men built themselves primitive hides and set out to trap specimens for the collectors and curio-hunters in New York and Paris : tarantulas, humming birds, the blue, russet and gold Menelaus butterfly.   At peak they exported 100 tarantulas a month to Paris, 10,000 butterflies a season.

" So many butterflies," Péan egged on his charges, " means so much in the bank."

For Péan saw all these as temporary expedients : his sights were set on nothing less than true freedom for all *libérés*.   The main problem was finance : a man was transported to Guiana at Government cost but even a single ticket steerage was 1,750 francs (about £22).   Out of his musings grew the coupon system that became the free man's reason for hope, his passport to living : twenty months' continuous work earned a man enough to buy a third-class ticket to France.   Once there Salvationists would feed him, clothe him, find him work.

To Péan, the crucial moment came when the first sixty-seven repatriates left Cayenne for the last time—among them Le Rouge, a boat-builder from Lyons who had served sixteen years for murder.   " The Salvation Army paid your passage for you," one loafer jeered as he strode towards the pilot boat—but at this, Le Rouge, fists bunched, swung round in white-hot anger.   " *Je l'ai gagné*," (I have earned it) he flung back in pride and passion.

Now the Door is Opening

Péan knew an aching surge of love and pity: he had witnessed the rebirth of a man's self-respect.

By February, 1936, the first repatriates shambled, like shipwreck survivors, down the gangplank of the mail-boat *Flandre* at St. Nazaire—some in stained pith helmets, others, North Africans, wearing turbans mocked-up from tea-towels. Now, as the months passed, Péan held his breath, for hostile pressmen foretold an imminent crime-wave sparked off by "Péan's Pariahs."

In fact, of the first 804 men repatriated, only three ever again fell foul of the police—but Péan knew anxious moments. One such occasion was at 5 p.m. on a bitter winter night when a young captain, sobbing with exhaustion, burst pell-mell into his Rue de Rome office. Twenty minutes earlier, at the Gare de Lyons, a repatriated man leaving for Annemasse, a tiny town on the Swiss frontier, had leaned from the coach window as his train steamed out to confide a secret: his claim that his family awaited his homecoming was a lie.

"I did twenty years hard for a gendarme's false testimony," he spat out, "and that man married my wife. So now you've bought my ticket, I can kill him."

Péan was electrified. All that frantic night he remained clamped to the telephone: one crime now, he knew, and The Salvation Army in France was finished. The Press would fan mob hysteria to frenzy, charging that The Army had flooded France with the scum of society. But the dragging hours brought him no crumb of comfort. At Annemasse, the chief of police knew only that the gendarme had quit the force and moved elsewhere. It was now late at night. Perhaps in the morning the police might trace him?

And so might the killer, thought Péan, hanging up.

Then came what Péan could see only as Divine intervention. All through that night the express ploughed through whirling blizzards and in just one third-class coach the heating broke down. Next morning at Annemasse the numb and swooning passengers were borne from the train and taken direct to hospital. Most had stamina to survive the ordeal—but not the man from Devil's Island. He died a week later of pneumonia.

" I have never in my life," Péan confessed later, " thanked God more."

Tirelessly, he shuttled from Cayenne to Paris, travelling all through France and Algeria, pleading passionately for abolition. Thousands flocked to the 600 lectures he gave and the nation's conscience was stirred. At last, in 1937, a Bill for the *Bagne's* abolition came before the Chamber of Deputies, but the wheels of the law ground all too slowly ; if the convict's lot became more tolerable he was still a deported felon. At long last, in June, 1938, the abolition of Devil's Island was official.

Then, with World War Two, all repatriation ground to a standstill. Forbidden by Nazi edict to wear Salvation Army uniform, Péan took up work in Paris among abandoned children. Unknown to him, General de Gaulle's government in exile was implementing most of his plans. In 1946, the Minister of Colonies, Paul Giaccobi, set aside a large sum for the repatriation of all free men and convicts and Péan and The Salvation Army were chosen to carry out the work. Péan was appointed the only non-government member of the High Council of Penal Administration.

In 1946, armed with the official warrant that wiped out the *Bagne*, he flew to Guiana. At Cayenne, Brigadier Edouard Chastagnier and his wife Helen, who had remained faithful to their trust for eight long years, awaited him. Then, on Good Friday, the boat took Péan farther inland, up the Maroni River to St. Laurent. No one knew he was coming. In darkness he made his way to The Army hostel. Through the lighted window pane he saw an Army captain, one of eighteen who, over the years, had worked in Guiana, telling the story of the Crucifixion to a group of enthralled and silent men.

On the Sunday they held a mass meeting in his honour. Convicts and free men came from miles around to spread a carpet of flowers before him. From a crude platform Péan looked out over a sea of walnut-brown faces—the men whose souls he had sought as zealously as William Booth had enjoined him.

Silence fell, as the crowds strained to hear his message, but

Péan, erect beneath The Army flag that for eighteen years had
streamed above St. Laurent-du-Maroni, could find no words
just then. At last he said : " How fitting that this meeting
should be held on Easter Morning." His audience knew they
must be content with that. Out of mingled triumph and travail,
Charles Péan was weeping as if his heart would break.

In 1952, the last officers leaving St. Laurent hauled down The
Army's flag. To-day it lies stowed in a brown paper wrapping
in Commissioner Charles Péan's safe at 76 Rue de Rome, Paris.
Sun and rain have bleached its red to umber ; all the elements
combined to colander it with holes. The hem is slashed and
ragged where a man dying of dysentery rent it to fashion a
primitive diaper. But to Péan it is a precious symbol of another
great Christian crusade fought and won.

To-day The Army has gone from French Guiana, yet the
work that William Booth bequeathed to them remains a
challenge for the years that lie ahead. On Hamburg's Herbertstrasse Major Walter Flade looks beyond the waxwork
silhouettes of the women in the windows and sees immortal
souls. Each night in Paris, 150 men would bed down hungrily
on cold stones save for the patience and piety of Major
Georgette Gogibus. The 25,000 alcoholics of New York's
Bowery have in common a shared sickness and two staunch
friends—The Army's Hazel and Franklin Hoffman. These are
the tasks that face The Army to-night and every night ; as
yet the war against sin and misery has seen no final Victory
Day.

Long ago an indignant citizen asked William Booth : How
dared he send his soldiers, and women especially, to work
among such degradation ?

Perhaps the old General would answer that query to-day as
he did then. His face assumed its most lugubrious expression,
belying the twinkle in his eyes. His hands outspread elo-
quently. With the woebegone drawl of a father whose
children are past all control, he confessed : " You see, I can't
stop them. *They will do it.*"

And he smiled.

FACTS ABOUT THE
SALVATION ARMY

ACKNOWLEDGEMENTS

BIBLIOGRAPHY

INDEX

Facts About The Salvation Army

Since its inception in 1865, few religious organisations have been more widely discussed, praised, vilified—and often genuinely misunderstood—than The Salvation Army. Even to-day, when the vast majority view their midnight-blue uniforms as synonymous with Christian endeavour, misconceptions concerning The Army commonly sprout like weeds.

With these in mind, here is an attempt to answer some of the questions most frequently posed in connection with The Army:

What is The Army's strength? A conservative estimate is two million Salvationists—the bulk of them men and women holding down workaday jobs, who don uniform only for Army duties, at week-ends or after office-hours. Among them are dockers, housewives, Cambridge dons, bank officials, solicitors, secretaries. In the year ending 1962, their full-time officer strength was 23,350 —18,914 active officers, 6,436 retired. But this tally mounts steeply when count is taken of over 115,000 Local Officers, 37,000 Corps Cadets and more than 307,000 Home League adherents.

Where does The Army work? Through federations of territories, The Army's sphere of operations has now scaled down to 71 countries—as against 86 in 1959. Though outlawed by Franco's Spain and all Iron Curtain countries, The Army believes that many Salvationists inside Communist-controlled territories remain faithful to their calling. Languages in which Salvation is preached now total 147—from Afrikaans to Yoruba.

Facts About The Salvation Army

What do Salvationists believe ? " Religion," as The Army's founder, William Booth, saw it, " is a very simple thing. It just means loving God with all your heart, and your neighbour as yourself." Other fundamentals in the Salvationists' credo include the Divine inspiration of the Bible, their belief in the Trinity, in the salvation of all believers " by faith through grace," in " the immortality of the soul, in the resurrection of the body, in the general judgment at the end of the world."

Salvationists strive continually to turn men and women to seek God ; they do not seek to wean true believers away from their existing faith.

How thriving is The Army's social work ? Despite only 3,600 full-time officers devoted to social work, astonishing results are commonplace—among them 23 million cut-price meals served each year, 11 million hostel beds supplied. During one year (1962), The Army's 51 employment bureaux found work for over 128,000 men ; their Missing Persons Bureau traced over 7,000 people who had dropped from sight. Prison workers helped 75,000 men and women released from gaol to make a fresh start in life. Over 16,000 unmarried mothers passed through Salvation Army maternity homes. In the U.S.A., their Harbor-Light Centres helped over 800,000 alcoholics.

What does The Army's medical work comprise ? Operating in thirty-two territories, The Salvation Army Nurses' Fellowship currently embraces 3,089 members—who are deployed throughout 31 general hospitals, 38 maternity hospitals, 70 dispensaries and clinics (serving over 165,000 in-patients, more than 728,000 out-patients), six leprosaria, 88 maternity homes for unmarried mothers.

What are the operational expenses of such work ? They vary from year to year and from territory to territory. For example, in 1964 The Army sought £300,000 to rebuild and repair men and women's hostels in Great Britain, £189,000 to maintain schools, outposts and hospitals in Ceylon, Burma, India and Pakistan. To maintain one rural overseas dispensary (mainly for out-patients) calls for £300 per annum ; to support the 1,300 lepers in The Army's care costs just under £20,000, roughly £15 per patient.

Facts About The Salvation Army

How does The Army raise the funds it needs? Much of The Army's funds are still raised through the Self-Denial Effort—which, in 1962, netted over £298,000 in the British Territory alone. But bequests of money and property from sympathisers are becoming increasingly common—notable among them the $2,000,000 that Mrs. Lyndon Perkins Williams, a New York widow, bequeathed The Army to build and maintain a home for ageing women.

Why is The Army's disaster work so often headline news? Mainly because The Army are still " the servants of all "—and while disaster relief work is only one facet of their war, their soldiers are usually first on the scene with food, shelter, boats and canteens. Operating in 30 major towns of New England during the floods of August, 1955, some units did not cease work for more than five minutes during an entire fortnight—supplying everything from 3,000 diapers, at two hours' notice, to 100,000 cups of coffee. More recently, The Army have seen front-line service in Cuba, Algeria and the Congo—and in the 1960 Chilean earthquake, according to a Santiago newsman, " went to places the Devil himself would be afraid to enter."

Does The Army stand apart from other religious bodies and welfare organisations? On the contrary ; the days when suspicion and prejudice forced The Army to plough a lonely furrow are long past. To take but a few examples : in the U.S.A., The Army's lay advisory boards, made up of business and community leaders, now count 50,000 members who consult with Salvationists on social programmes. Social work representatives are active in such groups as The American Hospital Association, The American Correctional Association, and the Child Welfare League of America. In Great Britain and elsewhere The Army is closely linked with the International Abolitionist Federation, the Ministry of Health's Advisory Committee on Mental Health, the International Conference of Social Work, the National Council for Social Service.

How does The Army select its leaders? Since 1929, The Army's Generals have been elected by a High Council, currently composed of 46 senior officers and Territorial Commanders. Each General must be elected by a two-thirds' majority and must retire at 70. Following General Bramwell Booth, The Army's second leader, successive Generals have been: General Edward Higgins (1929-34); General Evangeline Booth (1934-9); General George Carpenter (1939-46); General Albert Orsborn (1946-54); General Wilfred Kitching (1954-63).

The Army's eighth and present leader, General Frederick Coutts, was elected to office in October, 1963.

Acknowledgements

This book has been five years in the making. In the autumn of 1959, I first approached General Wilfred Kitching, The Salvation Army's seventh General, with a new concept : a centenary history of William Booth and the endeavours of his Army, to be told for the first time by a non-Salvationist, entirely for the lay man and woman. To General Kitching and his successor, General Frederick Coutts, therefore, goes my deepest gratitude ; their kindness and encouragement made it possible for me to make contacts and study records I would otherwise have missed altogether.

Much of the brunt of my search for material was borne patiently and cheerfully by sundry departments of International Head-quarters, London, and to many of its staff officers I remain eternally grateful. The late Commissioner Reginald Woods, then Literary Secretary and Editor-in-Chief, unfailingly bolstered my morale at times when the whole project seemed too vast . . . his successor, Commissioner William H. Grottick, saw that the wheels of research kept turning smoothly . . . Brigadier Cyril Barnes of the Literary Department not only guided me on a fascinating tour of William Booth's London but generously shared with me his unrivalled knowledge of Army lore, accumulated over a lifetime. Helpful, too, were discussions and consultations with Lieutenant-Commissioner Herbert Westcott, Lieut.-Colonel Bernard Watson, Brigadier John Moyse, Major Fred Brown, Major Marion Dunn and Captain Joy Webb . . . the expert musical knowledge of Lieut.-Colonel Charles Skinner . . . Colonel Albert Towns's conducted tour of The Army's instrument factory at St. Albans . . . the kindness shown by Lieutenant-Colonel Joseph Smith and Brigadier Albert Barnes at Hadleigh Land Colony. In the public relations sphere,

Acknowledgements

Lieutenant-Colonel Arthur Carr arranged visits and interviews and solved last-minute queries with tireless aplomb.

Especially opportune was the chance to talk with no less than five people retaining vivid memories of William Booth—General Albert Orsborn; the founder's grandchildren, Commissioner Wycliffe Booth, Commissioner Catherine Bramwell-Booth, Colonel Bernard Booth; and the late Commissioner George Jolliffe. As they reminisced and played home movies and gramophone records, the majesty and fervour of the old General seemed to come alive once more. But almost as invaluable in recreating those Salvation battles of long ago was the fascinating trip round William Booth's Nottingham planned by Brigadier Thomas Liptrott . . . the many nuggets of research mined by Senior-Major Elizabeth Marshall at the General's birthplace, now an Army museum . . . the late Brigadier William Fryer's help in reconstructing the Worthing riots . . . Brigadier John Mairs's superb curatorship of Clapton Museum.

Much of the research was, of necessity, conducted in the United States, and here my warmest thanks must go first to Commissioner Norman Marshall, former National Commander, his successor, Commissioner Holland French and to Commissioners Glenn Ryan, William Davidson and Samuel Hepburn. Their blessing for the project opened every door. At Territorial Headquarters, New York, the tireless labours of Lieutenant-Colonel Margaret K. Hale, Mrs. Ethel Logan and Captain Dorothy Breen, all of the Education Department, saved literally weeks of delving; other gems emerged through the indefatigable sleuthing of Colonel Rowland Hughes, Editor, and Brigadier Christine Macmillan of the Eastern Territory *War Cry* who also helped to provide photographs. Major Andrew S. Miller proved himself a worthy Public Relations Secretary for New York City; nothing was ever too much trouble. And others, all through the project, went to endless pains—to unearth a fact, to authenticate a detail or to present an image of latter-day Army endeavour. Foremost among them were Brigadier Hazel Hoffman of The Army's Bowery Corps, Brigadier Cora Nicholson, Brigadier Mary Honsburger, Major Ethel Renton, one of the last surviving "Doughnut girls," Captain Caryl Andrews, of the Brengle Memorial Library and Mr. Paul Parker. The secretarial aid of Mrs. Phyllis Phillips and Miss Leah Fisher was streamlined from first to last.

Other territories proved as rewarding. In Canada Commissioner Wycliffe Booth was not only a gracious host but his unedited tape-

Acknowledgements

deck of memories, supplied through the good offices of Lieutenant-Colonel Arnold Brown and the Canadian Broadcasting Corporation, was packed with fresh material. To supplement his gripping account of life on Devil's Island, Commissioner Charles Péan brought me face to face in the Cité de Refuge, Paris, with four who had survived that hell—and others who contributed materially to my stay in France were Lieutenant-Colonel Samuel Nicholson, Brigadier Edouard Chastagnier and Major Georgette Gogibus. In Germany, Lieutenant-Commissioner Gösta Blomberg, the Territorial Commander, gave me unrivalled opportunities to study the work of The Army at first-hand, along with Colonel Wilhelm Kiesel and Major Walter Flade. But so many other officers gave invaluable advice and help that I hope that they will accept the bare mention of their names as token of my gratitude : Commissioner Ragnar Åhlberg (Sweden), Commissioner Joseph Dahya (Southern India), Commissioner Charles Davidson and Lieutenant-Colonel Tamiko Yamamuro (Japan) for the facsimile and translation of the Yoshiwara *War Cry*, Brigadier Joaquin Diaz (Uruguay), Commissioner Alfred Gilliard (New Zealand), Brigadier Alberto Labut (Chile), Colonel Arthur Long (Madras), Major Jorge Nery (Bolivia), Captain Alegria Ortega (Brazil), Major Eveline Tournou (Argentine).

But many non-Salvationists took time and trouble to furnish unique material : Mrs. Harriet Dickson Reynolds who gave access to the unique " Circle M " collection in Houston Public Library, Texas ; the Chief Librarian, Rose Memorial Library, Drew University, New York, who produced the only surviving copies of the first Philadelphia *War Crys* ; Grace W. Bacon of the Olin Library, Wesleyan University, Middletown, Connecticut. In England, too, I owe singular debts to L. M. Bickerton, Chief Librarian, Worthing Central Library, Sussex ; W. R. Serjeant, County Archivist for Nottinghamshire ; the Chief Constable's Office, West Sussex Constabulary ; The Chief Librarian, the London School of Hygiene and Tropical Medicine and to Rev. John C. Bowmer for his lucid exposition of early opposition to Methodism.

Finally, those who worked most closely on the project deserve special mention. My wife, apart from handling the vast bulk of the United States research, resolutely produced a first typescript from handwriting grown well-nigh indecipherable. Joan St. George Saunders and her sterling research team traced up literally hundreds of queries, never admitting defeat, and other valuable on-the-spot

Acknowledgements

research was done by Mrs. Robin McKown in New York and by Ruth Fried and Ruth Johnson in London. Above all, I and my publishers owe an especial debt to Jemima Williams, my chief researcher, whose pioneer investigations enabled the final draft to be delivered on time.

Bibliography

All sources marked with a publication date only are printed by Salvationist Publishing and Supplies Ltd., London.

NEWSPAPERS AND PERIODICALS

All The World
The Bombay Gazette
The Christian
The Christian Mission Magazine
The Daily News
The Daily Telegraph
The Deliverer
The East London Evangelist
The Field Officer
Good Housekeeping
The Illustrated London News
Japan Daily News
The Ladies Home Journal
The Lancet
Life
The Literary Digest
Liverpool Protestant Standard
Look
New York Herald
New York Tribune

New York Times
Northern Daily Express
Northern Echo
Nottingham Journal
The Officer
Review of Reviews
The Revival
The Salvationist
The Saturday Review
Sheffield Independent
The Social Gazette
South Wales Daily News
The Statesman, Calcutta
Strathearn Herald
The Times (London)
The Times of India
The War Cry
The Warwick Gazette
The Western Mail
The Worthing Gazette & Shoreham and Rape of Bramber Advertiser

PRINTED AND MANUSCRIPT SOURCES

ABADIE, GILBERT. *Son of the South.* 1956.

Bibliography

ACTON, WILLIAM. *Prostitution, Considered in its Moral, Social and Sanitary Aspects in London and other large cities.* London: John Churchill, 1857.

AH KOW, ADELAIDE. *Arthur S. Arnott.* n.d.
From Maori Land to Wattle Land. 1930.
" Get That Army Girl." 1952.
Mary Layton. 1957.
Thirty Years in Indonesia. 1949.
William McKenzie, M.C.: Anzac Padre. 1949.
All about The Salvation Army. London: S. W. Partridge, 1882.

ALLEN, MARGARET. *Harvests of the East.* 1909.
Kingdom Makers in Shelter, Street and Slum. 1909.

ANDERSON, WILLIAM. *The Poor of Edinburgh and their Homes.* Edinburgh: John Menzies, 1867.

APPLEMAN, PHILIP, MADDEN, W. A. AND WOOLF, MICHAEL. *1859: Entering an Age of Crisis.* Bloomington: Indiana Univ. Press, 1959.

ARMSTRONG, RICHARD. *An Army of Gentle Warriors,* in *The Saturday Evening Post,* December 15, 1962.

ARTER, BILL. *Soldiers of Salvation,* in *The Columbus Dispatch Sunday Magazine,* May 19, 1963.

ASBURY, HERBERT. *The Gangs of New York.* New York: Alfred Knopf, 1928.
The Barbary Coast. London: Jarrolds, 1934.

ATKINSON, JOHN. *Black Star Shines Again.* 1943.
Tips from a Taxi-Driver. 1945.
Here Is A Man. 1954.
Always In Step. 1956.
Doctor Beer Returns. 1957.

AUSUBEL, HERMAN. *In Hard Times.* New York: Columbia Univ. Press, 1960
General Booth's Scheme of Social Salvation, in *The American Historical Review,* April, 1951.

AVERY, GORDON (ed) *Companion to the Song Book of the Salvation Army.* 1961.

BAIRD, CATHERINE. *William Stevens, Jeweller & Missionary.* 1944.
Pierrot on Wings. 1944.
Noel Hope. 1944.
God's Harvester. 1948.
" Little Doctor," V.C. n.d.

Bibliography

Irish Termagant's Last Fight. n.d.

Scot in Zululand. 1952.

BARLEE, ELLEN. *Pantomime Waifs, or A Plea for Our City Children.* London: S. W. Partridge. 1884.

BARNES, CYRIL. *Exile Always At Home.* 1959.

He Wanted To Be Rich. 1958.

Soldier of Peace. 1962.

Prophet in Prison and Park. n.d.

The Boy Who Didn't Count. n.d.

The Man With Two Lives. 1946.

The One-Legged Prophet. n.d.

" You Can't Stop Lawrance ! " n.d.

Called From the Plough. n.d.

He Conquered the Foe. 1956.

Every Inch A Missionary. 1962.

Princess in Army Uniform. 1957.

The Rising Sun. 1955.

BARNETT, ALFRED. *The Salvation Army In India,* in *The Royal Society of Arts Journal,* January, 1937.

BATDORF, EMERSON. *Fifty Years of the Sidewalk Soldiers,* in *The Cleveland Plain Dealer Sunday Magazine.* October 13, 1963.

BAX, E. BELFORT. *Reminiscences and Reflexions of a Mid and Late Victorian.* London: Allen & Unwin, 1918.

BECKETT, HAL. *Save-the-World Army.* 1947.

Some of China's Children. 1944.

BECKETT, VIOLET. *Worthy Citizen.* 1947.

BEGBIE, HAROLD. *Broken Earthenware.* London: Hodder & Stoughton, 1911.

Life of William Booth (2 vols.). London: Macmillan, 1920.

Other Sheep. London: Hodder & Stoughton, 1911.

BELL, E. MOBERLEY. *Josephine Butler,* in *Social Service Quarterly,* Autumn, 1962.

BENNETT, ALFRED. *London & Londoners in the Eighteen Fifties & Sixties.* London: T. Fisher Unwin, 1924.

BERTON, PIERRE. *Klondike.* London: W. H. Allen, 1960.

BINNS, L. E. ELLIOTT. *Religion in the Victorian Era.* London: Lutterworth Press, 1936.

BLACKWELL, H. B. *Ambassador Extraordinary.* 1961.

Fighting Sweep. 1962.

BLATHWAYT, RAYMOND. *Interviews.* London: A. W. Hall, 1893.

Bibliography

BOOTH, BALLINGTON. *From Ocean to Ocean.* New York: J. S. Ogilvie, 1891.

BOOTH, BRAMWELL. *Social Reparation, or Personal Impressions of Work for Darkest England.* 1899.
Servants of All. 1899.
On The Banks of the River : the last days of The Army Mother. 1894.
Echoes and Memories. London: Hodder & Stoughton, 1925.
These Fifty Years. London: Cassell, 1929.

BOOTH, CHARLES. *Life and Labour of the People in London.* London: Macmillan, 1902-3.

BOOTH, EMMA and BOOTH, BALLINGTON. *The Training Barracks, or Our London Homes.* 1884.

BOOTH, EVA and HILL, GRACE. *The War Romance of the Salvation Army.* Philadelphia: J. B. Lippincott, 1919.

BOOTH, EVA. *My Father,* in *The Saturday Evening Post,* December 8, 1928.

BOOTH, MARY. *With the B.E.F. in France.* 1916.

BOOTH, MAUD BALLINGTON. *Beneath Two Flags.* New York: Funk & Wagnalls, 1889.

BOOTH, WILLIAM. *How to Reach the Masses with the Gospel.* London: Marshall, Morgan, Chase & Scott, 1872.
In Darkest England, and the Way Out. 1890.
Emigration and The Salvation Army. 1906.
What is The Salvation Army ? in *The Contemporary Review,* August, 1882.
Doctrines and Disciplines of The Salvation Army. 1881.
A Talk with Mr. Gladstone at His Own Fireside. 1897.

BOOTH-CLIBBORN, KATE. *They Endured.* London: Marshall, Morgan & Scott, 1934.

BOOTH-TUCKER, F. *Muktifauj, or Forty Years in India.* London: Marshall Bros., 1912.
Life of Catherine Booth (2 vols.). 1892.
The Consul. 1903.
Colonel Weerasooriya. 1905.
William Booth, the General of the Salvation Army. New York, 1898.
The Salvation Army in the United States. New York. n.d.
The Salvation Army as a Temperance Movement. New York. n.d.
Our Future Pauper Policy in America. New York. n.d.
The Relief of the Poor by the Salvation Army. New York. n.d.
The Social Relief Work of the Salvation Army. New York. 1900.

Bibliography

Friends of the Poor, or the Winter Work of the Salvation Army. New York. 1902.

Darkest India. Bombay: Gazette Steam Printing Works, 1891.

BOREL, T. *The White Slavery of Europe.* London: Dyer Bros., 1880.

BOSANQUET, BERNARD. *"In Darkest England" on the Wrong Track.* London: Swan Sonnenschein. 1891.

BOSANQUET, HELEN. *Social Work in London, 1869-1912.* London John Murray. 1914.

BOURDET-PLÉVILLE, MICHEL. *Justice in Chains.* London: Robert Hale, 1960.

BOWMAKER, E. *The Housing of the Working Classes.* London: Methuen. 1895.

BRACE, CHARLES LORING. *The Dangerous Classes of New York, and Twenty Years Work Among Them.* New York: Wynkoop & Hallenbeck. 1872.

BRAMWELL-BOOTH, CATHERINE. *Bramwell Booth.* London: Rich & Cowan. 1933.

BREADY, J. WESLEY. *Shaftesbury and Social and Industrial Progress.* London: Allen and Unwin. 1926.

BRIDSON, THOMAS. *Lightening the Lepers' Load.* 1946.

BROWN, ARNOLD. *What Hath God Wrought?: the Salvation Army in Canada.* Toronto. 1953.

BROWN, FRED. *General Eva.* n.d.

BROWN, HENRY CULLINS. *Brownstone Fronts and Saratoga Trunks.* New York: E. P. Dutton. 1935.

BUEL, JAMES W. *Metropolitan Life Unveiled, or Mysteries and Miseries of America's Great Cities.* San Francisco: A. L. Bancroft. 1883.

BULLARD, HENRY. *A Missionary's Memories.* 1946.

BURROWS, WILLIAM. *The Curate of Onslow Square.* 1960.

Fiery Fiddler. 1945.

Black Into White. 1950.

BUTLER, A. S. G. *Portrait of Josephine Butler.* London: Faber and Faber. 1954.

BUTLER, JOSPEHINE. *The Salvation Army in Switzerland.* London: Dyer Bros. 1883.

Rebecca Jarrett. London: Morgan & Scott, 1885.

CAMPBELL, MRS. HELEN. *The Problem of the Poor.* New York: Fords, Howard and Hurlbert. 1882.

Darkness & Daylight. Hartford: A. D. Worthington. 1892.

Bibliography

CARPENTER, MINNIE. *Commissioner John Lawley.* 1924.

Three Great Hearts. 1928.

William Booth, Founder of the Salvation Army. London: Epworth Press. 1947.

Women of the Flag. 1945.

Kate Lee, "The Angel Adjutant." 1944.

Miriam Booth. 1920.

John Dean. London: Epworth Press, 1944.

Commissioner Henry Howard. 1926.

Some Notable Officers of the Salvation Army. 1928.

Central Criminal Court, Sessions Papers, 1885. *Vol.* 102. London: Stevens & Sons, 1885.

CHAMBERLAIN, JOSEPH. *Labourers 'and Artisans Dwellings',* in *The Fortnightly Review,* December 1, 1883.

Children And the Drink: Report of an Enquiry Conducted by a Committee. London: R. Brimley Johnson, 1901.

CLARK, G. KITSON. *The Making of Victorian England.* London: Methuen, 1962.

CLARK, HENRY. *History of English Nonconformity.* London: Chapman and Hall, 1911.

CLAUGHTON, LILIAN. *Charles H. Jeffries: from "Skeleton" to Salvationist Leader.* 1946.

Commissioner David Rees. (Unpublished Mss., Central Library, I.H.Q. Salvation Army.)

CLIMPSON, HERBERT. *Murder at Wairoa.* n.d.

COATES, THOMAS F. *The Prophet of the Poor.* London: Hodder and Stoughton, 1905.

COLE, G. D. H. and POSTGATE, RAYMOND. *The Common People.* 1746-1938. London: Methuen, 1938.

COOK, SIR EDWARD. *Edmund Garrett: a memoir.* London: Edward Arnold, 1909.

COPPING, ARTHUR. *Souls in Khaki.* London: Hodder & Stoughton, 1917.

Stories of Army Trophies. 1928.

Banners in Africa. London: Hodder & Stoughton, 1933.

CORNISH, WARRE. *A History of the English Church in the Nineteenth Century.* London: Macmillan, 1910.

COSSAR, JAMES. *"Lifted": the life story of Robert Cossar.* London: Pickering and Inglis, 1935.

COUTTS, FREDERICK. *Salute to a Mill-Girl.* 1942.

The First Salvationist. 1944.

Bibliography

Down in Demerara. 1944.

Short Measure : portrait of a Young Man. 1945.

The Battle and the Breeze. 1946.

Soldiership in the Salvation Army, in *Theology,* May, 1952.

Portrait of a Salvationist. 1955.

COWARD, ERIC. *Burglar With a Blue Scar.* n.d.

Clouds Across the Valley. 1957.

The Brick and the Book. 1960.

COX, ADELAIDE. *Hotch-Potch.* London : Unwin Bros., 1937.

COX, F. HAYTER. *He Was There.* 1949.

CROSS, F. L. (ed.) *The Oxford Dictionary of the Christian Church.* London : Oxford University Press, 1958.

DALE, PERCIVAL. *Fighting Mac.* n.d.

Salvation Chariot : the Salvation Army in Australia. Melbourne, 1953.

DAVIDSON, REV. RANDALL. *The Methods of the Salvation Army,* in *The Contemporary Review,* August, 1882.

DAVIES, EMMA. *Sure of Her Call.* 1952.

DAVIES, OLWEN. *Florence the Home-Maker.* 1962.

DE BECKER, J. E. *The Nightless City, or the History of the Yoshiwara Yukwaku.* Yokohama : Max Nössler, 1899.

DODD, GEORGE. *The Food of London.* London : Longman, Brown, Green and Longman's, 1856.

DOUGLAS, EILEEN. *Elizabeth Swift Brengle.* 1922.

DOUGLAS, EILEEN and DUFF, MILDRED. *Commissioner Railton.* 1920.

DRUMMOND, J. C. and WILBRAHAM, A. *The Englishman's Food.* London : Jonathan Cape, edn. of 1957.

DUFF, MILDRED. *Hedwig von Haartman.* 1904.

DWYER, PHILIP. *General Booth's Submerged Tenth, or the Wrong Way To Do the Right Thing.* London : Swan Sonnenschein, 1891.

DYER, ALFRED S. *The European Slave Trade in English Girls.* London : Dyer Bros., 1885.

EDMONDS, HENRY. *My Adventures with William Booth.* (Unpublished Mss. British Museum Reading Room, London.)

ERVINE, ST. JOHN. *God's Soldier* (2 vols.). London : William Heinemann, 1934.

Essays and Sketches : Phases of Salvation Army Work. 1906.

Bibliography

FAIRHURST, ANNIE. *From Pig-Pen to Parliament.* 1949.

FARRIE, HUGH C. *Toiling Liverpool.* Liverpool Daily Post & Echo Office, 1886.

Fighting in Many Lands : Memories of Pioneer Salvationists (3 vols.). 1960.

FLETCHER, LAURENCE. *Brother of All.* 1956.

The Fortunate Escape of the Prince Regent : narrative of Salvation Army work in many lands. 1929.

FRANKLIN, GORDON. *Lord Shaftesbury*, in Social Service Quarterly, Spring, 1957.

FRIEDERICHS, HULDA. *The Romance of the Salvation Army.* London : Cassell, 1907.

GAMMIE, ALEXANDER. *Underworld of a Great City.* London: Pickering & Inglis, 1942.

GAUNTLETT, S. C. *Social Evils the Army Has Challenged.* 1946.
Voiceless Inventor. 1943.
He Gave Sight to Hundreds. 1948.
Knight Errant's Crusade. 1960.
Queen of Protests. 1960.
John Murfitt : from Miner to Major. 1944.
" Never Seen the Like of That ! " 1945.
Once Upon a Time. n.d.
A Heroine of Reindeer Land. n.d.
Playboy to Convert. n.d.
Lady in Uniform. 1945.
His Money and His Life. 1950.

GELLATLY, JAMES. *He Joined Two Armies.* 1947.
Twice Saved By a Song. 1947.
The Better Fight. 1951.
Rags and Bones and Ballads. n.d.

General Booth : a Symposium. London : Thomas Nelson, 1912.

GILDER, RODMAN. *The Battery.* Boston : Houghton Mifflin, 1936.

GILLIARD, ALFRED. *All The Days.*
Married in the Salvation Army. 1955.
Gentle Eagle. 1955.
Sussex Yeoman. 1956.

GILLIARD, DORA. *Unto Me.* n.d.
General's Daughter—Soldier's Friend. 1943.

GINGER, RAY. *The Bending Cross.* New Brunswick : Rutgers University Press, 1949.

Bibliography

GODWIN, GEORGE. *Town Swamps and Social Bridges.* London: Routledge, Warne and Routledge, 1859.

Great Revivalists. London: Watts & Co., 1951.

A Good Shepherd, or What a Salvation Army Captain Should Be. 1884.

GOUT, RAOUL. *William Booth et Le Monde Ouvrier.* Paris: Editions Altis, 1955.

GREAVES, BRIAN. *Eighteenth Century Opposition to Methodism,* in Proceedings of the Wesley Historical Society, Vol. XXXI, 1957-8.

GREEN, J. R. *Stray Studies* (2nd series). London: Macmillan, 1903.

GREENWOOD, H. *General Booth and his Critics.* London: Home & Co. 1891.

GREENWOOD, JAMES. *Unsentimental Journeys, or Byways of the Modern Babylon.* London: Ward, Lock & Tyler, 1867.

The Seven Curses of London. London: Stanley Rivers, 1869.

The Wilds of London. London: Chatto & Windus, 1874.

GREGORY, BENJAMIN (ed.) *Heroes of the Free Churches.* London: Epworth Press, 1935.

GRISEWOOD, H. (ed.) *Ideas and Beliefs of the Victorians.* London: Sylvan Press, 1949.

GRUNER, MAX. *Revolutionares Christentum* (2 vols.). Berlin: 1954.

HAGGARD, H. RIDER. *Regeneration.* London: Longman's, 1910.

The Poor and the Land. London: Longman's, 1905.

HALL, CLARENCE. *Out of the Depths: the Life-Story of Henry Milans.* New York: Fleming H. Revell Co., 1930.

Samuel Logan Brengle: Portrait of a Prophet. New York, 1933.

The Man Who Conquered Devil's Island, in The Reader's Digest, March, 1947.

HALLIMOND, JOHN G. *Greatheart of the Bowery.* New York: Fleming H. Revell Co., 1925.

HAMILTON, MERLE. *Redhead on Fire.* 1955.

HAMLIN, FRED. *Land of Liberty.* New York: Thomas Y. Crowell Co. 1947.

Handbook of the Law Relating to Children. London: Ward, Lock & Co., 1887.

A Handful of Corn: the Tenth Annual Report of the Salvation Army in India and Ceylon. Bombay, 1892.

HARLOW, ALVIN FAY. *Old Bowery Days.* New York: D. Appleton & Co., 1931.

Bibliography

HART, REV. A. TINDAL. *The Country Priest in English History.* London: Phœnix House, 1959.

HART, SMITH. *The New Yorkers.* New York: Sheridan House, 1938.

HATCHER, MATILDA. *The Untouchables.* n.d.
Catherine Hine: " Teacher of Chinatown." 1943.
The Undauntables. London: Hodder & Stoughton, 1933.
The Uplifters. n.d.

HAY, JAMES. *Aggressive Salvationism.* Melbourne: 1951.

HEASMAN, KATHLEEN. *Evangelicals in Action.* London: Geoffrey Bles, 1962.

HENRIQUES, DR. FERNANDO. *Prostitution and Society.* Vol. I. London: MacGibbon & Kee, 1962.

HEWITT, MARGARET. *Wives and Mothers in Victorian Industry.* London: Rockcliff, 1958.

HILL, MICAIAH and CORNWALLIS, C. F. *Two Prize Essays on Juvenile Delinquency.* London: Smith, Elder, 1853.

HIRD, FRANK. *The Cry of the Children.* London: James Bowden, 1898.

HOBSON, J. A. *Problems of Poverty.* London: Methuen, 1891.
The Problem of the Unemployed. London: Methuen, 1896.

HODGES, S. H. *General Booth, " the Family," and the Salvation Army, showing its Rise, Progress and Moral and Spiritual Decline.* Manchester: privately printed, 1890.

Home Office Papers: The Riots at Worthing, H.O.45/9960(X2676). (Unpublished letters, Public Record Office, London.)

HOPKINS, ELLICE. *Social Wreckage,* in *The Contemporary Review,* July, 1883.

HOUGHTON, W. E. *The Victorian Frame of Mind.* New Haven: Yale University Press, 1957.

HOUSDEN, L. G. *The Prevention of Cruelty to Children.* London: Jonathan Cape, 1955.

HULME, SAMUEL. *Memoir of the Rev. William Cooke, D.D.* London: A. D. Ward, 1886.

HUME, H. S. *The Temperance Movement and the Salvation Army.* London: Strangeways, 1883.

HURREN, GEORGE. *The Street Fighter.* 1944.

HUXLEY, THOMAS H. *Social Diseases and Worse Remedies.* London: Macmillan, 1891.

HYLAND, STANLEY. *Curiosities from Parliament.* London: Allan Wingate, 1955.

Bibliography

HYNDMAN, H. M. *The English Workers As They Are*, in *The Contemporary Review*, July, 1887.

Illustrated Guide to the Salvation Army Land and Industrial Colony, 1926.
INGLIS, K. S. *Churches and the Working Classes in Victorian England*. London: Routledge, 1963.
International Social Council Addresses, 1911 *and* 1921.
Is It Worth-While ? : aspects of Salvation Army Social Work. 1933.

James Barker, the Prisoner's Friend. 1929.
JENKIN, A. K. HAMILTON. *Cornwall and Its People*. London : J. A. Dent, 1945.
JEUNE, MARY. *The Homes of the Poor*, in *The Fortnightly Review*, January 1, 1890.
JEVONS, W. S. *Married Women in Factories*, in *The Contemporary Review*, January, 1882.
JOHNSON, HARRIET M. *Children and Public Houses*. Nottingham : Licensing Laws Information Bureau, 1897.
JOY, DOROTHY. " *Orange Harriet.*" 1944.
JOY, EDWARD. *The Old Corps*. 1944.
Marvellous in Our Eyes. 1945.

KENYON, ALBERT. *Alive in His Coffin*. n.d.
Leonard Goes East. 1952.
Pied Piper of Odense. 1954.
Congo Crusade. 1955.
KIRSCHTEN, ERNEST. *Catfish and Crystal*. New York : Doubleday, 1960.
KITTO, JOHN F. *The Salvation Army*, in *The Churchman*, July, 1882.

LAMB, EDWARD G. *The Social Work of the Salvation Army*. 1909.
LARSSON, FLORA. *Always Ready to Sail*. 1958.
God's Man on Devil's Island. 1960.
Queen of the Barge. 1960.
Ruth goes to the Congo. 1961.
LAVER, JAMES. *Victorian Vista*. London : Hulton Press, 1954.
Edwardian Promenade. London : Edward Hulton, 1958.
Letters to the Centre : Some aspects of Salvation Army work at Home and Abroad. 1912.
LINGARD, MARTIN. *Chaplain on the Barrier*. 1963.
LLOYD, ARTHUR. *Everyday Japan*. London : Cassell, 1909.

Bibliography

LOCH, C. S. *An Examination of General Booth's Social Scheme*. London: Swan Sonnenschein, 1890.

LONDON, JACK. *The People of the Abyss*. London: Isbister, 1903.

LUNN, BRIAN. *Salvation Dynasty*. London: William Hodge, 1936.

LYLES, ALBERT M. *Methodism Mocked: The satiric reaction to Methodism in the Eighteenth Century*. London: Epworth Press, 1960.

MCGLASHAN, W. *England On Her Defence: a Reply to the Maiden Tribute*. Newcastle-on-Tyne: John B. Barnes, 1885.

MCKENZIE, F. A. *Famishing London*. London: Hodder & Stoughton, 1903.

Waste Humanity. 1909.

Serving the King's Men. London: Hodder & Stoughton, 1918.

The Clash of the Cymbals. New York: Brentano's, 1929.

Sadhu and Saint. London: Hodder & Stoughton, 1930.

MACKEEVER, S. A. *Glimpses of Gotham and City Characters*. New York: National Police Gazette, 1880.

MALLET, MRS. C. *Dangerous Trades for Women*. London: William Reeves, 1893.

MANNING, CARDINAL. *The Salvation Army*, in *The Contemporary Review*, September, 1882.

MANSON, J. *The Salvation Army and the Public*. London: George Routledge, 1906.

MATTHEWS, J. B. *The Law Relating to Children*. London: Sweet & Maxwell, 1895.

MAWBY, IVY. *Gold in the Torrent*. 1957.

MAYHEW, HENRY. *London Labour and the London Poor* (4 vols.). London: Charles Griffin, 1864.

MEYER, GRACE. *Once Upon a City*. New York: Macmillan, 1958.

MILSAPS, JOHN. *A Salvationist's Diary*, 1872-1932 (72 vols.) (Unpublished Mss., "Circle M" Collection, Houston Public Library, Texas).

MITCHELL, W. *Rescue the Children*. London: William Isbister, 1886.

MOON, GLADYS. *Conquistador*. 1946.

Bogey's Redemption. 1945.

MORRIS, J. *Our Sin and Our Shame*. Wimbledon: J. S. Amoore, 1885.

MOSS, FRED. *The American Metropolis* (3 vols.). London: Author's Syndicate, 1897.

Bibliography

MULHALL, MICHAEL. *Fifty Years of National Progress*, 1837-87. London: Routledge, 1887.

MURPHY, U. G. *The Social Evil in Japan.* Tokyo: Methodist Publishing House, 1904.

MURRAY, MARY. *The Salvation Army at Work in the Boer War.* 1900.

MUSPRATT, ALBERT. *The Salvation Army: is it a benefit to religion?* Ripon: William Harrison, 1884.

MUTHIAH, NARAYANA. *Triumphs of the Cross in Travancore.* 1946.

NEAL, HARRY EDWARD. *Hallelujah Army.* Philadelphia: Chilton Co., 1961.

NEEVE, ETHEL. *Her Father's Blessing.* 1954.
Nurse by Royal Command. 1958.

NEFF, WANDA. *Victorian Working Women.* London: George Allen and Unwin, 1929.

NELSON, WILLIAM H. *Blood and Fire.* New York: Century Co., 1929.

NEWMAN, F. W. *The Cure of the Great Social Evil.* London: Trubner & Co., 1869.

The New Papacy: Behind the Scenes in the Salvation Army, by an ex-Staff Officer. Toronto: A. Britmell, 1889.

NICHOLSON, RENTON. *Autobiography of a Fast Man.* London: Savill & Edwards, 1863.

NICHOLSON, WILLIAM. *The Romance of the War Cry.* 1929.

NICOL, ALEX M. *General Booth and the Salvation Army.* London: Herbert and Daniel, 1911.

O'CONNOR, RICHARD. *Hell's Kitchen.* Philadelphia: Lippincott, 1958.

OLIVER, SIR THOMAS (ed.) *Dangerous Trades.* London: John Murray, 1902.

On Salvation Battlefields. 1928.

Orders and Regulations for Field Officers. 1886.

Organised Empire Migration and Settlement. 1930.

ORR, J. E. *The Second Evangelical Awakening in Britain.* London: Marshall, Morgan & Scott, 1949.

ORSBORN, ALBERT. *The House of My Pilgrimage.* 1958.

OSBORNE, LORD SIDNEY GODOLPHIN. *Letters on Public Affairs,* 1844-88 (2 vols.). London: Griffith, Farran, Oreden & Welsh, 1890.

Bibliography

OTTMAN, F. C. *Herbert Booth*. New York: Doubleday, Doran & Co., 1928.
Outlines of Salvation Army History. 1927.

PAGE, JESSE. *General Booth : the man and his work*. London: S. W. Partridge, 1901.

PALMER, AGNES L. *The Times Between*. New York: 1926.

PARKER, EDWARD J. *My Fifty-Eight Years*. New York: 1943.

PATERSON, SIR ALEXANDER. *Across the Bridges, or Life by the South London Riverside*. London: Edward Arnold, 1911.

PATON, JOHN LEWIS. *Life of J. B. Paton*. London: Hodder & Stoughton, 1914.

PÉAN, CHARLES. *The Conquest of Devil's Island*. London: Max Parrish, 1953.

PEEK, FRANCIS. *The Workless, The Thriftless and the Worthless*, in *The Contemporary Review*, Jan.-Feb., 1888.

PENNICK, LILLY. *Robes of Renunciation*. n.d.

PENNICK, W. D. *In a Punjab Village*. 1947.

PERUGINI, M. E. *Victorian Days and Ways*. London: Jarrolds, 1932.

Phases of the Work of the Salvation Army. 1911.

PLOSS, H. H. and BARTELS, M. and P. *Woman* (ed. E. J. Dingwall, 3 vols.). London: William Heinemann, 1935.

PRESTON, W. C. *The Bitter Cry of Outcast London*. London: James Clark, 1883.

RAILTON, GEORGE SCOTT. *Heathen England*. London: S. W. Partridge, 1877.
Mother Moore. London: S. W. Partridge, n.d.
Behind the Pigeon Shop. London: S. W. Partridge, 1879.
Captain Ted. 1880.
Forward from Misery. 1912.
History of Our South African War. 1901.
Commissioner Dowdle. 1901.
The Truth About the Armstrong Case. 1888.
Twenty-One Years Salvation Army. 1889.
General Booth. 1912.

REDSTONE, J. J. R. *An Ex-Captain's Experiences of the Salvation Army*. London: Christian Commonwealth Publishing Co., 1888.

Bibliography

REDWOOD, HUGH. *God in the Slums*. London: Hodder & Stoughton, 1930.

RENDELL, DORIS. *Friend of the Desperate*. 1957.

Review of the First Year's Work for Darkest England. 1891.

RICHARDS, MIRIAM. *One of the Gang*. n.d.

RIIS, JACOB AUGUST. *How the Other Half Lives*. New York: Charles Scribner, 1891.

   Children of the Poor. New York: Charles Scribner, 1892.

ROBERTS, PHILIP. *The Dry Dock of a Thousand Wrecks*. New York: Fleming H. Revell Co., 1912.

ROHU, ETHEL B. *John Roberts—Evangelist*. n.d.

ROOPER, REV. W. H. *General Booth and the Salvation Army*. Bournemouth: Bright & Son., 1892.

Round the Clock: the Salvation Army in 1917-18. 1918.

ROWE, R. *Picked Up in the Streets*. London: W. H. Allen, 1880.

RYAN, W. P. *The Romance of a Motor Mission: with General Booth on his White Car Crusade*. 1906.

SALA, GEORGE AUGUSTUS. *Twice Round the Clock*. London: Houlston and Wright. 1859.

The Salvation Army Land and Industrial Colony: a brief outline. 1913.

The Salvation Army: its origins and development. 1945.

The Salvation Army and its Social Scheme, in *The Review of Reviews*, October-November, 1890.

The Salvation Army Year Book, 1906-64.

The Salvation War for 1882. 1883.

The Salvation War for 1883. 1884.

The Salvation War for 1884. 1885.

The Salvation War for 1885. 1886.

SANDALL, ROBERT. *History of the Salvation Army*, Vols. I-III. London: Thomas Nelson, 1947-55.

A School of the Prophets, by One of the Scholars. 1925.

SCHLOSS, DAVID F. *The Sweating System*, in *The Fortnightly Review*, April 1, 1890.

SEARCH, PAMELA. *Happy Warriors*. London: Arco Ltd., 1956.

SEKON, G. A. *Locomotion in Victorian London*. London: Oxford University Press, 1938.

SHAW, D. *London in the Sixties*. London: Everett & Co., 1908.

SHAW, WILLIAM. *An Affectionate Pleading for England's Oppressed Female Workers*. London: Swale and Wilson, 1850.

SHEARD, EDWIN. *Sergeant-Major in the Andamans*. 1957.

Bibliography

SHERWELL, ARTHUR. *Life in West London.* London: Methuen, 1897.

SHORT, A. R. and GAUNTLETT, S. C. *Clara Case—Nurani.* 1946.

SIEGFRIED, RUTH. *Missionary Diary.* 1956.

SIMEY, MARGARET. *Charles Booth: Study for a Portrait,* in *Social Service Quarterly,* Winter, 1955.

SLADEN, D. and LORIMER, N. *More Queer Things about Japan.* London: Anthony Treherne, 1904.

SMITH, FRANK. *The Salvation War in America for 1885.* New York, 1886.

The Salvation War in America for 1886-7. New York, 1888.

The Betrayal of Bramwell Booth. London: Jarrolds, 1929.

SMITH, H. PIMM. *Capturing " Crims " for Christ.* 1945.

Slow of Speech. 1953.

SMITH, J. ALLISTER. *Zulu Crusade.* 1948.

A Zulu Apostle. 1953.

SMITH, J. EVAN. *Booth the Beloved.* London: Oxford University Press. 1949.

SMITH, RODNEY. *Gipsy Smith, his Life and Work.* London: National Free Church Council. 1924.

Some Reasons Why I Do Not Sympathise with the Salvation Army. London: John F. Shaw, 1882.

STEAD, WILLIAM T. *A Maiden Tribute to Modern Babylon,* in *The Pall Mall Gazette,* July, 1885.

General Booth. London: Isbister & Co., 1891.

Mrs. Booth of the Salvation Army. London: James Nisbet, 1909.

STEELE, HAROLD C. *I was a Stranger.* New York: Exposition Press, 1954.

STRAHAN, JAMES. *The Maréchale.* New York: Doran Co., 1921.

STURGESS, CATHERINE. *This Quiet Man.* 1944.

SUTHERLAND, MONICA. *The San Francisco Disaster.* London: Barrie & Rockliff, 1959.

SYLVESTER, CHARLES. *Korea for Christ.* 1949.

TAINE, HIPPOLYTE. *Notes on England.* London: Strahan & Co., 1872.

TAYLOR, GLADYS. *She Avenged Her Father.* 1945.

So Sure of Herself! 1944.

TEICHMANN, SIR ERIC. *Affairs of China.* London: Methuen, 1938.

Bibliography

TERROT, CHARLES. *Maiden Tribute*. London : Frederick Muller, 1959.

THOMPSON, VICTOR. *Son of Sri Lanka*. 1953.
Wise Man of the East. 1956.

TILLETT, BEN. *Memories and Reflections*. London : John Long, 1931.

TOPLEY, EDITH. *No Coward Soul*. 1948.

TRACY, RUTH. *Marianne Pawson : the Zulu Queen*. 1944.

TREVELYAN, G. M. *English Social History*. London : Longman's Green, 1947. (4th Edn.)

UNSWORTH, MADGE. *Maiden Tribute*. 1950.
The Flower Called Faith-in-the-Night. 1946.
The Woman's Charter in the Salvation Army, in *The Methodist Magazine*, December, 1948.

VALLEY, ASTRID. *Marching Bonnet*. New York : Macmillan, 1948.

WALLIS, HUMPHREY. *The Happy Warrior*. 1928.

WALWORTH, DOROTHY. *General of the Army*, in *The Reader's Digest*, August, 1947.

WATSON, BERNARD. *The Sergeant Was Disgusted*. 1943.
Policeman Plus. 1947.
The Yorkshire Lad. 1951.
The Poet-General. 1955.
Olive in China. 1957.

WATTS, ARTHUR W. *Lion Hearts*. Gillingham, Kent : A. C. Burgess, 1929.

WELLS, ALFRED. *An Account of the Opening and Early Days of the Salvation Army on the Pacific Coast*. (Unpublished Mss. " Circle M " Collection, Houston Public Library, Texas.)

WESTERGAARD, KAARE. *Designer and Down-and-Outs*. 1945.

WEY, FRANCIS. *A Frenchman Sees England in the 'Fifties*. London : Sidgwick and Jackson. 1935.

WHATMORE, HUGH. *Autobiography*. (Unpublished Mss. Central Library, I.H.Q., Salvation Army.)

WHITE, ARNOLD. *The Problems of a Great City*. London : Remington, 1886.
The Great Idea. 1909.

WHITLOW, MAURICE. *Not Exactly a Birthright Membership*, in *The Friends Quarterly*, July, 1951.

Bibliography

WHYTE, FREDERICK. *The Life of William T. Stead.* Boston: Houghton, Mifflin, 1925.

WIGGINS, ARCH. R. *Lyons in the Jungle.* 1945.
Campaigning in Captivity. 1947.
Father of Salvation Army Music. 1945.
T. H. K. : a biography. 1956.
History of the Salvation Army, Vol. IV. London: Thomas Nelson, 1964.

WILLE, W. A. *Xeropthalmia : a deficiency disease,* in Transactions of the Far East Association of Tropical Medicine, Vol. I, 1922.

WILLIAMS, SIDNEY. *Punching Pride of Ancoats.* 1943.
Pudding and Policies. 1946.

WILSON, P. WHITWELL. *The General : the Story of Evangeline Booth.* London: Hodder & Stoughton, 1925.
General Evangeline Booth of the Salvation Army. New York: Charles Scribner's, 1948.

WISBEY, HERBERT A. *Soldiers without Swords.* New York: Macmillan, 1955.

WINSKILL, P. T. *The Temperance Movement* (4 vols.). Edinburgh: Blackie, 1890.

WOODS, REGINALD. *Unholy Joe.* n.d.
He Made Himself Mayor. n.d.
Two Men in the Snow. 1953.
A Desperado Transformed. 1952.
Brother of the Red Hand. 1955.
Harvest of the Years. 1960.
Wounded in the Warfare of Life : a report on Women's Social Work for 1900. 1901.

WYMER, NORMAN. *Dr. Barnardo.* London: Longman's, 1962.

Index

311

Index

Index

Index

Index

Index